Roderick Cavaliero is a writer and historian. He is the author of *Admiral Satan: The Life and Campaigns of the Bailli de Suffren*, *Independence of Brazil* and *Strangers in the Land: The Rise and Decline of the British Indian Empire* (all I.B.Tauris), as well as *Last of the Crusaders: The Knights of St John and Malta in the Eighteenth Century* and *Italia Romantica: English Romantics and Italian Freedom* (both Tauris Parke Paperbacks).

LIBRARY OF OTTOMAN STUDIES

Series ISBN: 978 1 84885 245 7

See www.ibtauris.com/LOS for a full list of titles

OTTOMANIA

The Romantics and the Myth
of the Islamic Orient

Roderick Cavaliero

I.B. TAURIS
LONDON · NEW YORK

Published in 2010 by I.B. Tauris & Co Ltd
6 Salem Road, London W2 4BU
175 Fifth Avenue, New York NY 10010
www.ibtauris.com

Distributed in the United States and Canada Exclusively by Palgrave Macmillan,
175 Fifth Avenue, New York NY 10010

Library of Ottoman Studies: 24

ISBN: 978 1 84885 106 1

A full CIP record for this book is available from the British Library
A full CIP record is available from the Library of Congress

Library of Congress Catalog Card Number: available

Designed and Typeset by 4word Ltd, Bristol, UK
Printed and bound in India by Replika Press Pvt. Ltd.

To Maria Schoina for putting the idea for this book into my head and to Glen Cavaliero for reading the result.

Contents

Preface

> **Myth**, a purely fictitious narrative usually involving
> supernatural persons, actions or events, and embodying
> some popular idea concerning natural or historical
> phenomena. Often used vaguely to include any
> narrative having fictitious elements.
> (*Oxford English Dictionary*)

I

ROMANTICISM HAD ITS roots in fantasy and was nurtured on myth. In revolt against the staid society of Europe, marked by religious conformity and royal rights, both in their turn living out the myth of their origins, it eagerly welcomed the solvents of transcontinental exploration, of colonisation and of scientific discovery, all of which were to manufacture myths of their own. In the appetite for encyclopaedic knowledge that characterised the eighteenth century, the myths and fantasies that surrounded the Islamic Orient came under scrutiny. They in turn derived from a mixture of past admiration and fear. The Romantics learned to reject the fear, but they preserved and perpetuated the myths. The people they thought they were studying were originally Turkic, but Turkey was only a geographical entity, and the term did not enter general usage until the twentieth century when Turkey became a nation and not a conglomerate. Before that, Turks and the races that lived beside them belonged to the empire of Osman, and were known as Ottomans. Distinctions among the Ottomans were mainly signified by religion, the Muslim and the non-Muslim communities, the one superior, the other inferior, but tolerated and useful.

The first myth the Romantics were to dismantle converted the Ottoman empire from a successful and viable imperial power to 'the sick man of Europe'. It supposed that its ruler was a tyrant, a Caliph/Sultan endowed with a will that commanded unquestioning obedience by the exercise of the power of life and death, exercised with ruthless efficiency, by an army of servants whose only *raison d'être* was to carry it out. As soon as this myth was unravelled, he began to appear weak and powerless. The Ottoman empire was never monolithic. Of all European states it resembled most the Austrian empire in the cosmopolitan nature of its subjects and loose arrangement of its dominions. It may have been conquered by armies that owed a loyalty first and only to their sovereign, but it was administered by diverse people that had a prime loyalty to their tribe.

The second myth was that half the population had no function but to service man, bear his children and delight his senses. In 1846, Thackeray was told by an Egyptian Pasha's son in Malta that 'the great aim of the women is to administer to the brutality of her lord, her merit is in knowing how to vary the beast's pleasures'.[1] Both myths were strongly supported by the subsidiary myth that *The Arabian Nights Entertainments* were an accurate portrait of the society over which the Caliph, in the person of the Ottoman Sultan, ruled. Underpinning these myths was the institution of slavery, without which his mighty palaces and the palaces of his satraps would not have been built. The Romantics did not invent these myths but their imagination created a web of legend about them.

Byron invented the myth of the Virgin soft as roses, in thrall to the social custom to love where she was told, but whose passions could not be controlled. He used it to create novellas with tragic, romantic endings, overtly to condemn the Ottoman tyranny of female subservience but also to hint that, in the West, customs might be different but the result was ultimately the same. Their enthusiastic reception among a readership of young woman suggested that they understood the message and hoped for better. The ultimate destination of Byronic love poetry was to be the tamed and dim household of Teresa Guiccioli, which resembled nothing more than Coventry Patmore's *The Angel of the House* (1854), and which Pierre Loti tried, towards the end of the century, to suggest was the true ambition for a woman in an Ottoman household.

Another land of growing Romantic interest was mysterious Egypt, the secret of whose longevity was hidden in a profound philosophic wisdom, controlled by passwords of which the key had been lost. The Ottomans now lorded it over the land of empires every bit in their time as mighty as their own, and they had died carrying their secrets with them. Faced with a huge Mameluke Arab army, that arch-Romantic, Napoleon, had rallied his soldiers with the thought that forty centuries looked down on them from the Pyramids. The time had come for those secrets to be revealed, and a new man born, and he was to be his avatar.

The land of Persia had never wholly succumbed to the Ottoman empire and remained in the imagination of the West a land of myth, of djinns and of peris and of a gymnosophism which Europeans were encountering in India. Its rulers demonstrated many of the characteristics of the Ottoman and Arab Caliphs before them, but Persians were heretics to the Sunni Islam of the Ottomans, and historic enemies of Arabs. Their Shia-ism seemed a repository of a more Romantic and eclectic religion. The land was after all the homeland of the Parsis of western India, its inhabitants the children of the magus Zoroaster who 'met', according to Shelley, 'his own shadow walking in the garden'. It was a natural setting for the English *Gil Blas*, the oriental Figaro, the barber Hajji Baba of Ispahan. Such a society, less threatening than the Ottoman's, was also the perfect location for a true Romantic dream: of poetry, magic, love and war, and of a virgin 'soft as roses', *Lalla Rookh*.

Hovering over all relations between West and East was the myth of the Crusades. Whether they were aggressive wars to carve out colonies or defensive struggles to roll back an alien conquest, to most Romantics they were a wasteful demonstration of ideological dedication, sanctified by the myth of chivalry. As most of them had lived through an era of almost total war, their view was that the past should now be replaced by an era of enlightenment, civilisation and amiability. Laughter should replace terror, and love replace force. As, on the whole, they repudiated organised religion, they gave little thought to reconciling alien religions to each other. Only Disraeli, an Anglican, who was also a Jew, thought in his novel, *Tancred*, that it might be possible.

2

A most elaborate dream of the Orient was forming in Coleridge's subconscious mind when he was summoned to the door by an importunate visitor from Porlock, one of the more famous interruptions in history. It centred on Kublai Khan, grandson of Genghis, whose dominions stretched from Korea to the borders of Hungary, and whose horde swept down to the Straits of Malacca and across most of the lands ruled by the later Ottoman empire. The Mongols had smashed the coalescing power of Arab Islam, contributing to the rescue of Christian Europe from conquest and conversion by the sword. But Coleridge did not dream of pillage, of mounds of skulls, of heathen or barbaric splendour, which had been hitherto the staple of travellers' tales, but of a stately pleasure dome in Xanadu, wrapped in the mist of oriental dreams: caverns measureless to man, the stately sinuous flow of a sacred river, a sunless sea, incense-bearing trees and forests virtually untouched by human hands.

The poem is an iconostasis of Romantic imagery. Coleridge imagines he is tempted to build a palace inspired by an air, sung by an Abyssinian maid playing on a dulcimer. As a paragon of sensibility with flashing eyes and floating hair, Coleridge defies the mundane world; he has fed on honeydew and drunk the milk of Paradise. He intended to but never did finish the poem, in which his mind, partially drugged by opiates against his indisposition at the time, peopled a Romantic land which ranged from the historic China of Marco Polo, about which he was reading when he fell asleep, to mysterious subterranean caverns and palaces of sensual pleasure which are so often the location of *The Arabian Nights*. An Ethiopian slave girl provides languorous music to accompany the magical banquets which djinns and houris provide in Paradise. For years the East had provided images of a world of sharp contrast to Renaissance and Enlightenment Europe, one where a shifting magic ruled, where sensual indulgence was steeped in idleness, where stuffs and foods were intricate in texture and vivid in colour. Turkish armies might press deep into Europe, the kettledrums might rimbombate, the sabres might flash, and death might preside with strange indifference over fate but, behind them, in the quiet enclosure of the harem gardens, the bulbul sang and the lute twanged, and there were, as Byron had it, 'virgins soft as roses'.[2]

3

Since the early eighteenth century *The Arabian Nights Entertainments* had been the source of oriental dreams in the West. Set in the caliphate of Harun ar Rashid, the Arab ruler from 789 to 809 of an empire centred on Baghdad which stretched from North Africa to Central Asia, they were the quintessential tales of Araby and Persia. A contemporary of Charlemagne and keen enemy of Byzantium, Harun admired the shadowy power of the first and the exotic culture of the second, and sought to emulate both in his own capital, creating an Arabo-Persian culture that became identified with Islam, and of which the Ottomans were heirs. Byron never penetrated as far as Persia, so that his virgins were all Ottoman, but Persia had for centuries been a land of romantic associations, ever since Tamburlaine had thought it was brave to be a king and ride in triumph through Persepolis. The eighteenth-century tales of magic and Magi, djinns and peris, of passionate love and wildly beautiful women, first translated into French, became instantly as popular as the fairy tales of Charles Perrault.

But behind the genial fancy there presided a ruler who epitomised the theory of absolute rule, the lordship of life and death, whose very gesture was law. One Persian ruler, Xerxes I, had crossed the Hellespont and, but for the heroic resistance of the Greeks, would in the opinion of the West have stamped the Balkans as a satrapy of an oriental despotism. Baulked first by Rome and then by Byzantium, the East in the person of the Ottoman Turks had finally in 1453 succeeded in transporting this despotism across the straits that divided Europe from Asia and had subdued the guardians of freedom. Inexorably, over the century that followed the fall of Constantinople, they built up a world empire.

Like all world empires, its very size and diversity, stretching as it did from the Danube to the Euphrates, determined its weakness and final dissolution. By the eighteenth century it was on the retreat. Since the annihilation of the Hungarian army at Mohacs field in 1526, Europeans had learned to resist, then to defeat, the formidable engine of war that was the Ottoman army and, by the end of the nineteenth century, the expulsion of the Turks, 'bag and baggage', from Europe did not seem the impossibility of a hundred years earlier. By then the Romantics had transformed the image of Turkey, from irresistible conqueror to sick man of Europe.

4

The schoolboys of Europe throughout the centuries had been fed the legends of the ancient world, creating powerful myths of an all-wise Hellas, nursery of democracy and democratic freedoms, and were all as a result, if Percy Bysshe Shelley is to be believed, at heart Hellenes. The Greeks had held Persia at bay at Marathon, and Greece had been the bulwark against the ominous East until, deserted by friends and allies, John Paleologus had fallen defending the walls of Byzantium in 1453. The Greeks had refused, however, to be absorbed into the Ottoman empire, which was never interested in absorbing them as long as they paid their blood tax and refrained from causing trouble. When Byron crossed into Ottoman Greece in 1809, he entered occupied country, where the Ottomans were intruders, satisfied, like good colonial administrators, if the revenue came in and the peace was kept. Ottoman policy was to allow the native Christians and Jews, believers in an incomplete monotheistic revelation consummated by Islam, to continue in their own ways, their religious leaders accepting responsibility for their good behaviour on pain of summary execution if it was bad.

Byron's eastern poems, by concentrating on conflicts between, on the one side, giaours, pirates and what we should now call resistance movements, and on the other Turkish pashas or renegade Europeans commanding Turkish armies, supported the belief that Greeks must be in the vanguard of liberation from an oppressive tyrant. Greece had thwarted Xerxes, and been engaged in almost ceaseless war with Persia until Alexander the Great added her to his vast empire. Now Greece was back in the front line, striving to throw off the Turkish yoke that had been imposed in 1453. Byron, however, was fair to his Turks. They were true to the qualities of their faith and to their honour, but as every English schoolboy had been taught to consider Greece his spiritual home from which he imbibed the feeling that he was uniquely independent and free, the Turk was fated to be the loser. This was particularly the case when what became known as Byron's *Turkish Tales* pitted true love against sexual slavery.

Shelley never crossed the Adriatic but, soaked in the liberation waters of that and the Aegean Seas, he readily accepted the Turk as loser. For him the Greek rebellion of 1821 was the rising of an enslaved people, inspired by their past glories to overthrow tyranny. It must triumph. For years the relentless rise of Russian power seemed to promise that she would be the nemesis of the Ottomans who had brought the East into Europe, but Turkey obstinately remained sprawled across the Balkans. Just as at Marathon the Greeks had thrown back the Persians, so now it was the destiny of the numerous subjugated Greeks of the mountainous highlands to cast out the Ottoman invader.

In Pisa Shelley, instructed by his Phanariot Greek friends, was right to mistrust the Russian agenda; but he also suspected that the British government was just as much not to be trusted. The fear that Russia had profound ambitions in the Balkans which would threaten Britain's security in

India, a fear which Wellington held very strongly, made the government's support for Greek independence seem feeble and half-hearted. An independent Greece as a satellite of Russia was as much an unwelcome prospect for Britain as it was for Austria. Metternich feared the contagion of revolution which, he warned the Tsar Alexander I, could infect the Russian empire herself. The British hoped that an arrangement acceptable to Constantinople could give the Greeks a sort of autonomy within the Ottoman empire short of total independence, and so help to avoid a major war between the Ottomans and Russia.

Romantic imagination not *realpolitik*, however, prevailed when Sultan Mahmud II, whose suppression of the Janissaries fatally wounded his power to resist Russian arms, called in Mehemet Ali's French-trained Egyptians successfully to reverse the early disasters of the Greek rising. Public outrage in Europe over his methods made intervention inevitable. A fateful agreement of the three admirals of Britain, France and Russia to deny supplies to Mehemet's son, Ibrahim Pasha, led to an unplanned but decisive sea battle at Navarino on 20 October 1827, in which the Ottoman armada was destroyed. Ibrahim's continued campaign of successful pacification and suppression could not be sustained.

Six years later, a Bavarian prince landed to take over a new kingdom, under the protection of Britain, France and Russia. The intervening years had been consumed in disputing the actual status of Greek sovereignty and finally, to avoid a dispute with Britain, the Tsar accepted that independent Greece should not be a Russian protectorate and renounced any territorial gains at the expense of Turkey. But in practical politics, Romanticism had been forced to equivocate, for the Greeks had, by the behaviour of their leaders and the unjustified ferocity of their fighters, all but forfeited the accolade of a new and idealised Christian state. Despite this, however, in the end it was Romantic enthusiasm that triumphed.

5

When the Napoleonic wars were over there was an attempt to revive the Grand Tour, but things had changed. Italy was no longer the cheap and enticing land which a man had to visit to finish off his education. The world had grown larger, horizons had expanded and adjustments were needed to survive in it. The Mediterranean, in particular, was no longer just the easiest way to get to Italy; it was the fabled sea that led to other fabled lands. What might have been Napoleon's dream of a passage for armies to reach India by land now seemed alarmingly feasible; and the great obstacle in the approaches to the East, the formerly dangerous and hostile lands of the Ottoman and Persian empires, which forced travellers to go to India round the Cape, had become weaker, friendly, almost welcoming. The Barbary pirates, moreover, who had for two centuries menaced the European Atlantic and Mediterranean ports were about to be tamed.

The glory that was Greece and the grandeur that was ultramarine Rome were now more accessible. Mighty Roman cities in North Africa and the Near East beckoned, and more ancient civilisations than the Greece of Thucydides began to expose their treasures. The study of ancient civilisation was no longer the monopoly of those who had a conventional classical education. A Scottish laird and coal-owner, James Bruce, set off to discover the sources of the Nile. Lord Byron embarked on a tour of Ottoman lands with no intention of discovering the soul of Greece. An Italian adventurer, by profession a circus strong-man, pioneered the discovery of the Egypt of the Pharaohs. Two aristocratic ladies sought the apotheosis of femininity in the Arabian Levant. From being the object of sporadic raids by Muslim pirates, Britain and the Netherlands were, after 1815, rulers in the east of Muslim populations larger than that of the Ottoman empire itself.

It was a new world and 'orientalism' was born. The Ottomans were at a moment in their history when they were weakest. Assailed by Napoleon in Egypt they had had to call on British assistance. Just as Europeans were dismantling the *pax Napoleonica*, the Turks were tempted to restore the *pax Ottomanica* which had been slowly eroded at its antipodes, by suppressing the stirrings of Greek revolt. It was a mistake. Though they had been doing this without interruption over many years a new spirit of nationalism had been born during the Napoleonic era, so that the Ottomans were assailed as tyrants oppressing the land where Liberty was born. It was a Romantic image, unreal but strong, and it proved too strong for the Turks.

For the Greek War of Independence became another crusade against a benighted power which, behind a tapestry of gorgeous colour and voluptuous pleasure, was seen to be basically hostile to the enquiring and thrusting intelligence of Europe. The Ottoman empire was ruled by a despot who was not enlightened, as the European despots claimed to be. Islam, moreover, which prevented it from embracing Enlightenment, was held to be as hostile as it had seemed to be throughout European crusading history, when resistance to invasive Islam was a Christian virtue. As a culture it had little to offer the investigative, arrogant *Weltanschauung* of 'enlightened' Europe. For the few whose sympathies with Islamic culture were profound there were many more whose views were born of prejudice and cultural alienation. The Romantic artists and poets of the day were affected by it, and Romantic travellers viewed its world either with a sinister focus, or with an air of ridicule and contempt.

6

For this, Romanticism itself was largely responsible. Prejudices are not born, nor do they die, quickly. On both sides of the divide today the notion of a crusade or jihad persists, though on the European side it is more utilitarian than ideological, more a matter of wishing rather than forcing attitudes, such as democracy or women's liberation, on Muslims. Muslims, for their part, are less offended by religious hostility – that has been the stuff of their history – than by ridicule. Ridicule is an attack on the roots of their culture. The Romantics found Muslim nations backward and unenlightened. They exposed them to mockery, their absurdities appealing to aesthetic dilettantes such as William Beckford, who wrote a whole fantasy novel pretending to be an oriental. The heroes of two Swiftian satires on human affairs were Persian barbers, the first James Morier's *Hajji Baba of Ispahan*, who gave us his picaresque autobiography as an oriental *Gil Blas*, the second George Meredith's Shigli Bagarat, court barber of Persia, who succeeded against powerful djinns and even more powerful thaumaturges in shaving the mighty sorcerer, Shagpat. Fantasy and mockery were, it was hoped, a more humane and peaceful way of disturbing ancient mores than force, but they did not help understanding.

Though he wrote only one novel actually set in the East, Walter Scott was fascinated by the conflict between East and West, less in the conflict itself, more in its effect on society at home. In one of his novels about the Crusades, *Ivanhoe*, the central characters may be crusaders but they are not on the Crusade, and in another, *The Betrothed*, they have not yet gone on the Crusade for which they had taken the vow. Only in *The Talisman* did Scott locate his characters on the Crusade itself, but set the novel in a period of truce between the two sides. In that way he could explore the characters of the two men who had fascinated historians since the Middle Ages: Saladin, and Richard Coeur de Lion.

In his unfinished last work, *The Siege of Malta*, he described Turks at war, the mode in which they were best known, but what interested Scott was whether the glories and follies of chivalry had survived into the early modern era. Its most shining exemplars, Ivanhoe and Saladin, are both driven not by ambition or religious enthusiasm, but by a desire to be champions of chivalry. Its two least worthy exemplars are Templar knights, for whom loyalty to an ideology is more important, if ultimately corrupting, than to a person or institution. Scott was ambivalent about crusading. In *The Betrothed*, he recognised that the Crusades were remote and irrelevant to the Wales of the thirteenth century; but in *The Siege of Malta*, he accepted that they had formed Malta's national consciousness. Scott's cool perception may have been modern in its day but his pen had set the imagination of Europe soaring into its medieval past, just as *The Arabian Nights* had awakened it to the magic of the East. Tannhauser, the crusader, was born of Scott from the head of Wagner.

7

The conquest of India only slowly had its effect on the British national consciousness. The romance of India was not immediately inspirational, since men went there to make money and hoped to survive to bring it home. The nabobs were not known for their patronage of the arts, but as new imperatives demanded a special breed of Company servant, so the nature of those who managed its affairs began to change. Relations with the Country Powers demanded language skills for trade and diplomacy; the lingua franca was Persian and the seductions of Persian poetry became as enticing and as well known to Persian learners as Catullus and Horace were to schoolboys who knew the Latin poets better than poets in their own language.

The appointment of William Jones as Chief Justice to the East India Company in Bengal was the high water mark of orientalism, when an enthusiast could claim, seventy years before Macaulay disclaimed it, that the epics of ancient India and the Persian treasury of songs were worthy to rank with the finest work of Greece and Rome. The hitherto largely philistine rulers of the ever expanding dominions of John Company in India now went into the field with Hafiz and Kabir in their knapsacks, while the more desk-bound pored over the *Ramayana* and *Mahabharata* for clues to understanding their puzzling Brahman subjects.

The end of the Napoleonic wars had established Britain's permanent interest in India, a land no longer in contestation with France but now threatened by the slowly encroaching Asiatic power of Russia. The Ottomans and Persians were not enough to be effective buffer states and so began the penetration by Company servants of the Persian and Afghan border lands to establish friendly emirates. It brought the British into the vale of Kashmir and the hinterland of Turkestan, where fresh breezes blew, roses bloomed and the bulbul sang of love between beautiful people. So sang the Irish minstrel, Byron's friend and biographer, Thomas Moore. Byron had given the world *Turkish Tales* which were intended to inflame the beating heart of burgeoning love set in the land of the harem.[3] Moore now did the same for Mughal and Persian India in *Lalla Rookh*. For authenticity he drew on the tales of travellers who had journeyed the hard way, and in doing so created a drawing room epic as popular and as ubiquitous as the images of India engraved by the Daniels, uncle and nephew.

8

Giacomo Casanova for a short time had an ill-defined official mission to Constantinople during which he was denied his usual access to women. Despite this frustration he admitted that the Turk was a gentleman, a point emphasised by Mozart and his librettist when the Pasha Selim behaved with generosity believed to be uncharacteristic in a Turk in his opera *Die Entführung aus dem Serail*. Lady Mary Wortley Montagu, wife of the British ambassador to the Sublime Porte at the opening of the eighteenth century, had already established that Turkish women were gentlewomen, and were sublime when naked at the baths or dressed in costumes worth a king's ransom. At the end of that century Constantinople was almost an amusing place to visit. Mozart wrote, in jest admittedly, protesting to his friend about bad verses he had written for Salzburg, that he 'was quite capable of going off to Constantinople, that city whose praises all chant.'[4] Moreover, the Turk was becoming amiable. He was even a figure of fun. When the Turk visited Italy, Rossini paired him off with his old flame, a gipsy, and when Isabella visited Algiers she made the Turkish Pasha join a drinking club and become a *pappataci* (a word Isabella invents, though its exact meaning is sand fly, a biting, itching *dipteroid* which infests Mediterranean shores).

The Turk, too, could even be a desirable husband, if he limited his appetite for women. If not a Sultan, a Pasha might be monogamous, and part of the attraction of the Sheik of Araby as a Romantic icon was that, though a champion cherisher of women, he could signify his devotion to one woman by eschewing others when there was no economic imperative to do so. Indeed, there might be powerful familial and clan imperatives to do the opposite. The battle for dominion and faith was becoming a battle of the sexes.

Yet despite the weakening of fear, the twenty-first-century doubts about secular Turkey becoming a member of the European Union stem from the persistence of a belief, left by the Romantics, that the divide between Christian Europe and the Islamic lands of the former Ottoman and Persian empires cannot truly be bridged, either by serious study or by good-natured humour. This belief originated in fear of Islamic military power, but it was stoked by the Romantic notion of Islam as an enemy of progress. It persists today because the clash of prejudice is taking place in European market places, schools and benevolent institutions. The attempt to conceal it beneath a shroud called multiculturalism is failing because it only conceals, not changes. The end of this conflict is not imminent, for it is stoked by Romantic images of femininity and freedom, which challenge the historic myth of the East, that man and his religion must rule, and this is the ineluctable will of Allah, otherwise known as God. In Malta, that most Roman Catholic of islands, the word for God is Allah. In modern multilingual Malaysia, the education department had to decree that it was permissible to refer to Allah as God and God as Allah as they were the same person and could not be belittled by either title.[5]

How these beliefs and fantasies were stoked by the Romantics is the subject of the chapters that follow. Kipling, who had a better insight than most into the phenomenon, averred that 'East is East, and West is West, and never the twain shall meet, / Till Earth and Sky stand presently at God's great judgment seat.' Mere earthlings are not God, but the more they know how the myths were created the better they may be able to discount them.

CHAPTER ONE

The Empire of Osman

The Turkish Myth

Turkey is a dying man. We may endeavour to keep
him alive but we shall not succeed.
(Emperor Nicholas I of Russia: 1825–55)

I

OSMAN (1259–1326) WAS a small chieftain's son from the upper Euphrates
who seized his opportunity when the Seljukian sultanate fell apart in
the wake of the Mongol horde. Establishing his base in the Anatolian hills
near the modern capital of Ankara, he gradually pushed back the Byzantine
colonies, until at his death he faced Constantinople itself across the Sea of
Marmara at Brusa. The empire of Osman, the founder of the dynasty of
Ottomans (which is the European rendering of his name), expanded in the
centuries that followed to become a world power and was by 1850 to last
another seventy years before Tsar Nicholas's prophecy was finally fulfilled
(see epigraph above). Its survival was largely due to the extraordinary nature
of the state of which the Ottoman Sultan had become the head. Despite his
Turkic origins, the Ottoman emperor, who had no hint of apostolic
succession to the Prophet, had assumed to himself not only the secular role
of king or sultan but also the semi-religious role of vice-gerent of God or
Caliph, leader of all Muslim peoples, which had been vested by the Arab
successors of the Prophet in rulers who traced a blood line to Mahomet. The
Caliph, as opposed to a mere emperor or king who could exercise his own
caprice, was to rule guided by Islamic precept and law. His task was to
protect the morals as well as the interests of all his people. The Caliphate was
intended to be a paradigm of good government, and to rule by divine law. It
had been located at various times in the past in Baghdad, Cordoba and Cairo;

by the sixteenth century CE it was in Constantinople, where the Ottomans exhibited both the strengths and weaknesses of Caesaro-Papism.[1] An awful power was invested in the person of the Sultan, moderated only by fear of his immediate entourage of wives, eunuchs and overmighty viziers.

At its apogee the Ottoman Empire was as powerful and extensive as had been the Roman. It stretched from the borders of Morocco to those of Iran, from the Indian Ocean to Belgrade and round the Black Sea to southern Russia. Its armies had reached the walls of Vienna. It dominated the eastern Mediterranean, the Balkans, the Near East and North Africa and only stopped short at the frontiers of five empires. One was the Empire of Morocco, ruled by a lineal descendant of the Prophet whom it would be an act of sacrilege to attack. Morocco had never been part of the Ottoman Empire; it was an Arab state subject only to Arabs. The second empire was the Persian which, through history, had aspired to the realms now ruled by the Ottoman. Iran had been once conquered by Arabs and evangelised by Muslims, but it had been Islamised, only lightly Arabised, and never Ottomanised. For centuries, even before and despite their conversion to Islam, Iranians had entertained a historic antipathy to Arab peoples.

The Ottomans, however, had been 'Persianised' by the letters and culture of a very ancient civilisation. As the Greeks were to the Romans, so Persia was to the central Asiatic Turks who had conquered Anatolia and the Balkans, who had subdued the Arab lands adjacent to the old Persian empire, the Levant, Mesopotamia, Egypt and North Africa. The Ottomans were also largely Sunni Muslims, the Persians Shi-ites, a distinction almost as great as Catholic and Protestant in the West. The Ottomans had enemies on both flanks.

The western flank was occupied by the third empire, that of Austria, the protector and champion of Catholic Europe, now steadily encroaching on the extended lands of the Osmanlis. A new and potentially lethal threat, however, came from the fourth empire, in the north. Since the time of Catherine the Great, Russia as the third Rome looked on the European lands which had once formed part of the Byzantine empire as *terra irredenta*, and the Empress dreamed of extending her dynasty to Constantinople and aspired to expand her territories into Muslim Asia. There the Ottoman Turks had originated, but it was now a vast land of petty chieftains who were not amenable to Ottoman, indeed to any rule, but that of their own khans.

The fifth empire was the empire of sand, and consisted of the huge, largely empty land from the south of the Barbary coast to the western shore of the Red Sea, so far unconquerable. The empires that had subsisted there had been asphyxiated for a millennium by drifts of sand, beyond which lay the mountainous stronghold of the stubbornly resistant Christian empire of 'Prester John' in Ethiopia, and the independent but Muslim, mainly Wahabi, pirate states of the Red Sea. Beyond to the east lay Hindustan, an empire ruled by descendants of the Asian Mongolian horde, for whom distant Rum or Constantinople was little more than a legend of splendour and power. The Mughals, a Turkic people who had been resolutely Persianised, looked east and not west and were, by the eighteenth century, suffering from a crisis of power in a sub-continent disputed by Hindu warlords and aggressive European mercantile companies.

The society of both the Ottomans and, to a lesser extent, Persians was largely urban, dependent on a hinterland of conquered and diverse peoples. The Ottomans relied heavily on Arabs, Turkomans, Jews, Armenians and Europeans, mainly Greeks, and on colonists imported from Asia, to work the land to feed them, to carry on trade to enrich them, to provide an élite fighting force to protect them, and to manage the intricate tasks of administration for which the Osmanlis had little stomach. The Sultan in Constantinople ruled a motley population of subject races who provided the sinews of the state and whose privileged servants had been converted in youth to Islam, the dominant though not the domineering religion of these people. To profess oneself a Muslim was comparatively simple, but it was impossible to deny one's faith once adopted. For those who were not, and did not wish to turn Muslim, there was a broad tolerance and dependence on their services, which were particular to their race. Jews and Armenians dominated the commercial and banking sectors, Greeks the marine trade and the fleet. Although every official of the empire was technically a slave of the state, and held his position from the Sultan, and could lose it and his life virtually at a whim, he enjoyed considerable liberty as long as he kept his place and demonstrated his loyalty.

A Pasha or local governor might be of any of the ethnic origins and might well be a renegade from his natal religion, provided that he was a Muslim. Those who were charged to collect the taxes had gradually acquired immunity from sudden or capricious change and had become a landed gentry, engrossing land from revenue they could cream off from tax farming. By the seventeenth century, as this class began to replace the specially trained and converted slaves, who were brought up to be creatures of the Sultan, and dependent on his will, the administration was beginning to exhibit both the strengths and weaknesses of a hereditary caste. By the end of the eighteenth century the administrators of the empire were more loyal to their caste than to their ruler.

Communities of the book – Christians, Armenians and Jews – had their own civic structures and laws and, provided they kept the peace and paid the taxes which fell more heavily on them than on Muslims, they were immune from persecution. The head of each community was bound over to keep his followers obedient and peaceful. When it was suspected they were not they paid the price, as at the beginning of the Greek War of Independence in April 1821, when the Oecumenical Patriarch, Gregorius V, was hanged at one of the gates of the Patriarchate. Even after the Greeks had, by the early nineteenth century, successfully wrested complete independence from Ottoman rule, their indispensable skills in translation, interpretation and negotiation meant that many of them never ceased to service the Ottoman Empire.

From 1570 the force that had seemed to have Europe in its fist had been less able to carry all before it. This was partly because the Europeans had become more united and able to resist Turkish armies, but also because those institutions, which had been forged to ensure the empire's triumph, were beginning to change their nature, and to decline from the high point of their efficiency. The empire at its best was basically a bureaucratic construct which was more pervasive and heavy handed that that of most European states as they changed from feudal into nation states. While the bureaucracy was relentlessly efficient, the Sultan was increasingly confined to his seraglio and became a prisoner of its bureaucracy, often a tool of court favourites, or of the eunuchs who clustered round a masterful Sultana. Oligarchs, headed sometimes by the Grand Vizier himself, or by an alliance of provincial governors who set up local dynasties, weakened the centre. Some, particularly the men who ruled the North African Regencies, owed as much loyalty to the Sultan in Constantinople as the Electors of the Holy Roman Empire owed to the Holy Roman Emperor they had elected.

Despite the nominal suzerainty of Constantinople, these north African Regencies – Algiers, Tunis and Tripoli – had for over a century been effectively ruled by virtually independent deys (Algiers) and beys (Tunis and Tripoli), sustained by the fruits of piracy and the ransoms paid for Christian captives. By the end of the eighteenth century the Sultan had also lost control of Egypt to the Mamelukes, descendants of Caucasian slaves originally imported to support the Caliphate in Cairo. The Ottoman writ no longer ran along the northern coast of the Black Sea, lost to Russia, and pirates menaced the shipping in the Red Sea and the approaches to the Persian Gulf. The Danubian provices had become virtually self-governing under native princes, while the industrialisation of Europe had reduced the market for Turkish exports. The cost of wars, especially with Russia, in which the Turks did not carry all before them imposed serious strains on the people, especially the heavy taxes imposed on a predominantly agricultural and thus demonetised economy.[2] The formidable, indeed once terrible, empire of Ottoman Turkey had become in one Romantic imagination little more than an Imperial cornucopia, like a food emporium, where

> Candied apple, quince and plum, and gourd
> … Jellies soother than the creamy curd,
> And lucent syrups tinct with cinnamon;
> Manna and dates, in argosy transferred
> From Fez; and spiced dainties, every one,
> From silken Samarkand and cedared Lebanon.[3]

2

As trade with Turkey grew, so Europeans acquired greater knowledge of a world which had formerly been both menacing and seductive, based on racial ignorance and religious prejudice. Even so, as late as 1840, a traveller crossing into the European dominions of the Ottoman Empire felt as if he were about to experience the Splendour and Havoc of the East. The Austrian customs officials would wring his hand and bid farewell to anyone so intrepid as to leave the civilised world, and march over the border, 'sternly prepared for death, for the Koran, or even for plural wives'. A dragoman, interpreter, *valet de voyage* and essential 'fixer', was there to see one through the Splendour and bore the tedium of oriental politeness and loquacity on the traveller's behalf. Not very far into Turkish Serbia the traveller would meet the Havoc, the skulls of rebel Serbs piled into pyramids, and the mortal remains of robbers, mostly impaled upon high poles, so that 'their skeletons, clothed with some white, wax-like remains of flesh, sat lolling in the sunshine, listlessly staring without eyes'.[4]

The Ottoman army that had once been the scourge and terror of the western world, was no longer invincible. The corps of Janissaries, founded in 1438 from the ranks of European and Caucasian children taken from their parents early and reared to be devoted slaves of the Sultan, ready for instant action in any theatre of war, had degenerated into a private army. The word Janissary meant, in Turkish, new troops, and since 1330 the hitherto irregular army of the Ottomans, which signed up for the campaigning season and otherwise acted as a sort of home guard, had been replaced by regiments of 'stolen children' forcibly impressed by recruiting parties that scoured the empire's Christian lands. In 1438 Suleiman the Magnificent had formed them into a *corps d'élite* at the personal command of the Sultan, and throughout the sixteenth century they became a feared and favoured army open to talent and sensational promotion. Christian parents were often only too happy to see their sons taken off to serve so powerful a sovereign, with so many rewards in his hand. But in 1700 taxes were levied rather than children, who were replaced by recruits. As the Ottoman Empire expanded in size so, too, had the corps of Janissaries, but as it declined the number of Janissaries did not diminish. When, in 1808, the Sultan Mahmud II abolished the order there were about 135,000 on the payroll, now stigmatised as 'a horde of over-privileged hereditary hangers-on with little or no military discipline'.[5]

In 1717 Lady Mary Wortley Montagu thought that the power of the Janissaries was pretty near unlimited. The one sent to attend on her ambassadorial presence offered her the head of the village chief (cadi) who had failed to provide pigeons for her supper. The brotherhood of Janissaries, she found, was such that 'the greatest man at the court never speaks to them but in a flattering tone, and anyone who wanted to preserve his estate took care to get himself enrolled in it.'[6] At their beginning Janissaries could not marry, engage in trade or escape military exercises for any reason but infirmity. They were, in secular terms, a sort of Muslim Society of Jesus, and their rules were remarkably similar. They vowed instant and unconditional obedience to their officers and through them to the Sultan and, abstaining from extravagant living, were always ready for action. Sectional competition was encouraged, so that each *orta* or division would vie with the others to be smarter, better drilled, more lethally armed, more prepared. Defeat in war or failure to suppress unrest spelled disgrace, so that, to ensure that they never failed, Janissary detachments acted with unbridled violence against both enemies and allies. The only way to avoid the oppression of the corps was by the payment of bribes, not so surprising when one considers that the Janissaries only received pay when on active duty, so that extortion, during extended periods of peace, became a necessary means of survival for all parties.

For all their devotion to the Sultan, the Janissaries by the end of the seventeenth century had developed a power they were often only too ready to exercise in their own interests. At best the corps was a limitation on the unbridled power of the Sultan, at worst it was a contumacious and potentially mutinous soldiery. In 1638 entry into the corps ceased to be by the impressment of 'stolen' and so, effectively, orphaned children, to be dedicated and trained to the service. They were replaced by the children, relatives or dependants of Janissaries themselves. Comparison with the Roman Praetorian Guard was frequently made as they became as effective an agent of disorder as they were of order. In Constantinople itself individual Janissaries took on other professions to augment their salaries and acted like a guild in defence of their own interests. The almighty Sultan himself was often helpless against their actions and in danger from them. Ambitious viziers would manipulate local Janissary garrisons; weak Sultans could be bullied into submission to their demands for largesse or immunity, or deposed, and a revolt of the Janissaries could block needed reforms.

The principal fear of the Ottomans, as it had been of the Byzantines, was that Constantinople was always in danger from the horde outside the walls. 'The very haughtiest of the Mussulmans believe that the gate is already in existence through which the red Giaours (the Russi) shall pass to the conquest of Stamboul; and that everywhere in Europe at least, the hat of Frangistan is destined to surmount the turban – the crescent to go down before the cross.'[7] During the Russian wars at the end of the eighteenth century the Janissaries had almost allowed this to happen, for they were no longer a match for their enemies. Many of them were too untrained to fire a gun, and they had to be replaced by regular troops, disciplined and trained in western methods. In 1807, for flirting with the French, Constantinople was threatened by a Russian army and a British fleet, and the Janissaries revolted against what they held was infidel influence on the Sultan over new uniforms, new drills and new soldiers. Two Sultans were deposed and murdered in the ensuing anarchy. It was the example of his Egyptian viceroy, Mehemet Ali – who had successfully destroyed the power of the hereditary Egyptian 'slave army', the Mamelukes (who nearly lost Egypt to the French in 1798) – that nerved Mahmud II, after initial insults and delinquencies, to destroy the Ottoman Janissaries.

The demise of the Janissaries started with a revolt on 10 June 1826. The war with the insurgent Greeks had gone disastrously badly. The Janissaries, to pre-empt possible retribution by showing their capacity for revolt, set out to kill their *aga* or commander-in-chief, were thwarted by his escape, ran amok and were finally shot down, burned out, and hanged by the regular troops against whom they had been waging virtual civil war. The slaughter lasted only a few days, and an order which had been the scourge and terror of Europe and the defender of the Ottoman faith and empire ceased to exist, destroyed by the new army which killed them under the sacred standard of the Prophet. The Sultan, who had sustained them over three centuries, had abandoned them.[8]

3

The Ottoman navy, which had produced a mighty armada to attack Malta in 1565, had never been a force comparable to the Janissaries, and in 1571 the annihilating victory of Lepanto showed that it no longer even ruled the waves of the eastern Mediterranean. Though the fleet soon recovered its numerical strength, it depended for navigation on non-Turks, mainly renegades, and was crewed by Greeks and by prisoners of war reduced to slavery. The precariousness of such dependency had been shown in 1748 when an Ottoman galley, with a provincial governor on board, was seized by its slave crew and sailed for freedom into Malta.[9] At the onset of the Greek War of Independence the Greeks who were Christians deserted Ottoman service, and became deadly privateers. The Greek islands that had plentifully supplied mariners for the Ottoman navy had enjoyed, as a result, virtual autonomy. Their devotion to the Greek cause meant that the Ottomans had great difficulty moving men or supplies from one sea to another, forcing them over the treacherous and mountainous inland routes, and thus contributing largely to the success of the early uprising.[10]

4

Despite thwarted territorial ambition, defeats in war, unrest at home and weak Sultans, the Ottoman Empire remained formidable until its end. Its many weaknesses had not damaged the unique source of its strength. Despite periodic occupation of the throne by sots, imbeciles, slaves to sensuality and triflers, no one until the early twentieth century attempted to change the institutional fountain of power: the Sultan in his seraglio. Few Europeans understood the dynamic of Ottoman society, and this was as much the fault of Ottoman lack of curiosity about the world as of the outsiders who observed it.[11] Persian and Arabic were the cultural languages of the empire, and Italian was the lingua franca that allowed Turks and Europeans to communicate. But on the whole the Ottomans were not interested in exchanging information and learning Western languages. They had plenty of ethnic interpreters for that. They were incurious about western advances in science and technology, and about the society of their enemies, for one day these enemies must deferentially acknowledge the supremacy of Islam, which taught all that one needed to know.

The Copernican cosmological theories only briefly came to Turkish notice towards the end of the seventeenth century and aroused little interest. There were few real accounts of Europe by Ottoman writers before the end of the seventeenth century, when the empire needed to know about Europe for its survival. Moroccans, having a powerful and implacable enemy on their borders, were more curious but though there were more Ottomans going to Europe than Moroccans, accounts of their experiences are far fewer. Europe, paradoxically, was the area of the world about which the Ottomans were least curious.[12] Even in the fourteenth century, at the apogee of Islamic intellectual dominance, Islam's most curious travellers, Ibn Batuta and Ibn Khaldun, had no desire or incentive to learn anything much about Christendom.[13]

Though European interest in the Ottoman Empire for two centuries of its history had not been much more enquiring, in the seventeenth and eighteenth centuries, as the quest for world knowledge expanded among Europeans, men of letters and historians began to enquire into the mysterious world of the Orient which began on the Serbian borders and on the shores of the Levant. Their embassies in Constantinople exchanged information and relayed it home. Much of it was inaccurate since it relied on interpreters and hearsay, for interaction with Ottomans themselves was slow to develop. European expansion into Asia had begun at much the same time as the fourth great Islamic empire was forming, on the fringes of the Ottoman and Persian empires, and one of the ironies of history was that the Europeans knew more about the Mughal Empire in Delhi than Constantinople ever bothered to learn. Relations between the two Turkic peoples were confined to little more than politeness.[14]

Merchants, missionaries and diplomatists had work to do on behalf of those who had sent them, and the reports to their principals, sometimes published, did not much extend the knowledge the West had of the Islamic lands. Theirs was the most extensive view of the Ottomans with whom there had been diplomatic relations since the sixteenth century, and of what was termed the Levant with whom trade had been lively for generations. Information was less extensive about Iran where trade was weaker, and very limited about North Africa, where the memories of ransomed prisoners of piracy were largely of their horrendous experience, often exaggerated to ensure generous contributions to their ransom money. Most of the travellers, however, who had no commercial business there were in search of the ancient world they had been taught about at school, with the intention rather of learning more about Hellas and the Hellenes than about the Ottomans that ruled there. By the middle of the eighteenth century when it was becoming easier, and safer, to visit the east, they were anxious to visit the Greek and Roman lands of Europe, Asia Minor and North Africa from which they had been deterred by the lure of Italy, fear of the plague and of having to spend quarantine in a noisome Levantine lazaretto. Moreover, the Ottomans until the end of the eighteenth century had been the enemies of 'Europe', and venturing into a war zone with different rules of engagement could spell trouble for friends and family.

Two things in particular were dismantling this barrier by 1800. First, the Ottomans had become, with Napoleon's invasion of Egypt, allies in the war against the French and, with Russia's defection from the second coalition, a bulwark against Russian hegemony in south-eastern Europe. Secondly, it was after 1801 possible to complete one's quarantine in Malta after the island had been freed of the French, spending just 14 days in relative comfort as opposed to a week in oriental squalor. Italy, moreover, was pretty nearly exhausted of treasures to buy or steal and her governments were making difficulties over acquisition. The comparative ease with which the British ambassador to the Porte, Lord Elgin, had been able to negotiate the removal of the marbles that bear his name indicated a whole new field of exploitation.

5

There was a general impression among simple people in Ottoman lands that English travellers were protected by evil demons, but all that was demonic about them was the length of their purse.[15] That purse could buy adventure without danger, uncertainty without catastrophe, and erotic excitement without assassination. These had all attracted Byron, but most travellers, like William Leake, who had a semi-official position in Albania when Byron went there in 1809, entered Ottoman lands primarily to find and identify the relics of the ancient Greek and Roman world which littered them. Few went purely for pleasure, but not everybody was in search of the classical past, to which Edward Gibbon had provided a historical guide. Alexander Kinglake, for one, in the 1840s did not share an antiquarian interest in ruins. His 'pagan soul's desire' was to live through this (ancient) world, as a 'favoured mortal under the old Olympian dispensation' and to 'believe for one rapturous moment, to speak out my resolves to the listening Jove and hear him answer with approving thunder'.[16] It was not to hear the thunder of Turkish army bands or the roll of those guns that had once echoed over Constantinople and Vienna.

Not that there was a great deal of thunder, even, from Jupiter *Tonans*. Travellers such as Kinglake remarked on the 'sad and sombre decorum that outwardly reigns through the lands oppressed by Moslem sway'. He attributed it to the stern and gloomy morality which 'made beauty their prisoner'.[17] Vivant Denon, going ashore at Alexandria when Napoleon's expedition entered Aboukir Bay in 1798, marked the silence and the sadness of the town, the only noise and activity that reminded him of Europe coming from the sparrows.[18] He did not attribute this silence to fear of the French invaders despite, or perhaps because of, their profession that they were in Egypt to support Ottoman rule. As a much later traveller remarked, there was little gaiety in Muslim lands, 'no *fandangos, siguiriyas gitanas* or *sevillanas*'.[19]

For the empire of Osman was ruled by its holy book, the Koran, by analects and sayings of the Prophet and by Shariah law as variously interpreted by its doctors, which united all Muslims in the *Sheikh-ul-Islam*. Ottomans, Arabs, Indians, Tartars, Persians, Chinese, Malays and African Muslims were subject to them. Despite its flexible, poetic text and its persuasive and reasonable injunctions on morality – in certain translations it reads as irenically as St Francis de Sales's *Introduction to a Devout Life* – the Koran had become as repressive and crabbed a repository of moral injunctions as the Old Testament, inhibiting that sense of enquiry that had once made Islamic scholars conquistadors of knowledge. There was the added claim that all that mankind needed to know was to be found in its pages, and from this there could be no deviation. It was the very word of God taken down in longhand. If the Prophet had added things of his own, they were still infallible pronouncements. Holy texts have a way of becoming a source of information they were never written to provide, – as for example when Biblical numerology provided Bishop Ussher with a date for the Creation in 4004 BC. Muslim divines could therefore tell Napoleon's zoologist, Geoffroy Saint-Hilaire, searching the Egyptian fauna for new species, that, as Mahomet had already listed all species that existed, Saint-Hilaire was wasting his and their time.[20]

6

For most of its time the Christian world had feared the empire of Osman rather than Islam, and throughout the Middle Ages and the Renaissance, scholars had studied Arabic and other oriental tongues, such as Hebrew and Armenian, and the works of Arabic thinkers. It was less for what they would reveal about the civilisation and peoples who spoke them, than for what light they might throw on the Bible and Biblical times. Because of this bibliocentric interest, many teachers were Jews, some of them claiming cabbalistic knowledge, and, because the study of the languages was seldom linguistically profound, scholars were quick to see linguistic links, patterns and derivations which later study could not support. As a result, there was little interest in the book holy to Islam apart from what the Koran might teach students about the Bible. Arabic was primarily used as a means of communicating with oriental Christians, mainly in an effort to reconcile them to Rome. But there were dangers in its study. Islam was commonly seen not as a rival religion but as a form of heresy, akin to Protestantism, or as a revolt against conventional Christianity. It could be fatal to the soul.

Much scholarly time and energy was spent trying to distance the usefulness of Arabic from its dangers. Translations of the Koran, whether accurate or not, were generally frowned on when not condemned outright as anti-Christian or, when produced by non-Catholics, as anti-Catholic. Depending on the church to which the writer belonged the 'errors' of Mahomet were likened to those of Protestantism or of the Papacy and were often cited as weapons in the apostolic blows and knocks of religious debate. Many of those who studied Arabic with a wish to translate the Koran, being mostly Catholic or Protestant minor clergy, wished either to promote their particular Biblical thesis or to support a syncretist or hermetic interpretation of the divine mysteries.[21]

The pernicious association of Islam with the devil during the early Middle Ages had derived, not from its persecution of Christians, – Islam had a good record of respecting the 'people of the Book' – but from its effrontery in claiming and occupying Jerusalem as its own sacred city. By the end of the thirteenth century the founder of Islam, the prophet Mahomet, had been consigned by Dante to the eighth circle of the Inferno, not for being a limb of Satan but for sowing discord among the faithful, being no more, in contemporary eyes, than a Christian schismatic. His punishment was to be ceaselessly split by a cleaver from 'the chin to the fart-hole', wallowing in his tripes and 'the sordid sack that turns to dung the food it swallows'.[22]

Islamic folk-lore endowed the Prophet with as many supernatural qualities and achievements as the Apocryphal Gospels did Jesus, but in the vulgar view one major distinction between the two religious founders stood out. For Christians the divinity of Christ, and his chastity, had been divinely safeguarded and were articles of faith. Mahomet, on the other hand, needed no hypostasis to differentiate him from other men and was no abstainer from women; by his own marriage he sanctified and applauded sex and the bearing of children. Hostile western myth, in its own preference for the sanctity of celibacy, however, endowed him with precocious sexual appetites and power, having a plurality of wives – certainly more than the four permitted to lesser faithful. One supposedly Arab source claimed that Mahomet sexually exercised eleven of his wives in one hour.[23] The animosities bred by the Crusades, which did not cease until the end of the eighteenth century, blinded Christians to the true image of a great religious leader who dared successfully to declare a new covenant for new faithful.

By the eighteenth century, however, saner opinions were beginning to emerge, largely as a result of closer contact with Islam and of scholarly investigation. When reasonably authentic versions of the Koran became available, and oriental studies more sophisticated, Mahomet was upgraded to an eccentric religious genius, much as were the Baptist cobblers and carpenters of working-class Protestantism who went to evangelise India at the turn of the seventeenth/eighteenth century. His simple message was submission to the word of God – which in the absence of a patriarchal, even papal, authority to interpret it – was the word of the Prophet. The reward for such total submission was seen to be carnal stringency on earth and carnal bliss in heaven. In place of the beatific vision offered to Christians, Islam appeared to offer the more tempting prospect of virgins of 'ravishing beauty' and, as there would be plenty to go round and their virginity was imperishable, a man could have any number in proportion to his merits. His wives, denied access to this particular heaven, would not be there to cause any trouble over the arrangement.

Early attempts in the West to have a better understanding of Islam were none too successful. The publication of an English translation of the Koran in 1648 ran into difficulties, for the book was popularly thought to be both Satanic and seditious. The Council of State attempted to suppress it but, as religious toleration of 'Turks, Papists and Jews' had been proclaimed as the inalienable law of Great Britain, no ban on the translation could be imposed. It immediately inspired a prolonged and defamatory campaign in which *The True Nature of Imposture, Fully Displayed in the Life of Mahomet*, ran to several editions, with the intention of deterring apostasy among anyone falling into the hands of the Muslim pirates of North Africa, who might be seduced by the false message of the Koran. One clergyman, Simon Ockley, vicar of Swavesey near Cambridge, spent his spare time in the Cambridge libraries translating works of Arabic theology and scholarship, before embarking on a *History of the Saracens*, which he published in 1718. Ockley believed that it was time for a better understanding of Islam, but his shy and hesitant manner did not find a patron, so that he died in penury.[24] It was with the expansion of the merchant companies in India that a better knowledge of Islam was to become the aim of men whose works could not be silenced by contempt and prejudice.

Gibbon was discouraged from learning Arabic at Oxford, partly because there was no one who knew the language well enough to teach him. Much of the material about Islam and the Arabs in the later volumes of *The Decline and Fall* was gleaned from d'Herbelot's Islamic encyclopaedia and the work of George Sale, a merchant's son who spiced the tedium of his legal practice with a study of Arabic and the collection of an Arabic library. Sale tried his hand at a translation of the Koran (1774), described in the 1911 edition of the *Encyclopaedia Britannica* as *paraphrastic* but which, following closely the Latin translation of an Italian cleric, proved surprisingly buoyant. Sale was the only prominent orientalist at the time not to be in holy orders, though he was invited to check the accuracy of the Arabic translation of the New Testament as a tool for conversion. Gibbon wrote his great work without the knowledge of any oriental language but Greek.

Gibbon's intention, however, was not to pursue the truth or otherwise of Christianity but to demonstrate by a dispassionate narrative that, in the irrationality of their beliefs and in their general behaviour, Christian and Muslim were pretty well indistinguishable. His view of the Crusades reflected pretty well that of Walter Scott's Wilkin Flammock (*The Betrothed*); they were as vain and unproductive as most territorial wars of the time nearer home, which most monarchs, Richard Coeur de Lion excepted, preferred to fight.

7

Gibbon accepted, if he did not share, the underlying conviction that Christians of both East and West had a peculiar title to the Holy Land and that they felt obliged to defend it from the impiety of their pagan and Mahommedan foes. That impiety was not religious but political. A study of the Koran should have cleared Islam of the libel of ignorance and bigotry, but Mahommedan princes were, for eighteenth-century observers, 'tyrants and usurpers'.[25] Writers and partial students of the East such as Montesquieu had built on this belief, attributing the despotism of Asian empires to the lack of any system of private property, which had acted as a baulk to western rulers. That conferred a legitimacy on a colonial power, such as Britain in India, to confiscate native lands in the belief that it was owned anyhow by the defeated ruler, and in this way they became tyrants in their turn.[26]

The European *philosophes*, having decided that their own holy book was a jumble of myths and legends, both pre-lapsarian and post-lapsarian, of more anthropological than theological interest, turned to consider another holy book in similar terms. To most of them the Koran was the most significant factor in underpinning the despotism of Islamic rulers, in particular the three Muslim rulers of Turkey, Persia and Hindustan. The Ottoman Sultan, secure in the isolation of the seraglio, seemed to have succeeded best in establishing single and undivided rule over his dominions. He appeared to acknowledge only one limitation on his power – not any notion of natural law, but the law enunciated by the Prophet in the Koran. The book, written by the Prophet at the dictation of the archangel Gabriel himself (like St Augustine's doves, hovering close to his ear), was accepted, far more than the Bible, as being literally true and incontrovertibly right.

It had no rival. Its precepts were as immune from criticism as the firman of any despot, who was, in theory as well as practice, God's lieutenant on earth and must be the Prophet's vicar.[27]

Western commentators tried to draw a parallel between the respective roles of the Sultan and the Grand Mufti, who was the supreme interpreter of Islamic law under which the Sultan was bound, and those of the Holy Roman Emperor and the Pope. The dualism that put constraints on both the power of the emperor and of the pontiff did not seem to apply to the Islamic monarchs of Turkey, Persia, Morocco and Hindustan. It was assumed that any religious pontiff was, in effect, a creature of the Sultan/Shah/Emperor, who embodied in themselves both the sacred and secular power. All were, however, subject to Koranic limitation, which in practice provided the only check to the madness of power and the caprices of omnipotence.

Travellers found the devotion to the Koran, to its letter rather than spirit, impressive. It was learned by heart in Arabic, though this was not the learners' mother tongue, just as Latin had been an essential feature of western education, as the key to divine commands in possibly inaccurate translation. The dedication to rules of life as complex and often anachronistic as those of the Pentateuch demonstrated a dedication often lacking in Christians, though many of the pious practices, such as using amulets with gobbets of sacred scripture to protect against evil or harm, were to many observers as superstitious as any Christian. They were convinced that the unchallenged obedience to comparatively trivial precepts bred in the subject an unhealthy acceptance of arbitrary rule. Those who were convinced that Christianity was also an irrational religion used this assumption to warn people that dedication to any irrational religion could buttress tyranny, since it encouraged a tyrant or despot to behave as if he were the 'shadow' of God himself and thus to command obedience.[28] God had become the supreme tyrant. That made Islam a false religion against which Enlightenment must fight.

8

The French *philosophes* began to warn that Osmanli despotism was the model for a society starkly alternative to the informed and participative democracy they were promoting. The basic information about Islamic societies which was now reaching Europe might, most of it, be reasonably objective based on observed and proven fact, but what most ordinary people knew about the East was the wonder world of *The Arabian Nights Entertainments*: a society into whose imagination flitted genii (djinns), and sorcerers (magi) and sorceresses with alchemical powers, who were transported on magic carpets, or by mythical monsters, and who guarded treasure beyond the dreams of avarice. *The Entertainments* might cast a genial light on the world of faery but the eastern world had long been seen as the home of necromancy and magic, through which the spirits of the demonic world, over which presided the satanic figure of Eblis, could be evoked. There was scarcely an oriental tale that did not figure a sorcerer, or a djinn, or a slave with a magic talisman. Many of these tales, too, evoked the image of a solitary tyrant who could determine life or death with the flick of his fingers, sitting in the most potent myth of all, in the heart and power centre of Islamic society, the seraglio.[29]

CHAPTER TWO

The Sultan in his Seraglio

The Myth of the Despot

His sons were kept in prison, till they grew
Of years to fill a bowstring or a throne,
One or the other, but which of the two
Could yet be known unto the Fates alone;
Meantime the education they went through
Was princely, as the proofs have always shown;
So that the heir apparent still was found
No less deserving to be hang'd than crown'd.[1]

(Byron, *Don Juan*)

I

UPON WHAT WAS this popular image of the Sultan in his seraglio based? The seraglio was supposed to be where a Muslim lord took his pleasures. The canny Venetians, who sent sharp-eyed men to represent their interests at the court of the Grand Signor, had known better for two centuries, and much of the information upon which the West had constructed its image of the Ottomans came from them. The seraglio was the inner quarter of any palace, where the most effective weapon of Ottoman control was forged. It was there that the Islamic virtue of submission was exercised with a secular thoroughness that was thoroughly oriental in its demand for total obedience and almost Japanese in its acceptance of sudden death. In 1533 the Venetian envoy Bernardo Navagero managed to learn enough of the four royal seraglios of Suleiman the Magnificent to report to his masters their true nature.

They were simply the best schools there were, and the pupils were chosen by the child-catchers who roamed the Ottoman dominions selecting children to be brought up there. Christians were preferred, largely because there were no laws or customs to protect them, but Navagero counted 14 different nationalities attached to the four seraglios at one time. They were usually the victims of war. Indeed, he maintained that the Ottomans kept up a state of almost perpetual war to ensure a constant supply of recruits for the seraglio. If there were any selection criteria on the part of the child-catchers they were the physical appearance of sound health and the impression of a sharp mind, and not all parents lamented for long their child's disappearance into the seraglio when they considered the prospects he might have there. Children so selected were not necessarily deprived of all contact with their natural parents, some of whom flourished when their son did well in the Sultan's service. The children of Caucasian families were well favoured in both the Ottoman and Persian courts. From this almost limitless supply of genetically sound young men were selected, and trained, the rulers of the Ottoman empire. Initially 'Mahommedanised', usually nothing more painful than circumcision, they were thereafter inducted in the religion and the lore of Islam. The rewards were usually immediate. Set apart by dress and privilege, waited on hand and foot by eunuchs, they could almost smell the career before them.

The handsomest and ablest graduated to the Sultan's inner chamber as pages. Their training instilled total dedication to the service of one man. The Sultan was never alone without a page to provide for his every need. The rewards for the most adept, wakeful and dedicated were many, the greatest that he might one day rise to become Grand Vizier. Most of them became senior civil servants, military and naval officers, or governors of provinces. Failure or backsliding might be met by sudden and nasty retribution but until the end of the seventeenth century there was a constant supply of young recruits to replace them if, for any reason, they failed in their role. Ottoman servants, at their best, were not drawn from a doubtfully loyal aristocracy, or from the chance workings of a career open to talents which brought Napoleon to power, but on the most thorough training in skills, wholly subordinated to one authority, the Sultan's, and one system, the Ottoman.

It was unthinking and unchanging, but under a strong Sultan, such as Suleiman the Magnificent, its deadly efficiency was felt from one border of the far-flung empire to the others. Under a weak ruler, the system tended to be most effective where the most able satrap held local power. By the end of the eighteenth century, the empire under a succession of weak monarchs was governed by pashas, deys or beys, sometimes almost autonomous, like the Pasha of Yannina (otherwise Janina or Joannina), whom Byron was to meet in Albania. He was Albanian and claimed, when it suited him, to be Greek. Few Ottoman rulers were pure Turks; their ancestral blood could be very mixed.

2

To western observers, this absolutism was most terrifying when under the control of a sultan such as Suleiman the Magnificent, for there was no aristocracy, no limited or constitutional government to hold him in check. Even under a weak sovereign, submission from birth to the concept of a single authority made it culturally difficult for a subject to contemplate rebellion or, if he contemplated it, to plan it. The Venetians recognised this. While they were amazed that so many of the Sultan's subjects had abandoned their personal freedom for a slavery of mind and body, and so were ready to offer their bodies to the torturer or executioner if that were the Sultan's will, they recognised that this was basically the source of the Ottoman strength.

That will, if it looked absolute to the observer, was in fact limited by the law of Islam. Even those who found Islam religiously unacceptable acknowledged that it had its own power to bind, a power no Pope or Potentate had been able wholly to exercise in Christian lands. It certainly bound the mightiest in the land; offences against Islamic law could meet with penalties that were horrendous, and which surprisingly did not arouse any revulsion against barbarism, as breaking on the wheel or burning at the stake did in eighteenth-century western Europe.

More secular behaviour was subject to the monarch's judgement, which was seldom disputed, and caprice often determined punishment for offences that he found unacceptable to his sense of dignity or security. Such penalties were imposed not by written law, but by the will of the sovereign, which was also law. The notion of an oriental despot was in this way epitomised in the rulers of the Islamic empires, of the Ottomans, Morocco, Persia and Hindustan. He could be a good ruler if he was a good Muslim, and a bad one if he was a bad Muslim. Otherwise, judgement of his reign was not subject to more worldly considerations of his capacity, humanity or clemency.

In the centre of this intricate web of authority western observers perceived a deadly venom in each of the four empires, the succession of a ruler was usually accompanied by a slaughter of possible family rivals or claimants. The ruling house was genetically revived through its female denizens, particularly when its seraglio was renewed by conquest.[2] The harem was, therefore, central to the seraglio. The jealous care of the women of the harem was both in conformity with Islamic precept and politically expedient, for one of the women there – coming from whatever part of the world, captured, enslaved or born into slavery, given as part of an alliance or treaty or tribute, or freely chosen – could be the mother of a future sultan. Usually the choice of the dying ruler was for a son of one of his seven Koranic wives, but sometimes the one who ascended the throne was the choice or victim of intrigue and violence within the seraglio. In the Ottoman empire, powerful influences at court, – they could be the presumptive heir's mother, ambitious viziers or self-interested Janissaries – played a predominant role in determining who occupied the Sultanate, the effects of which were usually masked by the efficiency and momentum of its general administration.

Christendom in the West was familiar with intriguing matriarchs and inadequate heirs, but as few reigning monarchs produced many heirs from a single spouse, and as the children of concubines were precluded by both law and Christian precept, a succession disputed by siblings was rare. The Osmanli dynasty tried to protect itself against this by leaving the Sultan to decide who was to succeed him and, once a sultan had ascended the throne, however degenerate or inadequate he might prove to be, he was almost (but not wholly) impossible to remove, so carefully was he protected by one faction or the other within the seraglio.

3

The weakening of Islamic monarchy was an inevitable result of seraglio-rule. It became rare for a sultan to travel beyond the confines of the seraglio, though notionally a supreme despot within. The apparatus of government could be manipulated by ambitious sultanas, eunuchs, Janissaries, viziers or a cabal that might dispose of a Grand Vizier or a pasha grown too big for comfort. Instant death became a feature of government, and in the Ottoman empire the ever observant Venetians saw the unnerving power of the Ottoman state change from a model of enlightened rule to one operating 'from top to bottom as a tremendous killing machine'.[3]

Travellers in the seventeenth century had picked up stories that showed the Sultan's forays outside the seraglio in a more sinister light. Sultans did prowl the streets incognito, trying to gauge popular feeling, behaving with the typical caprice of the All-Powerful, dealing out punishments or rewards on the spot. Some of these were heavy-handed. On being charged a price for a piece of meat above what he had established by *firman*, one Sultan summoned his executioner and had the butcher's head struck off immediately. Another, surveying the city from his vantage point in the seraglio, happened to pick out a voyeur who had his telescope trained on the women in the gardens. Within the hour, the agents of the sultan had killed him and hung his corpse from the window from which he had trained his inquisitive instrument.[4] Such stories were circulated to establish a healthy fear of a remote and deadly justice where courts of law, as the Europeans understood them, did not exist. The Sultan might be constrained by Islamic law as interpreted at the time, but in matters in which the law was no guide it was understood that any lesser mortal could be served with summary retribution for any offence against him at any moment.

Office-holders, even the Grand Vizier, could be required to relinquish office, and often with it life, without warning, for an offence or failure not invariably understood, the usual medium of warning being a perfunctory letter followed by instant execution. Observers noted that the recipients seemed to embrace death almost willingly, the decision of the Sultan being accepted as unquestionable, and the last service a man could give his master was to die at his whim. For Christians, this was like doing their duty to God. However they might walk in righteousness, He might chose to cut them off in full flight; and their duty was to accept what seemed to be His will by dying a Good Death. To the outside observer, oriental monarchy demanded unconditional acceptance of a duty to a, not necessarily omniscient, mortal authority in this world, endowed with God-like power to enforce his will.

The reaction of these observers was ambivalent. They admired the exercise of this power in ordering society but feared the arbitrary use of it to override the natural and man-made barriers against it erected by law, custom, rank and wealth. Their conclusion was that for a despot to be a just and effective ruler he must be benevolent. The problem with the oriental despot, however, was that he was not always just or effective, still less, it seemed, benevolent. Judgements leading to disgrace were capricious, so that an official in the field felt it prudent to accumulate sufficient wealth to see him or his family through it, and this was usually made at the expense of the people of whom he was in charge, a failing not unfamiliar in all single-ruler states, East and West.

4

The Sultan in his seraglio seemed, therefore, to be the walking and breathing role model for a despot. The word had acquired the sense of unlimited authority, but originally the despots were Greek tribal or clan chiefs who had become subject to the Grand Signor as he extended his rule over historic Greece. The title denoted a father of his people, who were his family, governed by the rules that were acceptable between the chief and his family. These despots might be hierarchical, arbitrary and oppressive but they were subject to tradition and custom, which could change and develop. A benevolent despot was the father of his people, and the question for admirers of the Ottoman system was whether the Sultan in his seraglio was benevolent. Was the emperor of the Ottomans, of Morocco, of Hindustan or of China, asked Voltaire, 'a ferocious madman who heeds only his own whims, a barbarian who has his courtesans lined up to prostrate themselves before him, who orders his satellites on an orgy of strangulation and impalement'?[5]

Many thought that, mostly, he was. The mysterious silence that surrounded the eastern monarch, the downcast eyes, the ritual obeisance, the protective cortège of castrated half-men, could hide, convincingly and without distinction, an imbecile or a genius. Even if he were neither, he was still likely to be a man with little general education, rotted by sensual indulgence, and probably in thrall to women or the half-men, the eunuchs. In short, with few exceptions, the man was a nullity; what preserved the empire was the myth that an all-knowing, all-powerful person was at the centre. He was the Wizard of Oz, exercising power with mirrors. For all that, his power, discharged by viziers, beys and pashas, could be terrible.

5

Until the eighteenth century what the West knew of the Ottomans came largely from the Venetians. Lady Mary Wortley Montagu, whose husband was sent as Britain's ambassador from 1716 to 1718, thought that Ottoman rule had been much maligned, and closer contact with French reports dispelled some of the opaque mist that surrounded the mysteries of Ottoman power. As a rule closer observers – for example the resident merchants such as James Morier, who had lived in the Levant – had no great opinion of viziers, for every new one,

> tried to establish his reputation for decision and create a wholesome fear. See him when he leaves the gate of his house, surrounded by a hundred servants and dependants; some watching the least turn of his head to catch a glimpse of his eye; others running at the side of his stirrup in officious haste to kiss his knee. Then if a poor wretch happens to obstruct the road as he is about to pass, how lustily the *ferashes* beat him!'[6]

He 'generally finds it necessary to begin his career by spilling human blood. He either decapitates a Christian merchant who is too rich, strangles a Janissary or hangs a Jew.'[7]

It was, however, one particular vizier who became almost a household word abroad, woven as he was into Byron's Romantic experience. Musing regretfully on his new-found Calypso, a girl he had met in Malta, Byron left Christian Europe to forget her by braving the terrors of Albania, 'rugged nurse of savage men' where 'the cross descends, thy minarets arise, / And the pale crescent sparkles on the glen'. He made of it a venture 'on a shore unknown, / Which all admire, but many dread to view'.[8] Facing perils which, as Childe Harold, he never shrank to meet, he finally greeted Albania's chief, 'whose dread command / Is lawless law; for with a bloody hand / He sways a nation, turbulent and bold.'[9]

Ali Pasha was likened in his time to Cesare Borgia, not so much as the true disciple of Machiavelli but rather for his ruthlessness, cruelty and treachery. Byron reported that in revenge for an insult 42 years earlier to his mother and sisters ('treated as Miss Cunigonde was by the Bulgarian cavalry'), he had 600 of the survivors of a town he had just captured – men, women, children and grandchildren – shot before his eyes.[10] Ali Pasha was the most successful free-loader in the anarchic society of Greece and Albania under Ottoman rule in the early nineteenth century. His family was either Turkish or Albanian, and though he could speak Turkish the language he used most was Greek; when he wrote Albanian it was in Greek characters.[11] After his father, a relatively peaceful chieftain, was murdered by rivals his mother, determined to recover his patrimony for her son, organised a revenge programme that was indistinguishable from brigandage.

Ali, like Cesare Borgia, learned the first lesson of survival in an unstable situation: if you cannot beat your enemies, join them, and then destroy them from within. He established his power-base in the impenetrable mountains of southern Albania, which then incorporated Epirus, and murdered both his mother and brothers as potential rivals. As he built up his personal power he adroitly pretended to do the business of the Grand Turk in Istanbul. He recovered some of his father's old fiefs and titles and, though undertaking to reduce lawlessness, allied himself in a booty-sharing arrangement with the bands of robbers he was sworn to destroy. His wealth was now enough to bribe his way out of trouble in Constantinople and finally, in 1788, he became the Pasha of Yannina in the Epirus mountains, in which capacity he began to receive visitors to his pashalik.

His ambition was to amass unassailable riches, which nearly always secured that Constantinople would turn a blind eye, and gradually to reduce the whole of the Albanian highlands, eastern Greece and the Peloponnese to his overlordship – even, in his wildest imaginings, to secure the Sultanate itself. To do this, however, he needed to command the narrow seas between Italy and Albania and this seemed to be made easier when France destroyed the Venetian Republic in 1797 and began to take an interest in him. For a time, like the redoubtable Haidar Ali in Mysore, the tyrant received French 'embassies', and professed to be a good republican waging war on local landowners, whom he claimed to be destroying in the cause of liberty and freedom from privilege. His support for France's occupation of Corfu, however, aroused the dismay of the two powerful naval powers, Britain and Russia. Ever a realist, Ali saw that the English were likely to be of greater use to him, turned against his allies and helped to clear the French out of Corfu, for which Nelson personally thanked him.

At this point the English decided to open a mission at his court and Alexander Ball in Malta, having a spare man at his disposal, sent William Leake to take him some guns. Leake reached the Pasha in January 1805 and was not overly impressed. He could not quite make out where, if to anyone other than himself, Ali's loyalties lay. He owed the effectiveness of his control of the Epirus round Yannina to the restraint he imposed on his followers; he could be as rapacious as he liked but their greed was to be moderated. He did not hesitate to cultivate the Orthodox hierarchy as his allies in extorting cash and supplies from the Christian faithful.

Despite his pretence to be a Greek among the Greeks, he had a very Turkish view of the nation. 'You don't know the Greeks,' he told Leake. 'When I hang one of these wretches on a plane tree, brother robs brother under the very branches. If I burn one of them alive, the son is ready to steal his father's ashes to sell them for money.'[12] He was, in his turn, just as unscrupulous, prudently amassing his wealth against any change in his fortune. He was also mean, refusing to pay his 'foreign advisers' a decent wage, forcing them to marry local girls to tie them to their, or rather his, apron strings, and rewarding them with clothes and petty cash mostly from loot.

Leake's distaste for the Pasha was exacerbated by the general style of finery in filth. Ali was approachable to all and not averse to vermin. In fact, they crawled over his clothes and hopped out of the velvet and cloth of gold which constituted his uniform of state. He was actually sharing command of Albania with two other Pashas, and more often at war – if the occasional sniping and pillaging by his gunmen constituted war – with them over territory. His Ottoman overlord was unable to prevent savage and expensive border affrays between them and was fearful of Ali's Albanian cohorts, who were both formidable and unpredictable at once. Ali himself, behind all the trappings of a primitive royal court, was both ruthless and predictable. Despite his own criminality he took a poor if capricious view of public immorality and, according to Leake, had the ladies of a well-known bawdy house drowned. For lack of sacks in which to put them they had to be thrown overboard and pushed under the waves by the oars of the Albanian boatmen.[13] Was Leake too credulous, believing too readily what the Greeks, who hated Ali, told him? Muslim law has never prescribed drowning in a sack or any other receptacle for marital infidelity, but this was another accepted 'fact' about Muslim practice.[14]

With the withdrawal of Russia from the Ionian islands after the Treaty of Tilsit, Ali pinned his hopes of support on the English, whose own interest in securing possession of Corfu meant that he was largely left untroubled to secure his hold on most of mainland Greece along the west and south as far as the Gulf of Corinth. He subdued neighbouring chiefs – 'some daring mountain-band disdain his power, and from their rocky hold / Hurl their defiance far, nor yield, unless to gold'[15] – and when Byron and his friend Hobhouse entered his domains in October 1809, he was engaged on such a task. It was Ramadan and the court that feasted every night at sundown: 'high-capped Tartars', 'bearded' Turks, 'lively supple' Greeks, 'high-kirtled' Albanians, 'swarthy Nubia's mutilated sons', 'crimson-scarfèd men of Macedon', prayed, smoked, whispered and gambled away the day until they came to life in the bustle and mingled din of the carouse after sundown. Many among the 'irregulars', Byron noticed, were *delis*, dubbed by James Morier as 'the enfans [sic] terribles of the Turkish army', desperados 'who had taken service with any local pasha who could pay them', and 'two hundred of whom, … with their cap of terror on, could cause more trouble than an army of ten thousand would in Europe'.[16] Byron had to go to Tepeleni, the former seat of Ali's father, to meet the Pasha in the tiled courtyard and around the fountain, a characteristic feature of Islamic architecture, even today. This man of war and woes wore his 'venerable face', hiding 'the deeds that lurk beneath, and stain him with disgrace'. But Childe Harold was not deceived; crimes 'have marked him with a tiger's tooth' for blood follows blood, and Ali rose to power, like Macbeth, in blood and kept himself there by blood.[17]

This was the court over which Ali ruled with pretensions to culture. It had a British resident, and the Pasha aped royal power.[18] Ali appeared to be impressed by Byron's title, no doubt emphasised by the British resident at his court who had made the arrangements. Byron made no complaint of his royal reception, which was generous and gracious. Ali received him standing, insisted on meeting all his expenses, greeted him like a son and remarked on his small ears, curling hair and little white hands, a sure mark, to Ali, of noble birth (and, Byron may have feared, homosexual predilection). Speculation on Ali's sexual intentions and Byron's reaction seems only salacious, but the sexagenarian pasha, small and fat, though blue-eyed and with a fine face and venerable white beard, could not be separated from his reputation for 'deeds that lurk beneath, and stain him with disgrace'.[19]

Ali treated Byron as an honoured, perhaps influential, English guest, who might persuade the English to give him some money. Childe Harold was impressed. He did not remark in his letters home on the astrologers, alchemists and poets at Ali's court, which would have medievalised the impression, and perhaps trivialised the memory. Instead, Hobhouse and he revelled in the colours and fabrics, in the costumes (which they bought as souvenirs), the gold and silver, the swords and daggers and the steeds that all conformed to the eastern myth of splendour amid squalor. The Pasha, too, satisfied all their imaginings of oriental despotism, accompanied by a

FIGURE 1   *Pasha Ali of Yannina. A painting on velvet in the Benaki Museum in Athens.*
This is how he would have appeared to Byron during this reception in 1809.

certain liberal cordiality and bluff talking that so often goes with men of almost unassailable power, such as Stalin and Hitler.[20]

In due course Ali overreached himself. When finally in 1817 the last enclave on the coast was sold to him by its British occupiers, he was without a rival except one. That was the Sultan Mahmud II himself, who decided that Ali's vast wealth and huge bribes would no longer protect him. The conflicting interests during the long war – which had the French, English and Russians jostling for primacy in Constantinople – had bred too many obstreperous, independent-minded pashas. Ali must go. Now in his eighties, Ali resisted the army sent to dispossess him, finally being forced to surrender. Having received the usual professions of immunity and esteem from the Grand Vizier who accepted his submission, Ali was stabbed in the back as he retired and his head despatched to the Sultan. So far everyone had acted as popular opinion felt they should.

6

The life of a Grand Vizier was seen, in the West, as being more precarious than that of most almighty subjects there, for whom loss of wealth and position was more common than execution. Aspirations beyond their station, displeasing the Sultan, falling out with powerful forces at court – sultanas, pashas, Janissaries – even expressions of popular discontent could lead to sudden death. Between 1644 and 1656 only one of 17 Grand Viziers was to die a natural death, but by the eighteenth century disgrace was more common than death, and careful husbandry over a period of power often ensured that disgrace would not necessarily mean penury.[21]

Byron used the figure of Ali Pasha as the model for the father of Zuleika in *The Bride of Abydos*. Giaffir, Zuleika's father, was content to trade his favourite daughter, issue of a favourite wife, to another warlord. That was the action of a tyrant and disgusted Byron. He was also disgusted, and hoped to disgust his readers, when he reported that Athens had become 'the property of Kislar Aga (the slave of the seraglio and guardian of the women) who appoints the Waywode [Voyvod]. A pandar and a eunuch now governs the governor of Athens.'[22] Pashas, Agas, and Voyvods oppressed the authors of our liberties and were the instruments of a regime that had disintegrated into petty local tyrannies. For Byron, the free world of the ancients had become the toy of voluptuaries and degenerates, the world was corrupt, both in the East and in the West, and only freedom could cleanse it. The Sultan, more than most monarchs, must tremble in his seraglio.

CHAPTER THREE

The Harem

The Myth of Sex

Every beauteous race beneath the sun,
From those who kneel at Brahma's burning founts,
To the fresh nymphs bounding o'er Yemen's mounts
From Persia's eyes of full and fawn-like ray,
To the small, half-shut glances of Cathay;
And Georgia's bloom and Arab's darkest smiles,
And the gold ringlets of the western isles,
Ah, all are there.
(Thomas Moore, *Lalla Rookh*)[1]

I

*I*SLAMIC TALES FROM a society that kept its women apart and veiled tantalised listeners with images of beautiful women, concealed in sensuous splendour, succubi to the man who owned them as slaves and chattels. Some of these beauties imparted an air of romance to what was otherwise seen as fatal imprisonment. Among them was Roxelane, the slave who captured the heart of Suleiman the Magnificent, the ruler of an empire at its most powerful from 1520 to 1566. She in her turn was the head of a household of as many as 300 women: wives, domestic servants and concubines. Later there was to be the creole beauty Aimée Dubucq de Rivéry, a cousin of Napoleon's first wife, Joséphine de Beauharnais, who was captured by Algerian corsairs and donated by the Bey as a diplomatic sweetener to the Sultan, Abdul Hamid I. Widely believed to be the mother of his successor Mahmud II (hammer of the Janissaries and would-be moderniser of that same empire from 1808 to 1839), Aimée was said to have influenced Ottoman policy in favour of France, despite Napoleon's invasion of Egypt.

What happened to women in Islam was the stuff of Romantic tales in the West for over a century after the first translation of *The Arabian Nights Entertainments* appeared in 1714. The passion of Ottomans for the tulip was a symbol of a secret world which revolved round The Woman. The six petals of a perfect tulip formed close guard round its anthers and ovaries only to open in the privacy of the private gardens to expose its vulva-like calyx and erect and arrogant pistil, awaiting the orgasmic triumph that set hearts racing.[2] On public display on ceremonial occasions such as the reception of an ambassador – a painting of the arrival of the Dutch ambassador, Cornelis Calkoen (1695–1764), at the court of the Sultan in Constantinople depicts rows of tulips tightly closed, – the tulip, it was believed, had risen miraculously from the blood of a Persian lover who, hearing that his love was dead, rode his horse over a precipice and was smashed to pieces. In Persia, redness in a flower signified that the lover was on fire with love, and the red tulip was a symbol of perfect love. After the tulip had wilted and died, the nightingale or bulbul and the rose were the summer symbols of love, wrapped in an erotic miasma, only a suspicion away from orgasm.

To the observers in the West the exercise of power had its roots in sexual predation and dominance, so that it was hardly surprising that they viewed the harem as voyeurs view pornography. Its lord and master picked wives, concubines and odalisques as a gardener picks roses, not for his table but for his bed. It was a place of unimaginable luxury, peopled by bored, intermittently pregnant but otherwise lusty beauties. It at once reflected the sardonic picture of the harem of the Grand Signor in Constantinople that Byron drew in *Don Juan*; it was also the ritualised brothel that Ingres painted for the soft eroticism of the Parisian salons, and the enclosed parlour Delacroix presented to would-be colonists of North Africa. It was to be a century before Pierre Loti tried to correct the image.

'No signs of odalisques nor of *narghilehs*, no sweetmeats in this Pasha's harem … with one or two exception every harem in Constantinople is of the same type … neither more nor less than the female part of a family constituted as our own families are, with the exception of their seclusion.' So wrote Pierre Loti in his novel, *Désenchantées*, in 1904. Anxious to do general justice to the country that had entranced him he went on that young 'Turkish damsels' in an upper-class harem 'talked German with no more difficulty than Italian or English', read Dante, Byron and Shakespeare in the original, 'had devoured alike ancient classics and modern degenerates, and in music were equally enthusiastic for Gluck, and for César Franck or

FIGURE 2 *Eugene Delacroix in presenting the ladies of Algeria at leisure in 1834 wished to present the harem as a place of chronic boredom rather than as a ritualised brothel. See also page 32.*

Wagner, and for reading the scores of Vincent d'Indy'. A hundred years earlier things were believed to be very different, and if Turkish, indeed all Muslim, society, *pace* Byron and the other Romantics, had a single major defect, Loti felt obliged to add, it was 'the thick veil worn out of doors and the improbability of ever exchanging ideas with a man, unless it were the father, or the husband, or a brother, or a very intimate cousin'.[3]

The harem became a major obstacle to East–West understanding, despite ever-increasing knowledge of Islamic society, as it never threw off the reputation it had acquired as an instrument of oppression more potent than Pierre Loti's mild rebuke suggested. He was right to state that the *harim* was the heart of a Muslim homestead, sacred to the essential family unit. It was not synonymous with polygamy, for by the end of the eighteenth century most Muslim homesteads could only economically support one wife, with all the other family members and dependants that a homestead might comprise. In Ottoman Egypt in the 1840s few men had more than one wife, though the practice of using a slave as a concubine was widely practised. Polygamy was largely confined to men of rank or wealth.[4] The harem was always intended to be a sacred and secret place and over the years it was accessible only to other women, the immediate male members of the household, to children and to eunuchs. What went on inside it became the subject of conjecture and myth, most of which clustered round the person and powers of its head.

The harem, however, was never the whole seraglio, though that name became identified with it in the West. Within the *serai*, the women's quarters (*haremlik*) were separated from the men's (*selamlik*) by those of the head of a household, who might require access to both. The intensely private quartering of women undoubtedly pre-dated Islam as it was more or less a customary practice throughout Asia (as witness the Hindu *zenana* in India) and it is a natural feature of societies that tend for all sorts of demographic reasons to have a superfluity of women. Despite the Jewish movement towards monogamy, which became increasingly the cry of the Biblical prophets, the use of concubines or serving girls to produce male heirs was widely practised and praised in the Old Testament. Rachel, being childless by Jacob, persuaded him to impregnate her handmaid, Bilhah, and claimed the resultant son as hers when the mother sat upon her lap to give birth. When Leah was also beyond child-bearing age, she used her handmaid, Zilpah, to give Jacob more sons.[5] The Jewish heroine, Esther, was celebrated because she rose from being a slave member of the harem, virtually kidnapped in a search for nubile young women for the Persian king Ahasuerus, to become his principal queen. It says much for the harem itself that this was not an uncommon progression in an oriental court.

2

The practice of keeping a household of women as bedfellows for a single man, though repugnant to Christian morality, was a not inhumane defence against childlessness (in effect sonlessness) in a philoprogenitive society, where not being married was a fate every woman feared. As the greatest hazards to all women, whatever their origins, were childbirth and 'defilement', either by rape or seduction, the harem protected women from both. Lady Mary Wortley Montagu was impressed by the desire, almost passion, of married women to have large numbers of children, which she attributed to the fact that the Prophet had promised no Paradise in the next world for women, so that sons provided solace as compensation in this, or that women were promised only a separate Paradise from their husbands: 'mais je crois que la pluspart n'en seront pas moins contentes pour çela'. One result was, she observed, that the cult of fertility and claims to a capacity to bear children long after child-bearing age left women prey to quackery. 'Proof of youth', she remarked acidly, 'is as necessary ... as it is to show the proofs of nobility to be admitted a Knight of Malta.'[6]

To ensure the continuation of the line of Osman, in an age when male child mortality was a natural hazard, it was necessary to keep the Ottoman royal harems filled. The enslavement of women, either in war or by sale, was common. The practice of enclosing in the harem women taken in war or piracy was one of the most powerful anxieties of Europeans in their resistance to Islamic conquest, and thus the source of sinister legend. For the most part the Sultan's harem was stocked with concubines, mainly of Indo-European race, who shared a single ambition: that one of them might be the mother of a Sultan or, if not a Sultan, someone socially superior. Though in all the Islamic empires the succession usually went to the eldest of the former monarch's sons, by a wife not a concubine, it was not always so. The seventeenth-century emperor of Morocco, Moulay Ismā'īl, waded to the throne through the blood of his siblings.

Few of those who might expect to succeed to the throne had any real preparation for the role, so that it did not appear to matter much who did succeed since the system ran almost automatically. Too many sons could, however, lead to a disputed succession and Sultan Mahmud II, on his unexpected accession in 1808, was reported to have had 200 women of his predecessor's harem drowned in the Bosphorus in case any of them produced a posthumous son round whom the Janissaries, whom he was resolved to destroy, could gather to dethrone him.

It was because the harem was such a closed thing that Byron was tempted to open it to erotic effect by inserting Don Juan, disguised as a girl, into the Sultan's own, to wreak seductive mayhem. He considered the harem to be no more nor less restrictive than marriage, western style. 'In the east they are extremely strict / And wedlock and a padlock mean the same,' the difference being that they do not 'knead two virtuous souls for life / Into that moral centaur, man and wife'. The Ottomans did well to shut their women up, as their chastity was not of that astringent quality as made 'our snow less pure than our morality', for neither the harem nor moral centaurdom was a guarantee against waywardness.[7]

Byron's version of life in the Sultan's harem was worthy of a women's magazine. Gulbeyaz was the Sultan's fourth if favourite wife, but 'she thought her lord's heart … / Was scarce enough; for he had fifty nine / Years, and a fifteenth hundred concubine.'[8] Being impatient and lusty, and provoked by Juan's epicene looks, she has him bought as a slave in the market, orders him to be dressed as a girl and introduced, as another Circassian maiden, into her quarters, where in private she demands from him passionate love. Don Juan, still pining for his Greek *innamorata* from whom he had been forcibly removed by her father and sold into slavery, declines the honour. Whereupon Gulbeyaz orders him to be disposed of in the usual way, by drowning.

Before anything is irreparably decided she receives a conjugal visit from the Sultan himself. The head eunuch, surprised at the strength of the Sultana's passion for the androgynous Juan, interprets her sentence as the result of temporary rage at being spurned and, knowing that she would want to try him again, as she was a lady with simple but single-minded tastes, arranges instead for Juan to be accommodated for the night in the women's quarters. He is unable, however, to make the sleeping arrangements, so that Don Juan is bedded with a buxom lass who rather noisily betrays her gratified alarm at his amorous if unintended groping. Byron was intent on mocking a female love of 'passion', but in real life the discovery of a strange man in the company of the women of a royal household would have met with instant death. The ever resourceful head eunuch arranges for Juan to be sent instead to the Russian warfront, a fate dreaded as much by the Ottomans in Byron's time as it was in Hitler's Germany in the 1940s.

3

Few observers of the harem shared Byron's sanguine view of it as a place of sexual diversion. There were many stories of brothers, fiancés or husbands trying to free their wives and lovers from incarceration in a harem into which they had been kidnapped or drafted as spoils of war. They became popular stories, among the best known of which must be Mozart's *Die Entführing aus dem Serail*. The plot was not original and Mozart's librettist, Gottlieb Stephanie, had 'borrowed' it from an earlier libretto by another author for another composer, who had in turn 'borrowed' it from an English comic opera, *The Captive*, itself an adaptation of a play by Dryden, *Don Sebastian*.[9] Added to the plot were borrowings from another English *singspiel* or play with songs, *The Sultan or a Peep into the Seraglio* by Isaac Bickerstaffe, which figures a harem custodian called Osmin and an involuntary English inmate, called Roxelane.[10]

The name Roxelane, or Roxane, appears many times in tales of the harem; one of whom, a Circassian, rose from the rank of concubine to be the Sultana of Suleiman the Magnificent (1520–66). Richard Knolles's *General History of the Turks*, 1603, gave her this name (her Turkish name was Hürrem), influenced by the story of Alexander of Macedon whose Bactrian wife, Roxana, schemed to make her son, also Alexander, the sole ruler of Alexander's extensive conquests. Roxelane or Roxana, however, was so popular a name used in tales of the harem that, after Daniel Defoe described a career of prosperous wickedness pursued by his *Roxana or the Fortunate Mistress* (1724), a concubine using sex to achieve her ambitions, the name became synonymous with whore, and the harem assumed in many minds the characteristics of a brothel.[11]

Libretto and overture (with only its triangle, big drum and cymbals to give it a Turkish air) apart, there is little that is eastern about *Die Entführung*. Osmin, the harem jailer, is a drunken buffoon, Blonde an arch soubrette (English of course), Kostanze a figure of tragic dignity, and Belmonte a wimp. It is the non-singing Pasha Selim who turns out to be the perfect gentleman, showing at the end the compassion, generosity and dignity Mozart found so often missing in his co-religionists and fellow countrymen. Mozart's *Enftührung* was predated by seven years by *L'Incontro Improvviso*, an opera by Haydn written for an Archduke's visit to Esterhazy. It has a similar theme and is set in Cairo. The protagonists are themselves orientals: a fictional Moor (Balsoran) and a Persian maiden, captured by pirates while eloping. The Persian ends up in the harem of the Egyptian sultan. *L'Incontro Improvviso* was an entertainment, mocking Turkish passions for forbidden things such as alcohol. The Sultan, however, turns out to be another Pasha Selim; the aristocracy of the Austrian empire was always respectful of rank. The plot reflects the growing taste for Turkish tales of the Seraglio, of which the best known were Gluck's *Pilgrimme von Mekka* (1764), Jomelli's *La Schiava Liberata* (1769) and *Adelheaid von Veltheim*, set to music in 1789 by Beethoven's teacher, Christian Gottlieb Neefe.[12]

There was barely a port in southern Europe that had not a tale to tell of female captives being lost in harems. *The Bride of Mosta* is a typical example of the kind of saga that studded the Mediterranean: the tale of a Maltese bride, stolen by a Turkish corsair just before her wedding, rescued by her fiancé who goes in hot pursuit of her and hears her singing 'their song' to the ladies of the sultan's harem. She is rescued from dishonour but not from death, and this, given the improbability of the fiancé's feat in crossing the waters that divide Malta from the North African littoral, was its inevitable end.[13]

Morier's tale of Yûsûf and Mariam and Mary Shelley's of Constantine and Euphrasia are better-known southern European stories. In Morier's tale, Mariam has been taken slave in a Turkish raid, and, to escape the sexual demands of her new lord casts herself from an upper-storey window of the building in which she was being held. She is providentially saved by a convenient tree into which she falls and then by her husband, who has traced her to the house. Morier's story was written in 1824, the year of Byron's death and three years after the Greeks had launched their bid for independence.[14] It bears a strong resemblance to the story of Constantine and Euphrasia, written by Mary Shelley in 1836 for the *Keepsake* (1838).[15]

The protagonists in Mary Shelley's tale are brother and sister. Euphrasia is rescued from the lusts of the pasha's son by Constantine at a moment when she is defying the whole repressive machinery of the harem into which she has been abducted. Killed by a stray bullet as she is being carried to freedom, she dies a martyr to the cause of wronged womanhood in Turkish hands. Such tales were an almost accepted cliché of the times – it was odd that Mary Shelley should have written hers three years after Greece had become an independent kingdom but she was almost certainly using the tale to illustrate not so much female escape from Ottoman tyranny as from the tyranny generally exercised over women's minds and persons by men in all societies of the time.[16] In the imagination of the monogamists of the West, being part of a seraglio really meant being in a harem, with all its connotations of sexual slavery.

The image of the harem as one man's brothel, providing the lord and master with a source of nightly pleasure at no cost apart from the provision of food and shelter, had a prurient fascination for those not accustomed to the system. Those who found it otherwise from personal experience belonged to the silent generation of women, so that the idea was not dislodged until later in the nineteenth century, when women became more articulate. That it spelled sexual slavery and intimidation proved one of the enduring myths of Romanticism.

Lady Mary Wortley Montagu in Constantinople was not among those looking for titillation when she remarked that 'the luscious passion of the seraglio' was, still, 'the only one that is gratified here to the full'.[17] The number of women in the harem was often not known by the master of the household himself, and the harems of the households of ruling figures were large. The Ottoman Sultan could have as many as seven wives, as a male heir was of supreme importance, and one sultan, Abdul Hamid II (deposed by the Young Turks in 1909), was credited with as many as 1,000 women in the *haremlik*. The reasons for this plenitude certainly included continuous sexual gratification but many women were there because of the interplay of politics, favouritism and protection, and the need to beget male heirs.

4

Western commentators on the travellers' tales coming out of Islamic lands saw only an oriental despot, treating the rest of society as he treated the women of his harem. The lordship of an Ottoman seraglio was a replication in miniature of the monarch's lordship of his country. The inner citadels of this maze were peopled by sinister maimed humans, dumb attendants skilled in the art of strangulation who carried out the despot's decrees of death, by dwarves collected for his amusement and, progressively less accessible as one approached its heart, by the despot himself, surrounded by cohorts of the weakest human beings, women, children and, most sinister of all, eunuchs. There he took his pleasure, which was total and uninhibited, providing the illusion of total power for which despots of all ages longed.

All who surrounded the intimate person of the monarch were sufferers of one kind or another. The Janissaries and court officials were originally 'stolen children', and had developed into an almost self-perpetuating closed society. Many of the women were denied the normal pleasures of marriage and motherhood. The individuals set to maintain the chastity of the harem were maimed, averred those who thought they had discovered the secrets of the harem, either 'simply cut or wholly shaved'. The simply cut were trusted and often comfortably ensconced servants of the seraglio, the shaved were those who had more intimate contact with the women; their entire male apparatus was removed so that they could introduce no simulacrum of the Sultanic penis to arouse interest or desire. These, so it was darkly said, were mainly black slaves who slept in the women's apartments to prevent lesbian attachments but who found pleasures among the women they were guarding while their lord was absent. One of the principal sources of information about all this was *The Arabian Nights Entertainments*, the oriental fantasy *par excellence*, in which, to prevent such infidelities, the Caliph killed every supposed virgin in his harem after he had deflowered them, so that they could never dishonour him, until Scheherezade put an end to the slaughter.[18] Even so, despite the emphasis that all entrants to the harem should be virgins, the Persian Shah Abbas II died of syphilis.[19]

The most helpless of the sufferers from this system were the children born in its midst. Though succession to the throne was not invariably accompanied by the wholesale slaughter of siblings the survival of many of the children of a royal harem beyond babyhood was problematic. The possible competitors for the succession were kept in a sort of perpetual nursery. Some were lucky enough to receive the same education as those who had been kidnapped to become servants of the seraglio, but for the sons born in a royal harem, even the eldest son of the Sultan, the closest relationship was not with the man who might have fathered them in what might have amounted to a one-night stand, but to their mothers.

5

The reigning sultan's mother had a despotism of her own, the virtual control of the harem. Her son's fortunes were, of course, hers, and after her ranking, as a poor second, came the mother of the expected heir. Until that expectation was realised, her position could be precarious. Parents were often the first victims of a palace intrigue or succession struggle. The relationship of the other Koranic wives to the slave mothers of sons and to the odalisques, a kind of domestic prostitute, was as complicated as any table of precedence thought up by the Almanach de Gotha. Among the duties of the chief ladies of the harem was the training and preparation of girls as dancers, musicians, make-up artists, and readers as well as *horizontales*. Hajji Baba in England is surprised that the King of England had 'only one wife and no dancing women, no story-tellers, no setters to sleep'.[20] Occasionally a 'favourite' might pierce the carapace of order and respect for status that prevailed within the harem, to become something more. At its best, the harem served as a kind of finishing school; at its worst as an employment agency, whence a woman slave might be offered for sale to another employer or owner. The slave herself was sometimes allowed a view on this matter, as Kinglake discovered when he wanted to see if he could buy a houri beauty and was offered a moon-faced lady of enormous girth, who in the event objected successfully to the prospect of sale to an infidel![21]

The harem was not a paradise of houris; they came in the afterlife to attend the Islamic blessed, or the male section of it. It was certainly a school for getting on with women penned up in a confined space, and sometimes a sort of permanent and pleasurable *conversazione*. When Lady Mary Wortley Montagu visited the Turkish bath at Adrianople she was delighted with what she found. For her it was one of the delights of a society that had created in her view many enviable pleasures. She admired the politeness of the women bathers, amounting to a lack of impertinent curiosity, except when she revealed her stays, which they assumed were a chastity belt to which her husband had the key. They sat in a perfect state of nature on the cushions and carpets that covered the sofas, accompanied by their slaves, who only revealed their status by having to stand. She found them in their movements as graceful as Milton described 'our general mother', and in shape and loveliness worthy of a portrait by Guido Reni or Titian. Their shining white skin and braided tresses, with strings of pearls or ribbons, reminded her of the Three Graces. This 'women's coffee house' with the teenage slaves serving coffee and sherbert, or braiding their mistress's hair, was a perfect subject for an artist.[22] Lady Mary was anxious to redress some of the libels about the life of Turkish ladies, suggesting that compared to their sisters in the West, they had not too bad a time of it.

Her enthusiasm led to a request to buy a slave, preferably a Greek, from a friend who fancied a life of voluptuous *houridom*. She declined on the grounds that the slaves on sale in Constantinople were not Greeks but Tartars, Circassians or Georgians, 'miserable, awkward, poor wretches' whom her friend would certainly not want in her domestic entourage. Moreover, as they were usually purchased when eight or nine years old, so that they could be trained in the arts they were to perform, good slaves were seldom sold away from their owner, except for a grave fault, and Lady Mary was sure her friend would not want someone guilty of crime or dereliction of service![23]

6

It was the existence of the Circassians, who were considered exemplary in the domestic arts, that provoked and titillated the interest of European visitors to Ottoman, Persian and other Islamic lands. They were fair-skinned Caucasians and, despite the Koranic embargo on enslaving Muslims, were often Muslims whose parents had sold them as slaves in the not entirely erroneous belief that life in the Ottoman or Persian capitals would offer more promise than in their bleak and impoverished mountain fastnesses. To the European eye, however, they were Christian and ethnic sisters under the skin, and their popularity as domestic servants or concubines was an offence against a womanhood born free.

The Circassian has been immortalised in the luscious and languorous odalisques of Dominique Ingres. It was Lady Mary Wortley Montagu's account of the baths of Adrianople, which appeared in a French edition in 1805, that inspired him to paint *Le Bain Turc* between 1859 and 1863, when he was nearly 80. But it was more the fantasy of the West than the reality of the East. The fame of the Circassian girls as beauties, rather than their plight, had already fired Alexander Pope, who wrote Lady Mary Wortley Montagu a sexually ambivalent letter asking her, while she was in Constantinople, to procure his dream slave, 'more amiable than the angels',

FIGURE 3A   *Two views of the harem. Amadeo Preziosi's watercolour of a Turkish lady attended by her Circassian, playing the lute, and her Ethiopian slaves, drawn probably from life between 1850 and 1860. By the time Preziosi was painting he could have had privileged access to a harem. The Circassian would occupy more the role of companion, the Ethiopian of personal maid.*

expressing a common dream of a beautiful, sexually accomplished but servile succubus.[24] It was only when Russia overran the Caucasus that the Ottomans looked to Africa, especially Ethiopia, for an alternative supply, so that in the late eighteenth and nineteenth centuries the place of the white ladies' maid was usually taken by a black slave.

The fate of Circassians was not always to be an odalisque, though Pierre Loti's heroine in the *Désenchantées*, of Caucasian origin, assumes that is to be her role when her husband takes another wife. There seemed plenty of them around even in 1906 when the Sultan's mother had an entourage of 'thirty or more little fairies – very young girl slaves, miracles of beauty and grace, all dressed alike like sisters'.[25] Loti probably knew more than most westerners what life in a harem was like, but rumours of what went on in a royal harem were legion. As the women were preserved for the single service of one organ in strict rotation, the more of them there were the less often did they perform their horizontal duties. Dark stories, thanks to *The Arabian Nights*, were attached to the elderly women, who supervised the younger and lustier wives, who were reported to be engaged in a constant

FIGURE 3B   *The same combination — woman at leisure, a Circassian and Ethiopian —*
set in Cairo by John Frederick Lewis in the winter of 1843.

search for any fruit or instruments that might be put to use in place of the
despotic and privileged priapus. 'Her office', wrote Byron, 'was to keep
aloof or smother / All bad propensities in fifteen hundred / young women,
and correct them when they blunder'd.'[26] A whole literature of lubricious
fantasy grew up around the prosaic and tedious life of the harem, and
tedious it was for the most part. Mirza Abdul Hasan, on his way to an
embassy in London in 1809, told James Morier of the principal occupations
of the women in a harem:

> They sew, embroider and spin; they make their own clothes; and my
> wife even used to make mine; besides that, they superintend all the

domestic concerns of the house; they keep an account of the daily expenses; distribute provisions to the servants; pay their wages; settle all disputes between them; manage the concerns of the stable; see that the horses have their corn and, in short, have the care of all the disbursements of the home.[27]

Senior wives, to discharge their domestic duties, learned to read and write, and take on household management. Had Jane Austen been born under another star she would have found her place in this system of things.

There was also a good deal of idleness and gossip, not unknown in households in the West, and it was not the odalisques of Ingres but the bored-looking, hookah-smoking, card-playing ladies of a domestic harem whom Delacroix was allowed to observe in Morocco who proved to be nearer the mark. The harem was a society as disciplined and hierarchic as a Christian nunnery. Indeed, Sydney Morgan, observing the convents of Rome at the beginning of the nineteenth century, made the comparison. The Sultan's mother was as reverend, in her own way, as any head of an enclosed female religious order, with as many as a thousand women to oversee.[28] Indeed the schedule of which wife or concubine would service the Sultan, often decided by his mother, was so rigidly kept that if the Sultan wished to vary the schedule, he often had to make an arrangement to meet the bedfellow of his choice away from his apartment, in an oriental *parc des cerfs*.[29]

The lot of female slaves was not altogether to be despised. Their treatment, provided they behaved themselves, was not unkind. They might learn to play musical instruments and to dance and they were better clothed than most domestic servants on virtually slave wages could expect in the West. Indeed, Pierre Loti thought that 'one wife of an uncompromising Western socialist might with great advantage come to a harem to learn to treat her maid, or her governess, as the Turkish ladies treat their slaves'.[30] They were often manumitted and given dowries on marriage, and if in royal service this stood them in good turn; former slaves like them 'had become great ladies by marriage'.[31] Often, but not always. Observers of the Shah's court in Persia could see that violation of the rules of the harem was something no man or woman undertook lightly. A girl who tried to upset the sleeping schedule and approached the Sultan's bed out of turn, or refused her 'scheduled night on duty' for no good reason, might be sentenced to death. Any man found, even by misadventure, in or near the royal harem or a royal conveyance could expect sudden death at the hands of the eunuchs. Hajji Baba's liaison with Zeenab, who met her death suspected of misbehaviour in the harem, was therefore more dangerous than Morier seemed to make out in his novel. Death was not always sudden, for it was said that in addition to being drowned in a sack, the burial alive of supposed interlopers was not unknown.[32]

In James Morier's *Hajji Baba of Ispahan*, Hajji tells Yûsûf, who has rescued his wife from the harem into which she had been sold, that he has committed a capital offence.[33] Thomas Moore was the source of a story that was to be the central feature of Byron's first Turkish Tale, *The Giaour*. In Constantinople Byron met a cortège going to the sea edge with a body in a sack, and assumed she was a Greek who was already dead. The story was later embroidered, however, to have Byron stopping the procession and at the point of his pistol, ordering that the girl be released on condition that she left the country. She ended up in a convent.[34] It is possible to cast doubt on this story – Byron does not deny that it might have taken place but behind it lurked his Turkish attitudes to life and death and his contempt for the treatment of women. As there is no Koranic authority for the drowning of unfaithful wives or concubines the whole episode may be more typical of his prejudice than fact.[35]

7

So it was generally held in the West that for the woman the harem constituted a prison, that 'once within (its) walls her husband becomes her sole lord and master, and then she eats blows, and devours grief, as a matter of course, for ever after'.[36] They could be transferred without being consulted from one harem into the harem of a friend or favourite. If for any reason a woman was thought to have disgraced herself in some way, she might be married to a menial or even sold into a brothel. They were the lucky ones. According to Chardin, girls in Persia who refused sex had been known to be shut in a chimney and burned alive, or beaten with rods.[37] In truth not all women taken captives in war or piracy found their way immediately to the captor's bed. Many became domestic servants, some did marry their 'owners', and most were usually manumitted or freed on his death or allowed to marry the man of their choice.[38] Despite the tales of ill-treatment, Lady Hester Stanhope, who met many harem ladies in Constantinople, was impressed by their general contentment. None was seething with fury at the ignominy of their status, or appeared to be used in any way as chattels.[39] Pregnancy for royal concubines could be something to be feared. Mothers of unwanted children might be turned out or otherwise disposed of. If an ageing woman were not the mother or grandmother of a prince, her fate was usually to become a janitor or tutor of the younger girls being prepared for the life of concubinage. Meanwhile, within the closed society, rivalry, jealousy, backbiting and envy were assumed to be the dominant passions.[40] The extraordinary degradation of human emotions shown on British television screens in 2005–06 by 'reality' programmes, such as *Big Brother*, are paradigms of the emotional life of a society whose orgasms are public and whose failures are so quickly realised. Life in the harem was prone to drawbacks but they were never exposed to the public or given any sort of publicity in authentic memoirs by female members of it.

There were happy marriages, devoted spouses and the development of real love within a harem, but happy and fulfilled marriage into the system by an outsider was rare. It was not unknown. In the harem of a strict Muslim, the Dagestan independence leader and Imam, were four wives, one of whom was a Christian captive, all of whom, bar the youngest and last married, were happy with the arrangement. Privation and solitude there certainly was but this was the accepted and inevitable custom.[41] Lady Mary Wortley Montagu tells of a Spanish lady from Naples, captured by the Turkish admiral, whose heart she won but only after she had suffered 'what happened to the fair Lucretia so many years before her'. When her family ransomed her she decided that her fall from grace could only result, back home, in confinement to a nunnery, so she decided to stay where she was, persuaded her Turkish captor to keep the ransom money as her portion and marry her, as honour demanded 'that no man could boast of her favours without being her husband'. The Turk was a true Selim Pasha, returned the ransom money, married her, refrained from taking other wives and died leaving her a rich and honourable widow. While she claimed to have been motivated solely by honour rather than love, she had nonetheless tapped a generosity often found among Turks.[42]

If women had little freedom of action, they did not necessarily repine in seclusion. Lady Mary Wortley Montagu, like Byron after her, was overwhelmed by the gaudy richness of the apparel worn by rich Turkish women, and by the richest of all, the Sultana. Despite the lady's strict seclusion, Lady Mary was able to make a detailed inventory of her clothes: her shift or caftan was buttoned by pearls the size of peas, or by loops of diamonds. A great diamond, the shape of a lozenge, formed its major fastening, while round her neck were strung strings of pearls or diamonds or emeralds, one of which might be as large as a turkey's egg. But her greatest wealth was worn on her hands, for the Eastern passion for rings as a portable bank deposit and visible demonstration of a husband's esteem was not confined to the Ottomans. She wore rings with diamonds shaped like pears as large as hazelnuts, larger than any diamond that Lady Mary had seen, rivalling the notorious stone, mined at Golconda, which, sold to the Regent of France, established the fortunes and the parliamentary careers of the two William Pitts. She calculated that one dress she had seen must be worth over a hundred thousand pounds, beside which the richest of most European queens would look very mean. Turkish dress hereafter became a popular travesty for masked balls and fancy dress. Men like Byron wore it for vanity, for comfort or to advertise their sympathies for the East, but for some women Lady Mary's account stimulated an erotic frisson to the passion for dressing up in Turkish clothing. Harlots wore it to stimulate men and wives their repressed husbands![43]

Ladies of lower rank and status were nearly as magnificently attired, even the household slaves being accoutred more handsomely than the domestic drudge in England. Lady Mary did not think that they found their very real confinement irksome, as they seemed to 'lead a life of uninterrupted pleasure exempt from cares; their whole time being spent in visiting, bathing or the agreeable amusement of spending money and inventing new fashions. A husband existed, at every social grade, to provide money for his wife to spend!'[44] Lady Mary believed that the privileged life she had observed in Constantinople represented a proper 'notion of life', for it was consumed in 'music, gardens, wine and delicate eating'.[45] *The Arabian Nights Entertainments* had described such a world but it was thought to be fiction. But so much of the knowledge the West had of the East had come to it in the imaginative form of fiction.

CHAPTER FOUR

Exotic and Erotic

The Myth of the Arabian Nights

De l'Orient arrive les plus beaux contes car on sait qu'en
fait de merveilleux, les Orientaux surpassaient toutes les
autres nations ... alors toute l'Europe fut avide de
l'entendre; alors les sultanes, les vizirs, les derviches, les
médecins grec, les esclaves noirs, remplacèrent
la fée Carabosse et la fée Aurore.

(Hazard, *La Crise*)[1]

I

*T*HE MYTHS OF the Ottoman Empire that flooded into Europe in the
eighteenth century were both exotic and erotic, and between them
they were as powerful as were the fear and dread of its military might. They
were composed of a ready mixture of mystery and quackery, of satanic
influences, of supernatural powers, and of sexual thraldom. In the eighth to
the thirteenth centuries CE, when the Arabs were the heirs to Greek
knowledge and sharers of Jewish kabbalistic lore – their rise to power and
conquest was, in the West, ascribed to demonic influence. Alchemy passed
into the language of post-Roman Europe as something peculiarly Islamic
and frightening, never to be quite banished by occidental and Christian
achievements in science and medicine. Hardly a tale of the Crusades was
told that did not include sorceresses and magicians, and almost as much of
Tasso's epic *La Gerusalemme Liberata* (1580–81) is spent in an enchantress's
wonderland as in fighting a furious battle for the deathplace of Christ.

The principal source of both the exotic and the erotic was *The Arabian
Nights Entertainments* or *The Thousand and One Nights*, which have presided
over the fabulous East ever since Galland published his translation into

French in 1704–07. *Entertainments* was the title that Edward Lane gave them in his translation of 1839–41. *The Thousand Nights and a Night* was the title chosen by Richard Burton (1885–88). Lane wished to de-sex the stories to make them acceptable to the taste of the time, and Burton thirty years later tried to re-sex them. *The Arabian Nights Tales* is the more general title by which they are known in the West. They were the thousand and one nights during which Scheherezade (Shahrazad, Shirazad) recounted her 'entertainments' to King Shahriya. They had to hold the interest of a king who, disgusted at the loose dalliance of his virgin wives with their black attendants during his absence from court, decreed that every one, after a night with him, should be killed. Scheherezade was the elder daughter of his vizier. When the supply of wives understandably dried up and the vizier was unable to find any more for his sovereign's bed, Scheherezade volunteered for the fatal night of pleasure. She carefully arranged for the king to overhear her stories to her younger sister Dinazade, and by stopping them at the most exciting or alluring point she managed to stave off her ritual slaughter for one thousand (or one thousand and one) nights. At that point, having given the king three sons, she sued successfully for an end to the killing and her acceptance as a permanent wife.[2]

Once published in French, *The Entertainments* quickly enthralled a society that had reason otherwise to fear the Islamic world. The collection also suited the taste of the eighteenth century; with pirated editions sweeping Europe, providing an exotic, almost cinemascopic 'treatment of sex, perversion, cruelty and corruption, their simple fantasies of wish fulfilment were all novel flavours that the reading public found greatly to its taste'.[3] The first translations, however, including those of Galland himself, did not set the *Nights* in the framework of the Scheherezade story, with its revelation of a king's obsessive cruelty, and of a voyeuristic younger sister taking pleasure from the story itself and, it was suggested, from the sexual encounter that followed when Scheherezade cut each story off at the most exciting part. This was clearly unsuitable for the general reader of the day, but by the 1840s the Romantic interest in perversity and the *fleurs du mal* had made a tale of barbarity in luxury not only attractive but a morality in itself. King Shahriya may have been the image *par excellence* of an oriental despot but one whom civilisation could tame, and Scheherezade metamorphosed into the 'chaste wife, wise, without debate' beloved of Victorian readers.[4]

The compilation, even composition, of these tales is still disputed. Though they purported to be of Persian origin, Coleridge detected 'a good deal of Greek fancy' in them and regretted the loss of what he considered to be their inspiration, the *Milesian Tales by Aristides* of Miletus, an ancestor of both the *Decameron* and *Heptameron*. Pretty well nothing is known of these tales, except that they were salacious, that Ovid wrote that they were translated into Latin and that they were read out in the Parthian senate house of Seleucia in order to insult the Romans. This was because, according to Plutarch, they were found on a dead Roman soldier during Crassus's last, fatal, campaign, and demonstrated to the Parthian senate how degenerate were their Roman enemies, who carried such scabrous works with them in their knapsacks.[5]

One Arab chronicler, referring to the collection in the tenth century, called it 'a corrupted book of silly narratives'.[6] Silly they may have been but like many silly tales they have survived as a source of oriental fable, an inspiration for pantomime, a quarry for opera, and an almost inexhaustible matter for anthropologists, textual critics and literary pundits.[7] Scheherezade's seemingly inexhaustible invention was exercised in the harem of a Persian monarch, and one ingenious student identified him as Esther's Ahasuerus. Shahrazad, in Persian Chihr-azad, was the name of the Jewish mother of Queen Humay, the daughter of Artaxerxes Longimanus, son of Xerxes, identified as Ahasuerus, since the Apocryphal chapters of the Book of Esther refer to him as Artaxerxes. When he sent out for virgins to sample after he repudiated Vashti his queen, Ahasuerus may, by his choice of Esther, have suggested the frame in which the *Nights* are set.

Their daughter was credited with authorship of the *Nights*, much as Marguerite de Valois has been credited with writing *The Heptameron*. The stories, however, whether set in Baghdad, Tehran, India or China, are not about Persians but about Arabs, the common core of all editions being almost certainly the fruit of the golden age of the Caliphate in Baghdad, between the eighth and tenth centuries.

A prominent protagonist is the Caliph Harun-Ar Rashid (the Abbasid Caliph between 763 and 809, and a contemporary of Charlemagne). The uncertainties about the original canon (and two of its most famous stories, Aladdin and the Lamp, and Ali Baba and the Forty Thieves, were not in the original collection), derive from the peripatetic habits of the professional story-tellers who carried them round the Arab world. The *Nights* were basically popular street literature, and this accounts for the inability of scholars to fix either the authorship, or the date, or the content of the collection. They were not considered part of the canon of classical Arabic letters.

Antoine Galland (1646–1715), who introduced the *Nights* to the western world, was attached to the French mission in Constantinople in 1670, having learned Arabic at the Sorbonne. The principal part of his job was to collect manuscripts for the university library, for which purpose he travelled throughout the Arabic-speaking lands of the Ottoman empire. He was later commissioned by Colbert to be the oriental expert of the newly founded *Compagnie des Indes*, and charged to collect and translate useful documents. In Damascus he found a collection of stories, now generally held to date from 1566, for most scholars accept the middle of the sixteenth century CE as the time when most of these stories were collected and written down in Arabic. One reason given for this dating is that there is no mention of coffee drinking, for coffee did not become a generally acceptable beverage throughout the Muslim world until the seventeenth century. Galland began to publish the tales as *Les Mille et Un Nuits* in twelve volumes between 1704 and 1717, when he was Professor of Arabic at the Collège de France in Paris. His text is still the standard French version.

The first English translation – from the original Arabic, not the French version – was that of Edward William Lane in 1838–40, and he put the date of compilation at 1517 to coincide with the Ottoman conquest of Egypt, where the habits of luxury and wine-drinking, which are a feature of the tales, were general. Linguistic hints, however, suggest that the core of the tales themselves date from between the fall of the Fatimids and accession of Saladdin in 1169 to the sack of Baghdad and the fall of the Caliphate at the hands of the Mongols in 1258.[8] Lane spent 16 years on the task, five of them in Cairo. He lived among the Arabs almost as a true believer, and his translation followed *The Manners and Customs of the Modern Egyptians*, his classic account of which appeared in 1836. Cairo was at this time the epicentre of Arab culture, and Lane's translation was sound and authentic.[9]

Richard Burton, who also translated the tales as part of his campaign for the sexual freedoms that he believed would liberate English women from frigidity, thought it 'garbled and mutilated, unsexed and unsouled'. Lane certainly exercised his own rigid censorship, excluding those tales that would, in his view, upset the morals of the generation that had just welcomed a virgin and nubile queen after twenty years' rule by adulterers, one of whom, William IV, had sired ten children by his thespian Scheherezade, Mrs Jordan. The collection of *Nights*, as annotated by Lane, constituted a sort of encyclopaedia of Muslim life and manners and Richard Burton, otherwise contemptuous of the sexual exclusions, admitted that between them the notes he and Lane provided to their translations would enable any reader to 'know as much of the Moslem East, and more, than many Europeans who have spent half their lives in Orient lands'.[10]

Among the later additions to the *Entertainments* were 11 tales told to Galland by a man from Aleppo. These enabled him to complete another volume. One of them, *The Tale of Abu-el-Hasan-al-Khalia*, in a slightly modified version, provided the story for a comic *singspiel* by Carl-Maria von Weber. It is one of the Harun-Ar-Rashid stories, in which the genial caliph is worsted by a man on whom he had himself played a trick. The trick was to make Abu Hassan Caliph for a day, in which he would be able to punish all those friends who, he averred, had treated him scurvily. The short one-act drama is devoted to the return trick that Abu Hassan plays on the Caliph, by pretending that both he and his wife are dead and so securing two funeral grants from the generous monarch. When Harun, checking up on this suspicious pair of deaths, asks who died first, he is informed by Abu Hassan that it was he. Harun, amused and endlessly tolerant, rewards Abu Hassan by making him his cup-bearer.

Weber was not the first to compose a Turkish comic opera. Apart from Wolfgang Amadeus Mozart, his music master, the Abbé Vogler, whom Schubert considered a charlatan and Browning rescued from oblivion, had also composed a Turkish opera, *The Merchant of Smyrna* (*Der Kaufmann von Smyrna*). Vogler may have failed in his ambition to rival Beethoven as an improviser on the piano but he succeeded in arousing in Weber that love of the exotic and irrational that led him to his later triumphs with *Der Freischütz*, *Euryanthe* and *Oberon*. At this point in Weber's life (1811) Abu Hassan was cast in the brilliantly playful and joyous mood that looked backward and forward to Mozart and Rossini. The work only reached London in 1825, almost a curtain-raiser for Lane's translation 13 years later.

2

Most of the oriental fables of the day were in French. Barthélemy d'Herbelot de Molainville (1625–95) learned his Arabic and other eastern tongues by consorting with mariners in Italian seaports. He became secretary and interpreter of Eastern languages to Louis XIV, ending his life as a pensioner of Colbert and Professor of Syriac at the Collège de France, and the author of *La Bibliothèque Orientale ou Dictionnaire Universal contenant tout ce qui regarde le connoissance des Peuples de l'Orient*. France had become the main source and origin of oriental knowledge. French artists moved naturally from fact to fairy tale to fable and magic. The Sun King had established a taste for finery, for *trompe l'oeil*, in which nothing was quite what it seemed to be, for masques and masquerades.

The Arabian Nights Entertainments spawned a prolific rash of orientalia, using the newly discovered Eastern world to point a moral and adorn a tale. For here were pegs on which to hang political criticism, authentic lands requiring no midgets or giants or flying islands like Lilliput, Brobdignag or Laputa to provide a locale from which to pass judgements safely on matters nearer home. Being lands ruled either by wise philosophers such as Mozart's and Schikaneder's Sarastro, or by cruel tyrants, like their Queen of the Night, they provided 'a sense of reality in the midst of unreality'.[11] What was essential was that they were remote, and the more closely the stories followed the style of *The Arabian Nights*, despite being condemned as 'extravagant, monstrous and disproportioned',[12] the more popular they were. Alexander Pope might deplore the existence of the hack who turned a Persian tale for half a crown but nothing could stop the proliferation of eastern make-believe.[13]

The extravagant fancies of Galland provided both an escape into a world of fantasy, an Orient so strange that cunning satirists such as Montesquieu and Voltaire could dress their criticism of contemporary society in the costumes of make-believe.[14] Voltaire's *Zadig* (1748) was set in Zoroastrian Baghdad, being the adventures of a man in pursuit of rational and unexceptionable behaviour in a world governed by 'les huit parties d'oraison, la dialectique, l'astrologie, la démonomanie'.[15] For a short time chief minister of the king of Babylon, Zadig is under no illusion that he is obeyed not because he is either rational or amiable but because 'il était premier vizir'. When his rational judgements and wise advice triumph over folly or crime, they do not lessen the envy, malice and prejudice of the men and women they have exposed to ridicule. Misfortune, therefore, dogs him throughout, for Zoroastrian Babylon is no different from Louis XV's France.

England's Grand Cham was to follow France's *bouleverseteur*. Samuel Johnson's *Rasselas* (1759–62) is, like *Zadig*, set in a land as fictional as *Erewhon*, Samuel Butler's *Nowhere*. Rasselas is the Prince of Abyssinia who, having lived in undemanding comfort and ease in 'a happy valley', seeks to broaden his experience by travel, and goes to Egypt, which in its turn is as real as pantomime. Babylon and Abyssinia, despite available Jesuit accounts to the contrary, are all remote, romantic-sounding places, where Zadig and Prince Rasselas could learn the vanity of human wishes.[16] (Rasselas is a black personage who shares many of the characteristics of Candide, the novel of that name appearing at about the same time; had Johnson ever practised manual labour it would have taught him that *il faut cultiver son jardin*.)

These oriental tales are oriental only in adventitious detail; their principal characters are embedded in the society of their time. *The Arabian Nights*, however, were the genuine article, set in the high noon of Arab civilisation, bringing 'the prime of good Haroun Alraschid' to every polite drawing room and displacing the Disney-like rocococity of wicked Carabosse and good fairy Aurora. One critic called them 'the fairy godmother of the English novel'.[17] Scheherezade had a novelist's skill in providing suspense at every pause in her narrative, but more to the point the picaresque adventures she was telling took place in a world as authentic to their protagonists as Henry Fielding's London to Tom Jones. The stories might be intricate, the characters extravagant, the *mis-en-scène* exotic but they did not moralise or preach a philosophy of life, like *Rasselas*, or expose it to mockery, like *Zadig*. The oriental background gave them a romantic flavour in contrast to the classical euphonics of Augustan London or pre-Revolutionary Paris. It was a world of cool, soft turf, shadow-chequered lawns, thick rosaries of scented thorn and Persian girls with

> argent lidded eyes,
> Amorous, and lashes like to rays
> Of darkness, and a brow of pear
> Tressed with redolent ebony.[18]

The poetic indication was that these were to be found by the lush banks of the Tigris, but Tennyson's *Arabian Nights* (1830) is a poem in which the exotic and erotic derive more from the Muslim gardens of Spain and the Alhambra, such as those then being created, under the influence of Washington Irving, on the banks of the Thames. The young poet was still fascinated by the incense-laden world of a Romantic imagination that was infecting western sensibility; 'the heroic romance had died and left no issue' but this:[19]

And many a sheeny summer morn,
Adown the Tigris I was borne,
By Bagdad's shrines of fretted gold,
High-walled gardens green and old;
True Mussulman was I and sworn,
For it was in the golden prime
Of good Haroun Alraschid.[20]

3

The Arabian Nights Entertainments was not solely responsible. Its most popular and perverse fruit was a tale that appeared in 1786. The supposed author was an American loyalist clergyman, Samuel Henley, who had left his post as Professor of Moral Philosophy at William and Mary College in Williamsburg at the beginning of the American War of Independence. After teaching at Harrow for a few years he was given the living of Rendlesham in Suffolk. His interests had already admitted him by election to the Society of Antiquaries; he had studied the controversial passages in the writings of Saints Peter and Jude on the Angels that Sinned, to see how far Milton had been justified in his portraits of them; and throughout his life he loved stray learning, making himself an expert on the poetry of Virgil.

At the request of a friend in 1784 he translated from the French and published what purported to be an oriental tale he had been given in manuscript form. The French version was, so word had it, itself a translation from the Arabic but, as its style was bold and original, its readers held that Henley had written the tale himself, so that he could append learned footnotes, in which he revelled, on the topographical, literary, linguistic and alchemic references with which the story was filled. Henley always insisted that he had not written the original, but as he possessed the only version of the French original, when he published it as an oriental tale, he appeared to be acknowledging authorship.

The real author had taken his family off to Switzerland and was powerless to substantiate his claim. In order to publish the tale in its 'original' form he put Henley's English text back into French, and then published the French 'original' three years later from both Paris and Lausanne. At last the real author emerged from the shadows: he was William Beckford and the curious story was *Vathek*.[21]

The oddly reclusive Midas knew no Arabic, and had no first-hand knowledge of the East other than what he picked up mainly from *The Arabian Nights*. Indeed, he had had no formal education beyond what private tutors could provide, and he had decided to write the tale in French, his mother tongue being English, to disguise its origins.[22] Beckford remained an enigma all his life. He claimed that he had not written *Vathek* in English owing to 'circonstances peu intéressantes pour le public' but no one really knew what they were. He never provided his own translation, believing that Samuel Henley's was good enough, though he did later translate an oriental tale from the French, titled *Al Raoui*. Despite the elder William Pitt's advice to him as a precocious and mercurial child not to read *The Arabian Nights Entertainments*, Beckford could not resist using the opportunity for embellished conceits about beauty, art and the world of the imagination provided by an ostensibly oriental tale. At the same time, he could not suppress a demurely satirical streak that was later to repeat itself in the work of Oscar Wilde and Ronald Firbank.

He claimed to have written *Vathek* in one continuous narrative, not punctuated by chapters, in three days and two nights while living in Switzerland with his wife. When she died he returned to his family home, Fonthill, and spent the rest of his career building, rebuilding and embellishing the house, collecting art treasures and books, and virtually beggaring himself. *Vathek* remained without a sequel, a solitary work of enthusiasm and genius masquerading as the authentic creation of an oriental world, a quarry for Romantic poets whose imagination luxuriated in nightingales and roses, butterflies of Cashmere and wine of Shiraz. *Vathek* was not their sole inspiration; Shiraz wine was the staple tipple of East India Company factories, while the other images flitted in an out of the Persian poetry of North India, being currently translated by Company officials.[23]

Yet Beckford's interests were not oriental, except in a lazy and circumstantial way. More they belonged to the rococo world, in which his cousin, Peter, had walked with Mozart's father in the gardens of the Villa Medici in Rome, and had persuaded Muzio Clementi to come to London. Beckford had undertaken the Grand Tour with his tutor in 1780–81 and kept a journal, published two centuries later and subtitled *Europe Before the Revolution Seen Through the Eyes of a Quizzical Young Man*.[24] *Vathek* is a rococo tale, the ornamentalism of its imagination winding in curlicues of fancy against a background of casual cruelty and darkening shadows, which seemed to epitomise the eastern world. Byron thought its descriptive detail, its sense of costume and luxuriant imagination made it hard for those who had visited the East to believe it was not the translation of an original oriental work.[25]

Its eponymous hero, the Caliph Vathek, is the grandson of Haroun el Raschid, so that the tale is set at some time in the tenth century CE, at a time when the Caliphate extended from Egypt to India. The action of the novel takes place in the Arabo-Iranian land between the Euphrates and the Caucasian mountain fastnesses. Most of it is set in a mountain landscape, round lakes and valleys, inhabited by a population of dwarves, ghouls, genii (djinns), and talking fishes. It is a no-man's land in which supernatural powers, none of them friendly to man, lurk to guard the hidden wealth of Soliman (Solomon), the magnitude of which beggars the imagination.

The normal conventions of the eighteenth-century novel do not apply to *Vathek*. There is no hero, no heroine; there is an unpleasant but colourful sorceress, much magical and supernatural intervention, but no real story and no conclusive finale to sort out all the puzzles. Most of the characters start as figures of fun; even the sorceress who, abhorring indolence, cannot resist curing the people whom she intends to die from the wounds she has caused to be inflicted.[26] Vathek himself, in a Firbankian aside, eats succulent fruit at prayer time, and 'calls for the Koran and sugar' to accompany it.[27] It is difficult at first to see past the ironical smoke-screen Beckford wove round the story. Was it the self-indulgent creation of a rococo fancy, or an elaborately disguised morality? The book is a celebration of perversity. Vathek's devotion to Islam is entirely opportunistic and, for the promise of unexampled wealth, he is only too ready to renounce it. He has a persistent anxiety about his next meal, which he expects to be a triumph of culinary art, and is over-anticipatory of the next dalliance with a woman, which he expects to be better than the last. So when the finale comes, it is with the shock of surprise.

A sinister element is first provided by Vathek's mother, Carathis, whom he dislikes but of whom he is afraid. With her one-eyed black Nubian slaves, mummified corpses, supernatural camel and power to talk to fishes, she is a powerful and single-minded sorceress. It is she who urges her son to seek Soliman's treasure with the aid of a sinister Indian *giaour*, whose object turns out to be the Caliph's soul. Beckford seems to have thought that a *giaour* signified the member of some Indian sect of saltimbanques. The word signified any non-Muslim, but acquired in the West a sinister connotation. A *giaour* was not only a non-Muslim but an enemy to Islam.

The orientalism of this tale, apart from its setting in an indeterminately Arabo-Persian frame, lies in the Islamic decoration Beckford gives it, belonging as much to the pantomime stage as to the books he collected and sometimes read. It pretends to be a satire on the vanity, not so much of human wishes, as of human desires. Organised religion is faintly mocked. There is a whole harem of unfortunate women who accompany the Caliph wherever he goes on his supernatural travels, confined to cages, from within which their only contribution to the tale are shrieks and giggles. Vathek has one reigning wife, Dilara, and is surrounded by eunuchs, the chief of whom, Bababalouk, tries to ensure a stream of good food and female comforts for the Lord of the Universe, when he embarks at last on his dangerous mission in search of Soliman's gold. On the way Vathek encounters the incredibly beautiful anti-heroine, Nouronihar, with her ivory limbs, and her light brown hair floating in the hazy breeze of the twilight. She has all the attributes of a houri, all the letters of which word are incorporated in her name. She turns out to be both a flirt and a gold-digger, and she captivates the susceptible caliph by her behaviour at bath-time as well as by her gourmet cooking.

The Reverend Samuel Henley had plenty to write about in his footnotes, as Beckford's imagination pranced about in fields of antiquity and curious lore. The treasure in search of which Vathek travels with his wives, concubines and eunuchs belongs to the Pre-Adamite sultans, the 72 kings who ruled over the anthropoid predecessors of man before God created Adam. Isaac de la Peryère, in 1654, was puzzled by the provenance of Cain's wife in *Genesis*, chapter 4, who seems not to be the daughter of Adam and Eve, and concluded that *Genesis* must have been concerned with the origins of the Jewish people, and that Cain's wife came from pre-Adamite people living in the land of Nod.[28] Most bore the name of Soliman, and Adam's non-evolutionary precursors knew both the power of magic and the value of filthy gold. The Biblical Solomon himself (Soliman ben Daoud) is entrusted with the guardianship of this treasure, as in his latter years, the Bible tells us, in addition to marrying idolatresses, he became obsessed by gold. Of the angels who sinned, about whom Samuel Henley knew all, perhaps more than all, Beckford appears to have been ignorant, but delinquent angels, known in the East as djinns or peris, are charged with protecting the treasure of the pre-Adamite kings.

This forbidding underworld is ruled by a Satan figure, Eblis, who has been commissioned by God to keep these angels exiled, with the treasure, in the furthest part of the earth. Hidden with the treasure is the Talisman of

Soliman, which Vathek's mother, Carathis, most wants, a ring very like that of Tolkein's *Lord of the Rings*, which will give the wearer entire command of everything, human, natural and demonic. The power of a talisman, both benign and malign, given to those who possess it, has exerted on the English imagination a strong attraction from the Holy Grail to Charles Williams's Stone of Solomon.[29] It is morally neutral, which is why its power is so important to control. It finds a wholly new existence in the popular programmes in which Dr Who has to protect his Tardis and in which Harry Potter is engaged on a cosmic contest for possession with the power of darkness. When Vathek finds the treasure, according to the *giaour*, he will be 'solaced with all kinds of delight.'[30]

The quest becomes clearer as it progresses, for *Vathek* starts to turn into a morality tale. The Caliph is too easily distracted from his quest, by a good meal, or by a girl like Nouronihar. His mother is more single-minded, being determined to secure the ring for herself and the rest of the treasure for her son. At long last Vathek, and Nouronihar, who cannot resist the lure of gold, and Carathis, the similarity of whose name to catharsis explains her fate, enter the subterranean world of Eblis. There they meet travellers who have nursed similar ambitions, and who are condemned to stalk the halls with their empty hand on the place where their heart should be. Theirs is the heartburn which results from lust and greed: a perennial flame in the place of a heart.

Having seen the halls of Eblis, Carathis orders all its treasures opened to her, which even the *afrits* and demons have never seen, and all the spirits to bow down before her as their chief. She is about to dethrone one of the pre-Adamite kings when her heart bursts into flames.[31] When they all meet Eblis, who speaks their doom, they see not a Satanic figure in the Dantean image or even a leader of the Dance of Death, but one 'whose person was that of a young man, whose noble and regular features seemed to have been tarnished by malignant vapours. In his large eyes appeared both pride and despair, his hair retained some resemblance to that of an angel of light.'[32] He is remarkably like a creature of William Blake who, while Beckford was writing *Vathek*, was writing his own first satirical works. Beckford ends his tale on a pious note: for the sake of empty pomp and forbidden power, Vathek (and all others like him, implies the author) will be prey to grief without end and remorse without mitigation.

There is only one happy person in this story: the epicene teenage lover of Nouronihar before she meets Vathek. He is blessed to live a life 'remote from the inquietudes of the world, the impertinence of harems, the brutality of eunuchs, and the inconstancy of women'. He enjoys what Beckford himself would like to have enjoyed, 'the boon of perpetual childhood'.[33] He was fortunate to acquire this state through supernatural intervention for, as Beckford tells us, whether in Christian Europe or in the Muslim East, no one in the way of nature can escape impertinence, brutality and inconstancy.

4

Beckford's hall of Eblis was an oriental nightmare, but Alfred Tennyson's Tigris was the dream of a golden past. When Tennyson came upon the 'great Pavilion of the Caliphat', he was safely evoking the 'golden prime of good Haroun Alraschid' and the innocence of *The Arabian Nights*, not the fearful power of the Ottoman superstate which had established both the caliphate and a secular empire ruled from Constantinople. There, for most people, the sultan personified, with his viziers, pashas and beys, the intricate splendour of Byzantium, which in its time anticipated the perfumed gardens of the Arabian Nights, and which also experienced the inexorable rule of a theocracy. Ottoman Constantinople was Byzantium revived, the only noticeable difference being the disappearance of the women and their relegation to the atrophying seclusion of the harem or child factory, where Islam held they properly belonged, and where they were invisible, in marked contrast to a former Byzantine empress, who was once a circus dancer. Of which emperor, one may ask, was Yeats thinking when he wrote of Byzantium 'of hammered gold and gold enamelling / To keep a drowsy Emperor awake', and of the bird 'set upon the golden bough to sing ... / ... Of what is past or passing or to come'.[34]

As Europe entered its age of enlightenment, or disillusionment, the East lost its minatory and supernatural power and became instead an exotic 'faraway' for strange and erotic adventures. These were married happily to the fantasies of the age that followed the Ottoman rebuff at Vienna. 'A western coquetry was projected onto the shores of the Bosphorus, reconstructed for the entertainment of the sophisticated upper classes ... which the seraglio's seclusion rendered highly seductive.'[35] *Turquoiserie* began to tempt Europeans to sample the exotic comforts that they had seen in Ottoman Turkey and which the English were acquiring from India. Baths, carpets, Turkish delight and, above all, coffee conquered where armies had faltered.

5

Coffee was Ethiopia's gift to the world. There it grew wild. The Arabs, at some time in the fifteenth century, commercialised the twin beans that snuggled in the cherry-like fruit of *coffea arabica*. Its energising, anti-soporific qualities (deduced from the behaviour of sheep grazing on the berries) aroused controversy among the faithful, for it was drunk originally, the mullahs suspected, to keep them awake through interminable sermons. Was it a stimulant, was it intoxicating, was it forbidden to Muslims by the Koran? Divine retribution might attend anyone who developed an addiction to it, but the menace of eternal damnation did not prevent the Arabian ports on the Red Sea, especially Mocha, from becoming *entrepôts* supplying the whole Muslim world. The story that the aroma of roasting coffee wafted from the Ottoman camp at the siege of Vienna drove the besieged to distraction is unproven, but it was not long before the coffee house in Constantinople had its counterpart in Venice. The first coffee house opened in London in Cornhill in 1652, and coffee-drinking spread across Europe in the latter half of the seventeenth century, its popularity contentious, too, in Christian lands, as authority feared that coffee houses encouraged loose talk and political disaffection. Leipzig had eight coffee houses when Bach composed his cantata in praise of the beverage. Official opinion was divided between fears for health and desire for revenue, a not unfamiliar tension throughout the ages.

So quickly had the drink become popular that Johann Sebastian Bach wrote a cantata in 1732 in which a young woman, whose father is seeking a husband for her, insists that she will not entertain any proposal unless she is allowed – in the marriage contract itself – *den Kaffee, wann ich will, zu kuchen.*[36] To meet the world demand, it was not long before the bean's cultivation had migrated to more congenial climates. An enemy to sleep, an aid to boredom, a stimulant to sedition, coffee may have caused anxiety among the authorities, but no medicinal, only moral, harm could be attributed to it. Its discovery and commercialisation by Muslims seemed confirmation to critical western observers that the Ottomans needed it to overcome the general torpor that appeared to afflict the empire in the century during which drinking it became almost a culture in itself.

Drunk in Turkish baths, on Turkish carpets, in Turkish silks and haberdashery, in the abandon of the Turkish harem, coffee added to the image of a people who preferred to loiter, who found sexual triviality more enticing than intellectual discovery, who believed that violent death was a more effective agent of control than justice, for whom intrigue was more exciting than diplomacy and who considered sucking on a *nargheel* less demanding than conversation. Lady Mary Wortley Montagu and Lady Hester Stanhope may have been pleasantly and publicly impressed by the charm and liveliness of Turkish ladies, but the society at home in which they used to move did not believe that this could be so. The western view of Turkish curiosity began and ended in the dragoman's interpretation of Alexander Kinglake's discourse on western technology. It was all 'whir! whir! all by wheels! – whiz! whiz! all by steam!'[37]

6

Vathek provided a wishful dream of the Orient, as much as a nightmare. It starts as a romance of a perfumed and luxurious idyll, and ends in a hell of Dantean intensity. It reeks of a drug-induced *cauchemar*, the kind in which, as de Quincey was to claim nearly forty years later, man was a weed, a strange amalgam of high culture and low barbarism, his dreams under opium of cancerous kisses by crocodiles, in which the dreamer, 'confounded with all unutterable abortions, lay amongst the weeds and Nilotic mud'.[38] Opium, which delivered these fantasies, was the oriental drug *par excellence*, and its narcotic monopoly, once the possession of the Muslim rulers of Bengal, was now a principal money-earner for the East India Company.

The real nightmares, however, did not emanate from opium but were the waking dreams of freedom, dreamed by those Europeans unhappy enough to become captives and slaves of Muslim states in Africa and Asia. There, if they did not join the company of apostates, life had little of colour and fantasies that only dreams could provide. The real nightmare in the West was the nightmare of captivity.

CHAPTER FIVE

Peri and Prisoner

The Myth of the Bagno

Barbary pirate ships are of little value, sufficient neither
for the subsistence of wounded mariners, nor for widows'
pensions, nor for gratifications to the captors, all expenses
necessary to keep sailors in the service of the Religion.
(Grand-Master of Malta to his envoy in Vienna, 26 April 1765)[1]

I

ONE OF THE greatest exploiters of womanhood was not a Muslim at all and, during all the time he spent in Constantinople as part of the Venetian embassy, Giacomo Casanova had only one sexual diversion. If we accept his memoirs as a truthful record of his exploits he was, on this sole occasion, allowed to view with a Turkish friend three women of his harem bathing naked, during which his host and he could only deflate their excitement by mutual fellatio.[2] Lady Mary Wortley Montagu, the ambassador's wife, and Casanova, the embassy secretary, unwittingly confirmed the general impression, being spread in the popular literature of the day, that a Turkish bath or *bagno* was only one step removed from a brothel. The image was certainly a powerful one, captured in the early nineteenth century by Dominic Ingres, who endowed his odalisques in the *bagno* with an air of expectant pulchritude, even lubricity, on which Lady Mary very properly did not remark. English poets and artists for their part preferred to remain chastely above it all.

Walter Savage Landor (1775–1864), in full lust of youth, but mindful of his chaste love for Rose Aylmer, allowed himself a cautious literary imitation of Casanova *voyeuring* in Constantinople. His early epic poem of

1798, *Gebir*, describes the queen of Egypt, preparing for her nuptials by taking a bath:

> Long she lingered at the brink,
> Often she sighed, and, naked as she was
> Sat down, and leaning on the couch's edge,
> On the soft inward pillow of her arm
> Rested her burning cheek:[3]

In so doing he inaugurated the archetypal image, so beloved of Alma Tadema and Lord Leighton, of the sexless odalisque tiptoeing into pellucid water, which ripplingly reflects her nubile limbs. Leighton in his Moroccan-style house in Holland Park Road, with its Damascene tiles, and sunken bath and fountain under a beehive dome, delighted in virgins soft as roses. Their peris, all bathing nudes, their shapely buttocks blushing pink and nipples rosy on their ample breasts, remained curiously sexless, as if exhausted by the effort of slipping their clothing. With these bathing beauties *Pudicitia*, ready to arouse but unwilling to inflame, had replaced the unashamed nakedness of Lady Mary's harem ladies at the Turkish bath. The Victorian odalisque was as oriental as an advertisement for loosely fitting underwear.

2

In the middle of the seventeenth century, however, the word *bagno* had for European readers a more forbidding meaning. It was where prisoners reduced to servitude in a perpetual war of religion were housed. One of the more bizarre features of Mediterranean history was the survival until after the Napoleonic wars of the institution of licensed piracy and prisoner slavery, masquerading as a religious war. On the Christian side, Spain, and its dependencies Naples and Sicily, were most committed to it, inhibited from making terms with the 'enemy' by the Crusade Bull, which was promulgated when the Spaniards were wrestling with Muslim occupiers on their own soil. Tuscany (with its licensed pirates, known as the Knights of St Stephen), the Papal States and Malta (with its licensed pirates, the Knights Hospitaller of St John) were committed to this war, part of the seven-centuries-old perpetual war to keep Islam out of western Europe.

Since the Ottoman empire and its dependencies pledged to its own form of *jihad* had become a naval force in those waters, the crusade had extended to those Christian ports which maintained warships, however small or light, who might successfully resist the advance of Islam on the sea and protect their shores against Turkish and Moorish raids and their merchants from depredation at sea. This war of hide and seek, to find, destroy or capture had been the special skill of the small galleys, really floating landing stages crewed by oar, which were light, manoeuvrable, of shallow draught, and viciously armed to grapple with, board and overcome their prey. They did not depend on wind or deep water. Their weapons were nautical skill, boldness and manpower. Because of the permanent need for the last, a heartless and vicious system of warfare had grown up, which meant that all prisoners taken in this war became slaves of their captor, largely to man the galleys, chained to a very probable death from a broken neck or drowning, as an opponent broke one set of oars by ramming. With the development of sailing vessels almost as manoeuvrable as a light galley, the need for oarsmen declined and slaves were put to public works, mainly building or improving the immense fortifications that protected the maritime cities on both sides of the Mediterranean, or were sold to private citizens as domestic servants.

There was no Geneva Convention to protect the rights of prisoners of war, but a system of reciprocity had grown up whereby the treatment of slaves was regulated by custom, breach of which could invite reprisals. The Ottomans had largely by 1700 withdrawn from this type of warfare, replacing it by diplomatic representation. The most prominent nation with whom they had diplomatic relations was France, but the French court always stressed that this did not make it pro-Muslim.[4] But the Ottoman Regents, the Beys of Tunis and Tripoli, and the Dey of Algiers were virtually rulers of self-governing states and a law unto themselves. The Sultan of Morocco was not an Ottoman dependant, and his country faced the Atlantic as well as the Mediterranean, but piracy and slavery were also the props of his economy. To Christian seamen, Morocco and the Barbary Regencies – which occupied the coast line once the exclusive homeland of the Berbers, a Caucasian but Islamic people (Arabic *barbar*) – all posed an anarchic threat to the freedom of the seas.

Front-line states such as Malta had enough prisoners to ensure that this convention was kept in North Africa and reciprocity protected the continuation of slavery, so necessary to the domestic economies of these states. Being sparsely populated by a mainly nomadic people, the Barbary Regencies, ruled by Turkish adventurers, depended on an involuntary but skilled workforce to complete their public works, at first protective walls and ditches and later grandiose mosques and palaces. The Sultan of Morocco between 1672 and 1727, Moulay Ismā'īl, intent on rivalling his contemporaries the Sultan in Constantinople and Louis XIV, employed with singular brutality a workforce of Europeans, largely taken, like Robinson Crusoe, by the corsairs of Salé either on the high seas or in daring shore raids. Some of these prisoners came from far-away Iceland, and many from the Cornish peninsula.[5] Similarly, slave labour from North Africa helped to erect the mighty bastions of Malta.

Any of the major naval powers could have put an end to this perpetual war at any time. Indeed, Cromwell's Admiral Robert Blake in 1654 had already shown them how it should be done. That it lasted until 1816, when Lord Exmouth battered Algiers into ruin to persuade the Dey to honour the treaty he had signed abolishing Christian slavery, is a testimony to the vested interest the littoral states, both Muslim and Christian, had in keeping the Regencies in being. Great Britain, having recently acquired Tangiers, Gibraltar and Minorca by treaty and conquest, relied on Barbary to keep their garrisons supplied with food and water, and was reluctant to enter into any forceful arrangements to protect her shipping or release her subjects from slavery. France put greater importance on her diplomatic alliance in Constantinople, reckoning that the advantages of its treaties with the Porte were worth the survival of the Regencies as pirate states. Spain was the one major nation to take her Christian mission of war with the Infidel too seriously to contemplate more than a local truce from time to time, but her European wars demanded more naval resources than could be spared for peripheral activity. For most of the century Spain controlled Naples and Sicily but, when she no longer did so, the Kings of Naples were engaged in more important survival games than antagonising the nests of buccaneers across the water.

3

The rank and value of a Christian captive taken in this undeclared war once established, assisted by a little judicious torture by bastinado if he was thought to be diminishing himself, he was available for disposal by sale. In

FIGURE 4   *A Turkish slave, detail from the tomb of Grand Master Nicolo Cotoner (regnavit 1663–80) in St John's Co-Cathedral, Valleta, Malta, ascribed to Demenico Guidi. The characteristic moustache and shaven head with topknot identified the wearer as a prisoner of war/slave.*

Algiers the Dey took one in eight of able-bodied men for public works and often more if he thought they had particular skills. The remaining seven were sent to the slave market and paraded like cattle to attract a buyer. As the presence of a large captive population in a small city port was often barely exceeded by the indigenous population, it had to be distinguished by physical appearance, by dress and by shackles, and lodged securely until ransomed in dungeon-like strongholds, which took the name of the baths they so closely resembled.

Christian captives, taken in conflict, or by pirates in landing parties, often far away from the pirate's base in North Africa, were the chattels of the captor(s) who could negotiate their ransom or sell them to another owner. He was free to transfer any women slaves into his own or another harem (which was how Kostanze in Mozart's opera ended up in Pasha Selim's household[6]), or treat them as unpaid domestic servants. Consigned to a bagno on a ration of three small loaves of coarse black bread, such as was sold to poor Muslims, the slave was required to labour through the hottest days from dawn to dusk, allowed only holy days off to look after himself.

Religious orders, like the Redemptorists, assumed official consular roles to arrange and provide a mail service from Christian prisoners to their families, while a Turkish or Moorish cadi, often a mullah, filled the same role in the Christian ports. Even when the French consulates in Barbary were recognised by treaty, priests were attached to the consulate to carry on the business of ransoming slaves, since the religious orders controlled the funds. Ransoms varied with the rank or physical condition of the slave, payable in piastres or sequins of Barbary. The piastre was worth about four French livres so that an average ransom was 150 piastres (£30 or £40 of the day), but an influential or richly connected slave would command a much higher sum. A special redemption mission might negotiate a cheaper rate for slaves in bulk, and private treaty could bring the price demanded down, but slaves so redeemed had often outlived their economic value. As all observers remarked caustically: money was all that Barbary was interested in.[7] The ruler took his percentage from the ransom, which in a pirate state was one of the principal sources of revenue.

The treatment of slave prisoners varied according to whether their families were able to meet the ransom demanded. Richer captives might even be housed as guests in the captor's household if the arrival of the ransom seemed only a matter of weeks; others less fortunate lived in the *bagnos*, clothed in rags, poorly fed, and often brutally treated, while a charitable collection for his ransom might take years; in the meantime the prisoner to be ransomed might be purposely maltreated to speed up payment.

The poorest often disappeared into slavery, either meeting death chained to the oar of a galliot or worn out by privation. They might, if lucky or considered specially deserving, be recipients of local charity and often kindness, some slaves actually setting up families in captivity. Those who changed faith were not necessarily freed or subject to better conditions, since it was not to the advantage of their owner to lose the ransom, which was not paid for those who changed their faith. Sometimes apostasy paid rich dividends, but the richest went to those who became Muslims freely. Casanova in Constantinople met Osman, Pasha of Karamania, the *ci-devant* French Comte de Bonneval, who certainly took his conversion lightly. His library and seraglio consisted of an array of bottles of fine wine, cunningly disguised behind latticed doors. All he said he had to do was say that "'God is God and Mahommed his prophet" and the Turks do not bother their heads over whether I thought it or not.' He lived in style, employed a renegade French cook and a renegade Neapolitan gardener, entertained his guests in Italian, the lingua franca of polite discourse with foreigners, and because of his age left his two wives unmolested in comfort.[8]

Though the captive renegade from either faith never, unless formally manumitted, lost the status of slave or confinement at night to the bagno, his conversion, particularly to Islam, often opened the door to a privileged position. Byron, in his poem *The Siege of Corinth*, put a disaffected and thus renegade Venetian in charge of the Turkish army. In Algeria renegades were considered Turks who, despite being mainly the riff-raff of the Ottoman empire, assumed lordly airs and claimed the right to any office that was going, even the position of Viceroy of the Sultan, or Dey. Less exalted renegades such as Thomas Pellow in Morocco became military officers, and Greek renegades, because of their sailing skills, could rise to command ships in the battle fleet. The Regencies relied heavily on them, the native Arab or Moor being often deficient in technical skills of many kinds.

Bond slavery, which is what this amounted to, continued in both Christian and Muslim lands until after the Napoleonic wars. Treaties between the Ottomans and major Mediterranean powers, such as France, often decreed a mutual immunity from depredation, and were by and large respected by both sides. The English negotiated a pact with Algiers, which gave immunity to licensed British ships from attack and sequestration by Muslim corsairs. The ships of lands which had no such licences continued to provide the Regencies with slave labour.

Mirroring Islamic slavery was Christian slavery, especially in the front-line states such as Malta, Naples and Spain, only a few nautical miles from Barbary, all of them engaged in a perpetual crusade with Islam, and it with them. In the most exposed of all, Malta, there was a civil correspondence with the Barbary Regencies. Incoming Beys and Grand

Masters welcomed each other with politeness, often the gift of a few released, usually aged and thus less valuable, slaves as a goodwill gesture, and a wish that existing conventions should continue to apply. On 13 January 1703, the Grand Master invited his ambassador at Rome to assure the Pope that slaves were always treated well in Malta, to ensure that the Turks did not ill-treat missionaries and members of religious orders in their states. Grand Masters frequently protested to the rulers of the Regencies that because slaves might be ill-treated elsewhere that was no reason to take it out on their Maltese prisoners.

The treatment of slaves likewise mirrored Barbary practice. They wore the same chains, were locked in similar *bagnos*, and if they were slaves of the state they worked similar hours on public works. By and large a kind of common-sense usage prevailed. Slaves were allowed a reasonable opportunity to raise their ransom money by working for gain, in European lands by hiring themselves out to do dirty jobs, or by setting up booths to sell fruit and vegetables; in Barbary by operating taverns to sell liquor to non-Muslims. Some employed servants to mind their businesses. Even so, redemption was often slow. Many had borrowed money as starting capital, usually from the sizable Jewish communities, so that raising their ransom money could be a long process while they paid off the debts they had incurred. At night all slaves, except those in private service, were secured in the *bagno*.[9]

4

A steady but not immense number of Britons were the subject of ransom appeals, mainly by various Protestant denominations. The amount involved was, for its time, quite substantial, the average ransom being estimated in the 1670s at about £60.[10] Most of the information about their condition came from accounts by the victims themselves and from missionary reports. Of disinterested and observant visitors to Barbary there were few. At a time when the anthem of Thomas Arne's *Alfred* (1740) was proclaiming to the world that 'Britons never, never shall be slaves', many were. One estimate put the number of captives from the British Isles in the early decades of the eighteenth century at 8,000. At the time of the Moroccan emperor Moulay Isma'il, there was an army of 1,500 European renegades in his service.[11] Slavery with privation and even torture was a risk especially accepted by seamen, but there might also be intolerable persuasion to apostasise. If anyone did, his chances of redemption with public money were much reduced. If redeemed as the result of a charitable appeal, the former slave was expected to take part in public displays wearing slave clothes, and sometimes shackles to stimulate the pious generosity of others for their fellow countrymen still unredeemed, and suffering barbarian cruelty. In April 1751 the Covent Garden Theatre under John Rich exhibited a chain gang of redeemed slaves, rattling the fetters that secured their legs and arms. Rich had a penchant for prison dramas, having earlier produced *The Beggar's Opera*.

Roman Catholic countries staged more elaborate appeals to piety, and the ransom business was efficiently undertaken by religious orders, who were the guarantors that a ransom would be paid. The efficiency of their ministration to captives was only matched by the efficiency with which they collected money for their redemption. The Catholic littoral had, of course, many more captives to redeem, and as Catholic monarchs tended to have sensitive trade or political relations with various Islamic states, they were happy to leave the negotiations to religious charity. Public funds were seldom used to ransom slaves, though a ruler might make a gift to a religious order in order to help with the ransom of an important person, or to reimburse an owner for a slave who was returned to his homeland by treaty or as a goodwill gesture. The English had to depend on much less organised arrangements, but the accounts of redeemed slaves not only raised money for further ransoms but served to educate Britons of the 'truth' about conditions in Islamic countries.

5

The worm's eye view is inevitably skewed, but tales of persistent barbarity were essential to keep public interest alive. There was a tariff of punishments: refractory slaves, engaged in sedition, could be beheaded or impaled, and they could be bastinadoed for offences against public order or for attempts to escape.[12] And escape from Muslim captivity became a feature of the many ballads and stories told of captivity. A beautiful Turkish maiden becomes enamoured of the captive and helps him to escape; in one ballad she becomes his wife in preference to his fiancée, not unassisted by the fact that she accompanies him on his escape with a jewelled belt worth enough to set them

FIGURE 5   *Two views of Barbary. Officers of the Grand Seraglio Regailing, and A Turkish Warrior Richard Tully's Narrative of a Ten Years' Residence at Tripoli in Africa, London 1817. This would be the standard early nineteenth-century vision of Rossini's* The Turk in Italy *and of* Mustafa in The Italian Girl in Algiers.

up for life.[13] Many of the claims to have escaped from Barbary captivity were invented by beggars who mutilated themselves to avoid being arrested for vagrancy; others, while genuine enough, were written so long after the event for their accuracy to be suspect. True or not, they all contributed to the prevailing view that slavery in Islamic countries was an inhuman experience and that it was the duty of governments to negotiate an end to the perpetual *guerres de course* that exposed their citizens to it.

In northern Europe it was not until the plight of prisoners in the Barbary states became more highly publicised that people began to understand exactly what being a slave in Islam meant in suffering or deprivation. In 1740 Thomas Pellow published the narrative of his 23 years as a captive in Morocco. He had been taken while playing truant from home on his uncle's vessel at the age of 11. The book exhibited all the characteristics of journalism in recall, but tried to tell the world the truth about Morocco. Pellow was unfortunate enough to be taken captive during the reign of the Moroccan emperor Moulay Ismā'īl (1672–1727), who had in many ways the characteristics of Idi Amin, late ruler of Uganda. For both of them devotion to Islam concealed a paranoid sadism. Ruthless ambition brought them both to rule through a sea of blood – in Moulay's case, that of his siblings, and a regime of methodical frightfulness kept them there. Consciously modelling his court on those monarchs he envied for their sun-like splendour, Moulay was a builder of monumental palaces, mainly constructed by slave labour, using the technical skills of a workforce largely collected by shore raids and piratical attacks on shipping by the Saletine Rovers.

Pellow's narrative was written to stir the national conscience but his experiences were not uniformly bad. As a renegade he was privileged, but he had to play down his apostasy after he had escaped to England, because it would have diminished sympathy for his plight and that of others like him. Moulay Ismā'īl was more interested in the building skills of his slaves than their ransoms and, since they comprised his most experienced building force, he was reluctant to lose any, using every expedient from bribery to torture to encourage his slaves to abandon their faith and put themselves beyond redemption. As the repudiation of Christianity only involved the raising of one finger to show that one denied the Trinity, and if circumcision was painful it was less so than torture, many of the work force 'turned'. A new name and new clothes, however, signified little since a convert continued to be a slave, and the new garments soon became as verminous and ragged as the statutory *djellaba* given to all prisoners when consigned to public works. But they also brought hopes of improvement. Pellow, once converted, rose to command a fighting unit. Like Idi Amin, Moulay could be genial, even generous, but his paranoid anxiety that someone was getting the better of him made him unreliable in keeping to agreements or fulfilling promises. In the face of diplomatic missions he could appear relaxed and, if the gifts were right, he might there and then release a few captives.

It was not only the slaves who suffered from often persistent sadistic treatment by their black supervisors, one rank up in the ranks of the unfree. Merely to satisfy a sadistic or megalomaniac whim of Moulay Ismā'īl, anyone who approached him too closely, or who offended him in some way, might be decapitated on a signal to one of his *bokharis*, a black foreign legion which acted as a personal guard. These were effectively black Janissaries, like them stolen children, taken in slave raids on the deep south and reared to be the Sultan's personal protectors. Moulay's lust for women became legendary but, nevertheless, he allowed himself to be hag-ridden by one black concubine whose influence was certainly successfully used by Commodore Stewart on his official mission in 1720 to secure the release of all English slaves in Morocco who had not turned Muslim.[14] Their number was uncertain as he only obtained the release of 293 slaves, but these were those who had not died of their mistreatment, or apostasised.

The number included no women, since the disappearance of any into a harem could not be established. Saletine corsairs in the sixteenth and seventeenth centuries had made extensive raids on Cornish seaside towns and taken off men, women and children, most of whom were never seen again but, until the public conscience was raised, such fates were accepted by coastal people, who made their living from the sea, as no worse than they could expect from the forces of nature, from wartime forays by the French or from the Inquisition in Portugal. But what people knew of North Africa in the eighteenth century gave Islam the name of an unrelenting and malevolent religion, so that it began in England to replace Roman Catholicism as the ideology to hate.

6

The national myth was that Englishmen were above making an accommodation with the enemy, and 'never, never would be slaves' or allow themselves to be reduced to such ignominy as to adopt an alien faith.

Robinson Crusoe (1719) was captured by Moroccan pirates who took him to slavery in Salé, and though not badly treated, he resolved on escape. That was what was expected of those captured by pirates. A further horror to emerge from these stories was the possibility of buggery. Was Robinson Crusoe, being 'young and nimble' and 'fit for his business', desirable? Women might fear enforced seclusion in a harem, but men faced unspeakable violation by their captors. It was widely accepted that homosexuality was so universally practised in Arab and Ottoman lands that it fuelled the appetite for slaves, especially in Morocco, where sodomy was 'reckoned only a piece of gallantry'.[15] Its practice was so extensive that a continual supply of young men who were not unfamiliar with the practice on board ship was required to bolster an otherwise declining population. Throughout the Judaeo-Christian world this was an anathema even more heinous than apostasy and, with the increasing number of north Europeans venturing into the Mediterranean in pursuit of gain, the fear of both sexes grew with what it fed on.

There were few women captives in North Africa; at least there are fewer records of them, as most of those taken in shore raids on Christian shores disappeared into harems, either as concubines or domestic servants. One exception was Elizabeth Marsh who, falling into the hands of Moroccan corsairs at the age of 21, published her account, *The Female Captive*, in 1769, ten years after her captivity. By the time she came to write it, her rather ordinary experiences had grown into a story worthy of a woman's magazine. In it she is propositioned by the Prince of Morocco, and her stout Kostanze-like resistance earns his respect and her immunity from molestation. In 1769, captives in Islamic lands of either sex were expected to experience the hazards of sexual rapacity, and as rape implied, at that time, consent of a sort, it was to be avoided either by death before dishonour, or by escape.[16] By the end of the century, however, Mediterranean women had become more familiar with Turks, and were well able to deal with them, like Isabella in Rossini's opera *L'Italiana in Algeri*.[17] Among northern Protestants, the sexual myths, when they took root, stuck fast.

7

By the beginning of the nineteenth century the Ottoman Turks had long been full members of the diplomatic world, but the vice-royalties along the Barbary coast were too dependent on the booty gained by piracy and

FIGURE 6 *An oriental gentleman smoking a pipe, watercolour by the Rev. David Markham, on a visit of Malta in 1845–46. The Turk had long since ceased to be the perpetual enemy and was a familiar sight in the streets of the island.*

slavery and had to be chastened from time to time, usually by bombardment and assault by the navies of France, Spain, England and, latterly, the USA. As long as the rules were observed, the practice of enslaving each other's captives could be tolerated. Damage to trade could not. When the French Revolutionary and Napoleonic wars filled the Mediterranean with warships of all nations, the age of the corsairs died unlamented.[18] Public opinion concluded by 1807 that the transatlantic slave trade was both immoral and unjust and that slavery of all kinds was similarly obnoxious, but it was not until the end of the Napoleonic wars that European states decided that the anarchy of perpetual wars of religion and prisoner of war slavery were a great nuisance and should be finally ended. Slavery itself took longer to eradicate.

In far-away Britain, there was no holy war to be waged against Islam. British interest in the Mediterranean had been spasmodic at best but already by the beginning of the eighteenth century England was the principal supplier of naval and military stores to Algiers, for which service her consul was allowed to be appointed by the British government. Both France and England had arrived at official understanding with the Barbary Regencies, especially Algiers, whereby licensed shipping was exempt from piracy. But the agreements were precarious, since the Anglo-French wars occasionally affected Muslim property or passengers at sea, at which the Regencies would take retaliatory action. They were often, moreover, at war with each other or with Morocco, as well as with other Christian powers, and in the morass of shifting alliances, in which adventurism of a particularly independent, anarchic-minded ruler might spill over into offensive action against Christian ships, the role of the Consuls – not among the hierarchs of a diplomatic service – could be sorely tested.[19] Barbary was still considered too dangerous for visitors to extend their journey from Naples to see the Roman remains in North Africa. It was time to consider what could be done about it.

CHAPTER SIX

Virgins Soft as Roses

The Myth of Lord Byron

Where the virgins are soft as the roses they twine,
And all, save the spirit of man is divine.
(Byron, *The Bride of Abydos*)[1]

I

HEN BYRON CROSSED into Asia in 1809 he was not in pursuit of Roman remains. He wanted to see for himself what the Ottomans were like and how Greece was faring under 'barbarous' misrule. He had been fascinated by the Ottomans since his childhood so that the seeds of his journey to the Levant were sown in his teens. Isaac D'Israeli claimed Byron told him that 'all Travels, or histories or books about the East he could meet with he had read'.[2] He may have told people that he wanted to make the desert his dwelling place, but Kinglake, who had heard him make this claim, was sure that, had he ever decided to adopt the life of the Arabs, he would have made a terrible fuss. The partitioned tents were not designed to separate Childe Harold from his ministering spirit but from the 20 or 30 brown men 'who sit screaming in the one compartment from the fifty or sixty brown women that scream and squeak in the other'.[3] Byron could, at least, claim that he had been East and like a previous traveller whom he much admired, Lady Mary Wortley Montagu, he was keen to present it as he had found it. To show that he was not a benighted traveller he supplied copious notes on Turkish ways and Islamic religion to impress his readers.[4]

Speculation about whether or not Byron was tempted during his time there to become a Muslim is upheld only in a letter to his estranged wife, in which he told her he was 'very near to becoming a Mussulman'. It is unlikely that Byron, having discarded conventional Christianity, would for no good social reason have adopted a faith every bit as restrictive, but he was fair-minded and not prejudiced from the outset.[5] He liked the dress, the simplicity of manners, the virility of the men, the beauty, such as he saw of it, of the women – his source here was almost certainly Lady Mary Wortley Montagu – even the uncomplicated acceptance of buggery. Principally he liked the landscape, for this was the Graeco-Roman world he had studied since childhood. Greece, even Albania, was the real thing: 'the land of the cedar and the vine / where the flowers ever blossom, the beams ever shine'.[6] It was not the imaginary highlands of Ossian or the Hindu Kush of Thomas Moore. He would make the Ottoman lands as vivid and real as Wordsworth was so successfully making the Lake District.

The fruits of his Levantine journey began to pour from his pen in 1813. He was in the strongest lyrical form; verses seemed to flow ready made from his brain; he composed in a fever of creativeness, with a mind, he confessed, confused about his future. The four oriental or *Turkish Tales*[7] are all set 'in the land of the sun', where 'all save the spirit of man, is divine'.[8] They were to fix an image of the Levant in the western mind that continued until the death of Jane Digby in 1881, when the western tentacles had so wound themselves round the Ottoman empire that it was about to die of suffocation. Byron's picture of the Levant in 1813 was, despite all the exotic evidence of Byzanto-Turkish splendour, of a place of dereliction and oppression. The *bulbul* or nightingale might woo the rose in perfumed gardens,[9] but beyond their curtain walls, sudden and violent death stalked the countryside, the mountains were lowering, the pathways deserted, a sullen enslaved people were restive under a despot's rule.

Francis Jeffrey alone of contemporary critics was impressed and wrote in *The Edinburgh Review* that Byron 'spread around us the blue waters and dazzling skies – the ruined temples and dusky olives – the desolated cities, and the turbaned population, of modern Attica'.[10] Byron had seen it all: the wild dogs tearing at dead bodies beneath the walls of Constantinople, the body in the sack on its way to a judicial drowning, Athens under the heel of a slave, the *delis* or irregular Turkish troops tyrannising the countryside in the service of one of the Sultan's contumacious pashas. The Aga, a slave of the seraglio and guardian of the women, was reputed to be the overlord of Attica, and he had appointed another slave to be the *voyvode* or governor of Athens, – 'a pandar and a eunuch'.[11]

2

The *Turkish Tales*, like the country in which they are set, are dark and menacing. The voice of the piccolo, of lyrical beauty, is deafened by the bray of Byron's brass. The energy is that of despair, revenge and finally death. They are all, nevertheless, love tales, but tales of a love across forbidden frontiers: of a *giaour* (that is, a non-Muslim) for a Muslim, of a brother for his supposed sister, of a Turkish concubine for her *giaour* deliverer, of a besieged Christian girl for her besieger who happens to be the Sultan himself no less, the leader of the Turkish army. The lovers are all doomed. Do not fall in love across race or religion, Byron is saying; as the Italian proverb has it, *mai mescolar vino o sangue* (mix neither wine nor blood).

He dedicated the first tale to Thomas Moore, soon to be the acclaimed author of *Lalla Rookh*. *The Giaour*, Byron called him a Venetian, is bent on the rescue of Leila – a name which in the Levant can denote either a Christian or a Muslim girl – who is the conventional, or about to become the conventional, image of eastern beauty: her 'fair cheek's unfading hue / the young pomegranates blossom strew', her hair is 'in hyacinthine flow', her feet gleam 'whiter than the mountain sleet', she is like 'the loveliest bird of Franguestan' (that is, a Circassian).[12] Hasan, in whose harem she is the choicest flower, has discovered that Leila has a lover, a *giaour*, an infidel, whose intentions are to steal her away. Before she can be abducted he has her drowned. When the Giaour discovers what Hasan has done he vows that one or other of them will die. Through a land that had become familiar to Byron in Albania, Hasan and his Tartars hunt the Greek and his henchmen, until they are themselves caught and slain by them in an ambuscade.

The Giaour stands over Hasan's dying body, content that he has despatched him to the 'maids of Paradise', impatient for his arrival at 'the Heaven of the Houris' eyes'.[13] Though he is not perturbed by the death of Hasan, absolving himself with the thought that a Muslim killed at the hands of an infidel is assured of Paradise, the Giaour is racked by guilt over the death of Leila, for which he believes he is responsible. He becomes an archetypal Byronic hero, inconsolable, restless, cut off from salvation, oppressed by thoughts of self-destruction, all of which showed so much in his 'dusky scowl', that the superior of the Franciscan convent, in which he enrols himself as a lost soul seeking salvation, fears that if he approaches St Francis's shrine all 'may dread the wrath divine'. Finally at the brink of

FIGURE 7 *One of Byron's virgins 'soft as roses'. Leila from* The Giaour, *an engraving of a painting by Edward Parris (1793–1873), engraved by H. Crook from* The Poetical Works of Lord Byron *with an introduction by the Rev. W. L. Bowles, no date, about 1830.*

death, the Giaour confesses his sense of guilt for the disasters caused by his love for Leila and is content to be buried where no 'prying stranger' nor 'passing pilgrim' may read his story.

Byron tells this in a series of flashbacks. He says he heard it from a Turkish story-teller in a coffee house, and part of the story is in the words of the teller. He prefaces the poem with a lament for Greece 'but living Greece no more. Hers is the loveliness of death.' He stands as he writes these words, so he says, near Thermopylae where the 'servile offspring of the free' have succumbed to 'villain bonds and despot sway'.[14] Byron tried to be neutral between Christianity and Islam, as he did not wish to subscribe to either, but not between Greece and Turkey. His 'religious' affiliation was to pre-Christian and pre-Islamic Greece, where morality was guided by the sense of honour and not by a sense of sin, where sexual and religious as well as political freedoms were highly developed. The Turks had smothered Greece, with oriental characteristics that rendered her a pale shadow of her former glory. Byron's belief in the unique values of ancient Greece, and thus of the superiority of western culture, reflected the prejudice of his day, and revealed that *The Giaour*, for all its profession of oriental sympathy, was still a pro-western tract. Like most of his readers, he believed that 'the barbaric Orient is by nature inferior to Western civilisation and religion'.[15]

Yet, despite Byron's obeisance to a land in which western interest was being awakened, this was not a poem of liberation. The Giaour might be a Venetian, and his accomplices Greeks, Maniote seamen who crewed and navigated the Turkish navy when they were not being pirates, but the Giaour does not strike a blow for national, but for sexual freedom. It is a poem about revenge and the desolation of grief. The heart of it, the failure to liberate Leila, is the cause of the Giaour's nihilistic cafard. Despite its complexity and its wayward overtone of self-destruction, the poem was an instant success. Its imagery and sense of huge horizons was like the onset of technicolour in the film industry. Byron had pedestrianised through mountains 'where vultures whet the thirsty beak',[16] and found dark passion and wild love; the spark his feet struck from the flinty soil burst like a firework, causing frissons of excitement.

3

Byron followed *The Giaour* with *The Bride of Abydos* (also in 1813), a less complex story, written in rhymed couplets at high speed; he said he finished it in four days.[17] Giaffir, a warlord said to be modelled on the one warlord Byron had met, Ali Pasha of Yannina,[18] proposes to give his favourite daughter, Zuleika, in marriage to another grizzled warlord. This is too much for Selim, his supposed son by a concubine, who loves his half-sister. On protesting to his putative father about the proposal, Selim is abused for having the soul of a Greek, who would rather 'watch the unfolding roses blow', than strike 'one stroke for life and death / Against the curs of Nazareth'.[19]

Unknown to Zuleika, who returns Selim's ostensibly incestuous passion, Selim is not her half-brother but her cousin, the son of Giaffir's brother, murdered by Giaffir, like Hamlet's father, out of jealous ambition.

Selim is actually the leader of a gang of 'curs of Nazareth', Greek brigands or what today would be called freedom fighters, and he now resolves with their help to abduct his cousin from the seraglio. The attempt is thwarted, Selim and his followers are overwhelmed and killed and Zuleika, who witnesses the failure from a convenient cave in which she is hidden, dies of grief. It is not the heroism of Selim, or his protest at the blind will of a tyrannical father that makes *The Bride of Abydos* remarkable, but the passionate depiction of Zuleika. Byron had in the first draft left the two lovers as half-siblings but, recognising that incest was rather more frowned upon in the West than in the East, changed them to cousins. Selim might be the bloodless caricature of a man in love but Zuleika expressed a passion few women had been allowed to express in verse before. Some found the torrent of love too open and dangerous to be decent.

Zuleika is the second of the virgins who 'are soft as the roses they twine', 'fair as the first that fell of womankind', 'the majesty of loveliness'.[20] Her love for Selim is unconditional: she must, and will, share with him the Paradise reserved for women, of which she had dreamed, and which her Prophet had disdained to reveal, for what 'Houri (could) soothe him half so well?' Zuleika may not have been sure whither her soul would go, or whether there was no heaven at all for women, but Byron believed that one third of Paradise was reserved for well-behaved women.[21] In the place where they died, the enchanted bird of Islam, the bulbul, sings, 'soft as harp that Houri strings / His long entrancing note'. The nightingale was a much used Persian trope, made popular by Sir William Jones, who was translating Persian verse in India, but here it is the soul of Zuleika, mourning her thwarted love.[22]

It could also have been Byron's lament for Augusta, but if that is hinted at by his original intention to make Zuleika and Selim half-siblings, he was too intent to create an authentic oriental story to wish it to be an allegory of his own passion. But one cannot resist the allegory of love represented by the women in these tales; it is pure for, if the Muslim cherishing of women provoked the western myth of connubial concubinage among men, it allowed no doubt about the purity of women. Mere suspicion of this could lead, as it did Leila, to death by drowning, in what Byron called 'the sack'. But within this purity existed also the purity of passion which finds its apotheosis in Zuleika. Muslim women experienced passion no less than Christian but it was subject to constraints that, for Byron's readers in the West, made it more intense, enticing and dangerous.

Those constraints lay, Byron implied, in the arrogant conviction that man was the superior being. This was the straitjacket that was imposed on men's emotions by the characteristics of the despot: pride, a sense of honour, defiance to death, deafness to argument, expectation of instant obedience. Despite all these, a man could be as tender to a woman as stern Pasha Giaffir to his daughter, hailing her as his 'Peri ever welcome here, / Sweet, as the desert fountains wave / To lips just cooled in time to save, / Such to my longing sight art thou.'[23] To Byron, being effectively fatherless, such inflexibility led to tragedy. His Romantic dream was to dissolve that inflexibility, the attribute of a male God, male lawgivers and male prophets. The allegory of passionate love in the *Turkish Tales* was that it was a potion that led inevitably to death.

Byron wrote *The Bride of Abydos* while his mind was in such a state of fermentation 'that he was obliged to empty it in rhyme', holding that only writing it had kept him sane.[24] His public, attracted by the poem's intense authenticity, accompanied by a learned commentary on eastern mores, was thrilled with excitement. The first printing sold 6,000 copies, orientalia had become a best seller, a fact not lost on Thomas Moore, and a new discovery of the Levant was under way.

4

In the next tale, *The Corsair*, which sold 10,000 copies on the first day of publication, Byron is less interested in the women, who may have been 'virgins soft as roses'. It is the masculinity he admired in eastern men which obsesses him. Can love break it? It is both the most straightforward and simple of the tales, shorn of ambiguities and shifts in time, with a narrative that wasted little time in Byronic musings on the condition of his mind. Conrad and his gang of desperadoes are *giaours*, pirates who live in an impregnable island from which they foray out to wreak havoc on the Ottomans. Byron gives his corsair leader qualities of a passionless courage, daring, and ruthlessness, only humanised by his love for his wife, Medora.

Conrad and his fellow pirates attempt a daring raid on the mainland where the Ottoman garrison and fleet under Pasha Seyd are gathering to attack him. Dressed as a dervish, Conrad enters the Pasha's presence in his palace while the Muslims are celebrating their forthcoming victory in advance; the pirates attack, fire the ships and Conrad disrobes to lead the assault. The attack seems to be a success when fire spreads to the palace and Turkish reinforcements begin to overwhelm the marauders. Conrad loses valuable time in making his escape when the conflagration threatens the harem quarters, for rather than leave the defenceless women to roast alive he orders their rescue, and leads them to a place of safety. He himself rescues Gulnare, the 'pomegranate flower', favourite concubine of the Pasha, but in doing so he is taken captive. Clapped in irons, Conrad composes himself for the dreadful death by impalement he is bound to suffer on the following day, but philosophically composes himself to sleep, as he will need all his strength to face the ordeal.

While he sleeps he is visited by Gulnare, who with disarming ease has stolen Seyd's seal of authority, his ring, to get past the guards. In Conrad's cell she pours out her love, inspired by the way in which he had rescued the harem women from a dreadful death. ''Twas strange – that robber thus with gore bedewed / Seemed gentler than the Seyd in fondest mood.'[25] Though Conrad gently refuses her love, for he only loves Medora, Gulnare will still do what she can either to have his execution commuted for the exchange of his hoards of loot, or to assist his escape, if they can leave together. She has no love for Seyd; she is but a slave and 'the Pacha' (sic) 'wooed as if he deemed the slave / Must seem delighted with the heart he gave'. Instead she 'felt, I feel, love dwells with – with the free'.[26]

She pleads with Seyd to spare Conrad, only to be accused of suspicious sympathy for the attackers and fears that she too is now likely to die with Conrad. 'There yawns the sack and yonder rolls the sea.'[27] She resolves on Conrad's escape and, as it means passing through the married quarters, and as Conrad will not, she stabs Seyd to death. Their escape is made; the Corsair and Gulnare return to the pirate's lair where she is hailed as his deliverer. But Conrad's return is too late, for Medora, believing that Conrad has been killed, has perished of grief. Conrad cannot accept the love of Gulnare, stained as it is with murder committed when her lawful husband, no matter how tyrannous, was asleep. He disappears to be heard of no more. Love for Conrad has either conquered or failed; both ends are open to conjecture. But for Gulnare it has failed.

The improbabilities of the tale did not worry its readers. If Conrad were such a ruthless and abandoned sinner, would he have taken such care to rescue the harem women; would he have had so much compunction about killing Seyd; would it have taken him very long to recover from Medora's death to live with his saviour, Gulnare, to whom he is physically attracted? Gulnare, for her part, has her ambiguities too. She did not seem to have any trouble leaving the harem to enter the prison which held a male prisoner, nor was it too difficult to hire accomplices and arrange an escape. One wonders why, if she hated her slavery so much, she had not done it before. These conundrums did not interest Byron. His foray into the Orient had showed that love does not conquer all, change everything, awaken the spirit of magnanimity. Passionate love was not the supreme prophylactic for the Byronic cafard; it was in itself a form of death-wish.

Conrad had 'a laughing devil in his sneer' and 'where his frown of hatred darkly fell / Hope withering fled – and Mercy sighed farewell.'[28] In this he was no better than Seyd. If the positions were reversed and Conrad had Seyd in his power, Seyd could have expected no mercy. Conrad could not blame Seyd for planning an execution of peculiarly Ottoman frightfulness. Impalement meant death by thirst, for the damage to the organs from having a stake thrust through one's entrails meant that drinking led to more fearful pain, and it took several hours, even days, before the end. Revenge was an emotion that dominated both men, and Byron gave Seyd a whole stanza to plot the awfulness of his revenge on Conrad. What, in Byron's eyes, was to redeem Conrad was that he would not appeal to God for help. 'I have no thought to mock his throne with prayer / Wrung from the coward crouching of despair.'[29] In his self-control and sense of personal freedom he represented not the Christian, but the Byronic West.

Byron did not wish to paint the Muslims in a worse light than Conrad, but Islam, whose very name meant submission, was not the religion of the free: another good reason why Byron resisted any temptation to 'become a Mussulman'. He was quite ready to show that Christians were no better than Muslims, and he was portraying an Islam he had experienced at first hand. As a society it was irredeemably stained by the violence of power: power over human destinies, over women's lives, over human freedom. In true Shakespearian mode he ended all the oriental tales with death. He did not bring the faithful Medora into contact with the more fascinating and seductive charms of Gulnare; that would have been dramatic but not Romantic, more in the spirit of Don Juan. At this point Byron still nursed, along with his palpitating readers, high hopes for passionate love.

5

The fourth of the *Turkish Tales* was *The Siege of Corinth*, published by John Murray in 1816. This siege was that of 1715 when, after Sobieski's relief of Vienna, the Venetians wrested control of Corinth from the Ottomans and appointed a governor, Minotti, to hold it. The vizier in charge of Byron's siege was the latest conqueror of Greece, Coumurgi ('till Christian hands to Greece restore / The freedom Venice gave of yore')[30] who was to perish two years later in Eugene of Savoy's victory at Belgrade in 1717. The poem is the strongest indication yet of Byron's preoccupation with the fate of Greece at the hands of the Turks.

Minotti has a daughter, Francesca, and like all Byronic, indeed all Romantic, daughters she loves the wrong man. He is the leader, no less, of the besieging Turkish army, Lanciotto or Alp, the renegade. He and Francesca had fallen in love before Lanciotto had been expelled from Venice for crimes unspecified and, as a renegade, he had achieved high command in Ottoman service. Alp has to justify his betrayal of Venice, his fatherland and his religion, by destroying Corinth, but he is prepared to spare Francesca whom he knows to be in the besieged town.

While musing on the seashore and contemplating the city he will attack on the morrow, he is confronted by Francesca, who suddenly appears before him. He renews his forlorn suit; if she promises to leave with him after the battle they will depart for ever from this place of dreadful war. Francesca in her turn tries to induce him to return to the faith of his fathers and to his countrymen; he refuses, and she vanishes, having promised that he will die on the morrow and be damned. Battle is joined and, while the father is defending himself, Alp learns from him that the girl he met the night before was a wraith, come to save his soul; in fact, she was already dead. While defying Minotti, he falls from a random shot, Francesca's prophecy is fulfilled and, after the guardian of the vaults promises that the spirit of Leonidas will again animate the enslaved spirit of Greece, Minotti torches the city arsenal and everyone goes up in an enormous bang. Byron did not know that in fact an army of 70,000 men had besieged Corinth defended by 600, who, after the arsenal blew up, were overrun and slaughtered almost to a man.[31]

In 1810 Byron was on his way through Epirus, 'where freedom still at moments rallies, / And pays in blood Oppression's ills.'[32] He had stood on Acro-Corinth's brow and looked on the city, envisioning its dreadful siege.

The Siege of Corinth fulfils its battle scenes magnificently, but the love between Alp and Francesca is sterile as well as hopeless, because she is already dead. It is not a poem about the unsurpassable barriers that culture and destiny put between people, but about the equally unsurpassable disgust with lands that deny their sons, as Venice denied Alp and Byron deemed England had denied him. For Alp, Venice had long ceased to 'be her ancient civic boast – "the Free"' and unnamed accusers in the dark had placed 'a charge against him uneffaced'.[33] Irreconcilable in hatred of the land of his birth, he was prepared to destroy all he could find within the walls of Corinth, sparing only Francesca and her father, but not at the expense of his military duty to destroy the Christian stronghold.

On his way to the Levant, Byron had visited Malta, victim of a terrible Muslim assault in 1565 which the island had successfully resisted, and had not the thrall of Greece begun to possess him at the time *The Siege of Corinth* could well have been *The Siege of Malta*. Alp's lonely contemplation of the opposing walls, strewn with the bodies of his warriors being gorged and growl'd over by wild dogs, 'their white tusks crunching' skulls peeled 'as a fig when its fruit is fresh'[34] is so cinematic it could have been filmed courtesy of the Malta Tourist Board, but it also reflects the poet's distaste for the unsung horrors of war. In 1810, while Byron's ship skirted the sea walls of the Seraglio in Constantinople, the travellers beamed their telescopes on the gardens in the hope of seeing a beauty or two, but what they did spy were two dogs gnawing at a dead body.[35] Though treading over the 'tombless dead, a feast for lesser living things', is a ghastly experience, 'There is something of pride in the perilous hour / Whate'er be the shape in which death may lower.'[36] Byron, despite his eulogies about the Greece that was past, is suitably disinterested about the fate of the battle. Alp, renegade though he was, has his job to do and, like Hasan, and Giaffir and Seyd, his role to fulfil. Byron had no quarrel with that: Alp commands his men, as any good commander would, with stirring words of encouragement. The business of a soldier is to make war, live or die. Corinth is not too distant, as the crow flies, from Thermopylae, but this time

> Corinth's sons were downward borne
> By the long and oft renewed
> Charge of the Muslim multitude.
> In firmness they stood, and in masses they fell,
> Heaped by the host of the infidel.[37]

Like a later fateful bomb, the smoke from the explosion 'assailed the eagle's startled beak / And made him higher soar and shriek.'[38] The din on that fateful day could be heard 'o'er Salamis and Megara, even unto Piraeus' bay'.[39] Megara, home of Euclid and his school, was a neighbouring rival to Corinth, who might have expected to hear the explosion with mixed feelings.

6

The popularity of Byron's four *Turkish Tales* was in their appeal to stereotypical fantasies. The women – Leila, a Circassian; Zuleika, the daughter of a slave; Medora, a Greek; Gulnare, a slave – are all beautiful victims. The men are all driven by a primal male duty of revenge, the Giaour for the abduction of his love, Selim for the casual disposal of his woman as a chattel, Alp for the false accusation of treachery, Seyd and the Corsair for the wrongs perpetrated by unlicensed piracy, all exhibited the characteristics of a Satan licensed by God to act according to their nature, as in the *Book of Job* and the *Koran*. A man had to confront his fate, whatever it might be, and not complain of inevitable disaster. In Islam's predestinarian attitudes Byron found a clue to how he hoped he would face his own destiny. He passes no judgements on Christian or Muslim protagonists, as they act according to their beliefs and natures, against which they were not battling,

As for his attitude to women, who both fascinated and annoyed him, they had to accept the results of their affections and their passions, as well as living up to their reputation for beauty and pulchritude. Byron set his tales in lands where the normal restrictions of western morality, which he stigmatised as cant, induced by Christianity, did not apply. Similar behaviour to that he was describing may have been evident in earlier centuries in the western world, but the effects of Reformation and Enlightenment had smothered them. His journey to the East had liberated his mind.[40]

Byron returned to the East in *Don Juan* but he had quite a different purpose in doing so. The 'Virgins soft as roses' were now confined to the harem, which had become to Byron a subject of subtle mockery. Don Juan did not end in a sack. The Sultan was almost a benevolent old gentleman. Juan was sent to the Russian front, Byron's interest now in how the

Ottomans faced the Russians in war. He may not expressly have recognised that this was a theatre of war as serious as the Peninsula War had been in forging the future of Europe, but one episode of that war caught his imagination as worthy of the epic treatment that had been given to Christian assaults on Muslim strongholds by Pulci, Ariosto and Tasso in their poems.[41] Byron however was writing rather a pastiche than a paeon in praise of courage in battle. No higher motive inspired the Tartar Khan to battle to the death with the Nazarenes he hated than 'the black eyed girls in green, / That make the beds of those who won't take quarter', the houris, who 'have a natural pleasure / In lopping off your lately married man, / Before the Bridal Hours have danced their measure.' At least, before he died, he would see Paradise. It might not be distinguishable from the 'Prophets – Houris – Angels – Saints – described in one voluptuous blaze' but, if ultimately absurd and futile, it was still amazing what a black-eyed virgin could achieve.[42] In the last analysis they were more potent than virgins soft as roses. They might not be as enticing but they were more dangerous.

7

It was not long before *The Siege of Corinth* was translated into French and twelve years later was to find progeny in another work of art, in a medium for which Byron's poems were almost natural fodder. Rossini's opera of the same name received its first performance in Paris on 9 October 1826 and for this, his first work for the French capital, he hurriedly adapted an earlier composition, *Mahomet II*. The two sieges of Corinth are not the same siege. In Rossini's opera, Mahomet II, after subjugating Constantinople, sets out to capture Corinth in 1458. The opera was written for the San Carlo opera theatre in Naples in 1820 and the libretto owed nothing to Byron but was taken from a play, *Anna Erizzo*, by Cesare della Valle, Duke of Ventignano. In this play, the daughter of the Venetian governor of Negroponte is in love with a man she met in Corinth, who turns out to be Mehmet the Conqueror. She rejects Mehmet/Mahomet's offer of marriage, chooses the side of her father, goes demented at the turn of the battle and kills herself. In the version performed at La Fenice in Venice, the Greeks defeat the Turks. The *prima soprano* was out of voice and the Venetians barracked the performance. So the changes Rossini made were prudent. French support of Greek freedom was running high, and Rossini had already raised 30,000 francs for the cause at a benefit concert. Many of the composer's earlier works were pillaged for numbers, and he so strengthened the forces of wind and brass that he was accused of introducing noisy orchestration to French audiences.

As Parisians were getting tired of trouser roles, he turned the soprano into a tenor. It was a triumph. Curtain calls for the composer lasted half an hour, and after he had left the theatre, musicians gathered under his hotel window to play the finale of the second act. *The Siege of Corinth* then played the round of metropolitan opera houses: Barcelona, Brussels, Budapest, St Petersburg, Prague, Mexico City, London (at the Haymarket in 1834), and New York. Its Italian premier was in substitution of an opera called *Alfred the Great*, but greeted with less wholesale enthusiasm, as singers began to select and insert arias to suit themselves. When the pro-Greek enthusiasm had died down, the music was set to a new libretto called *Nabucco*, but it never rivalled the Verdi version, which captured the sentiment of the Italian sigh for freedom.

Rossini's siege actually took place under one of the Greek warlords who, after the fall of Constantinople five years earlier, were now vassals of the Ottomans. Irked by his behaviour as an Ottoman satrap in the Morea, first the Albanians, and then the Greeks revolted against him and invoked the support of the Venetians. To assert the overlordship of his client, Mehmet (Mahomet) II sent an army to destroy the epicentre of the trouble at Corinth. The principal characters of Byron's poem and Rossini's opera perform essentially the same roles. In Rossini, the governor of Corinth, Cleomene, has a daughter, Pamira, and she loves the Sultan Mahomet himself, whom she has met under the name of Almanzor, incognito, in Athens. There the plots diverge. Because she loves Almanzor, Pamira will not marry the man her father has chosen for her, the leader of the besieged Greeks. Mahomet is the gentlemen throughout, and is prepared to marry his lover and spare her family, but she cannot desert her people in their hour of need. She leaves him to join the man her father wants her to marry and side with the beleaguered Greeks.

Both poem and opera then come together as the assault starts. Mahomet makes one last effort to spare the Greeks and win Pamira, to be defied by the father and her betrothed, and the victor is denied his spoil by the mass suicide of the women of Corinth, which brings down the curtain. Rossini's finale is as rumbustious and noisy as Byron's. The enthusiasm for the Greek cause was noisy. Though Byron's poems pre-dated the actual Greek rising by five years, when it came and the spirit of Leonidas appeared to have entered the souls of the Greek people, Byron was held to have been prophetic. Rossini's opera was the apotheosis of his prophecy.

Rossini and Byron were uncontested meteors in their art, but their trajectories did not meet. By the time *The Siege of Corinth* came to London, Byron had been dead for ten years. At the same time it was clear that both men had a soft spot for the Turk who was to be found in Rossini's comic operas of earlier years (*Il Turco in Italia* and *L'Italiana in Algeri*) and in Byron's *Don Juan* and *Beppo*, not the jealous tyrants of sexual and military domination but figures of fun that belied their frightfulness.

In truth Byron was inclined to believe the Turk was a better Christian gentleman than the Christian gentlemen he had encountered. His espousal of the Greek cause was not visceral; it was lodged more in his brain than in his heart. His Greece was not peopled by men and women who practised the sexual and political freedoms he craved, for they had been rendered craven, he believed, by the centuries-old domination of theocracies, both Christian and Muslim. The effects of those theocracies were to be found in his *Turkish Tales*, into which he interpolated laments for what Greece had once been. They were not a call to return to her former splendour, but a lament for its irrevocable passing. Rossini and Byron both felt that they should express some response to the Philhellenism that was then a popular cause. Shelley for his part wrote as if he had invented it.

CHAPTER SEVEN

Ghastly as a Tyrant's Dream

The Myth of Resurgent Greece

Victorious Wrong, with vulture scream,
Salutes the risen sun, pursues the flying day!
I saw her ghastly as a tyrant's dream,
Beneath which earth and all her realms pavilioned lay ...
(Shelley, *Hellas*)[1]

I

D E QUINCEY WAS sure that the Ottomans, like the Byzantines before them, had a persistent fear that Constantinople was always in danger from the horde outside the walls, 'that the very haughtiest of the Mussulmans believe that the gate is already in existence through which the red Giaours (the Russi) shall pass to the conquest of Stamboul; and that everywhere in Europe at least, the hat of Frangistan is destined to surmount the turban – the crescent to go down before the cross'.[2] For the mighty if shambling Ottoman empire was now being challenged by a people who in their time had seen off the Persian threat to Europe, the threat, as they saw it, of a dark theocracy snuffing out the nascent liberties of the Greek soul which was emancipating itself from the thrall of wilful and despotic gods.

A new war between East and West had begun; it only needed a second Lepanto to seal the inevitable. The battle of Navarino Bay (1827) led directly to the liberation of Athens, the Jerusalem of the Philhellenes, and Greece became a latter-day Crusader state. Many poets had added their prophetic voice to the chorus that was swelling as the Greeks took to arms, but one was more excitable and more vicious in his antagonism to those Gods, or to that God to which they were all subsumed. Percy Bysshe Shelley – unlike Byron, virtually unread in his lifetime – had defined an Islam against which he sought, as he did with Christianity and all established order that was founded on kings and clergy, to foment a revolt.

In 1817, Shelley wrote his longest poem – it was also one of his most puzzling. It was, eventually, entitled *The Revolt of Islam* but its inspiration owed nothing to Islam. The principal protagonists, Laon and Cythna, the radical poet and his principal female follower, were in revolt against Othman (Osman?), representative of ancient and oppressive authority, whose reaction to radicalism is violence. The poem was written when Lord Liverpool's government was taking increasingly draconian measures against radical thought. William Cobbett had been forced to flee the country; William Hone, editor of the *Reformists Register*, had been beggared in court; James Leigh Hunt had just served two years for slandering the Prince Regent. Shelley was cautious about espousing his dialectic openly, so that *Laon and Cythna*, the poem's original title, was a masquerade of careful 'political speak', seeking readers among the general British public. Like his earlier *Queen Mab*, it denounced the authority of throne and church as evil. A poem which clothed its ideals in talk would, Shelley hoped, be enough to distract, even confuse, their representatives, while giving his radical ideas an airing.[3]

These were not modest. The poem's ambition was to awaken an 'immense nation from their slavery and degradation', and its programme was to replace 'the faithlessness of tyrants, the consequences of legitimate despotism, civil war, famine, plague, superstition and the utter extinction of the domestic affections' by tolerance and the benevolence of true philanthropy. In short, it promoted the final and inevitable fall of oppression, which had presided over the sorry history of the world, allowing the triumph of evil over good. Men had seemed unable to distinguish between them, except for the time

> (w)hen Greece arose, and to its bards and sages,
> In dream the golden-pinioned Genii came ...
> ... And oft in cycles since, when darkness gave
> New weapons to thy foe, their sunlike fame
> Upon the combat shone – a light to save,
> Like Paradise spread forth beyond the shadowy grave.[4]

In 1817 Shelley believed that the earth had become once more the 'tyrant's garbage', and Greece was in fearful danger from the archetypal despot, the tyrant in Constantinople. Its early readers were almost unanimous in savaging the poem, but what they condemned was that Laon and Cythna might have been incestuous lovers. Scott's biographer and son-in-law, Lockhart, alone seemed to pick up the Graeco-Turkish connection, and he thought 'our ideas of Greeks ... struggling for freedom in the best spirit of their fathers' were realised in the two lovers.[5] Shelley could only deal in abstracts and, nervous that his poem was going to result in oppression's usual riposte to criticism, he tried to spin over it a protective veil by suggesting that its subject was the overthrow of Muslim rule.

Four years later, in 1821, that suddenly seemed possible. Turkish rule in Greece had been creaking badly since the repulse from Vienna in 1683. Outside the centre, power seemed to have leached away to pashas and beys who acted as if Constantinople were on a different planet. Ali, Pasha of Yannina, for example, when Byron met him, behaved like an independent sovereign. There had been unrest for years in the Greek highlands which the Ottoman state seemed unable to suppress methodically. Communities, related by kin and held together by tribal loyalty, behaved as brigands. The forces of law and order, mainly drawn from indentured Christians, turned a blind eye to breaches in both in return for a fee greater than their annual pay, and local governors, like Pasha Ali, profited by conniving with whomever paid them best.

2

One major power had a special interest in the fate of Greece. According to prophecy Russia, the home of the red-haired race, the Russi, was to save the Greeks. The Byzantine emperor, Leo the Wise (896–912), had promised opaquely that the Turks would be driven out of Constantinople 320 years after its fall, and when in 1774 by the Treaty of Küchük Kaynajar the Russians assumed a solemn if undefined protection of all Greeks in Ottoman lands, that prophecy seemed about to be fulfilled.[6] Russia's ambition had long been to control the Black Sea entrance to the Mediterranean, which meant in effect the occupation of Constantinople, and in 1781 Catherine the Great had hatched a secret plan with Austria to partition Turkish lands, reviving the state of Byzantium under her son Constantine. Expatriate Greeks, if not the simple *klephts* or brigands who had resisted Ottoman rule because it was there to be resisted, dreamed ambitious dreams of an independent state.

So strong did this sentiment grow that Pasha Ali, actually an Albanian, but who spoke Greek better than Turkish, made a bid for total independence from the Sultan. He professed himself a Greek, put a tricolour cockade in his turban, drank the health of Mary Theotokos, Mother of God, joined the Greek association for would-be liberals, the Philike Hetaerea, and hoped for international recognition as ruler of a virtually independent Morea. His immediate objective was to control the Adriatic by securing the possession of Corfu and the other Ionian islands, which had never been conquered by the Ottomans, and he hoped by flirtation with revolutionary France, which had overthrown the Venetian republic, to be given them as a reward. That design was thwarted by the English when it established a protectorate in 1815. By 1821 the Corfiotes had become dissatisfied with the arrangement and Ali hoped to capitalise on local unrest. What he managed to do, however, was to ignite the touch-paper of insurrection in Greece itself. The Archbishop of Patras raised the standard of revolt and a force, plentifully supplied by Russia, invaded Moldavia, that part of Romania which had been radically Christianised and which was ruled by Christian princes as Viceroys for the Ottoman sultan.

Shelley devoted himself at once to being a clarion voice for Greek freedom, though in the event few listened to him or even heard him. His poem *Hellas* — which was inscribed to Alexander Mavrocordato, Prince of Wallachia, whom the Shelleys had met in Pisa — was written in the year of revolt, 1821. It was inspired by the *Persae* of Aeschylus, the glorious model for 'the glorious contest now waging in Greece', whose 'final triumph' would be part of the 'cause of civilisation and social improvement'.[7] But for Greece, Europeans would still be savages and idolators, along with the stagnant and miserable state of the unfree institutions in China and Japan.

Unlike the contemporary Italians, among whom Shelley had lived for nearly three years, the contemporary Greeks (with whom he had not lived) were, in his view, worthy descendants of their illustrious forebears, matching their sensibility, enthusiasm and courage. Shelley did not wait to see how the Greeks went about their war of independence, for in his mind they were all Attic heroes, wearing the halo of Thermopylae, not bloodthirsty peasants armed with scythes, knives and bludgeons and the occasional firearm. The largely defenceless Muslim population in Greek lands – men, women, children and animals – was rounded up and slaughtered, and soon the countryside was pretty well empty of them, except for those who managed to escape to the protection of Ottoman garrisons. By May the Turks were pent up on the Acropolis in Athens, as one by one their garrisons were overwhelmed. In Tripolitza, the nerve centre of the Morea, the Greek brigand and now patriot commander rode to the citadel through streets carpeted by Turkish dead and presided over the systematic slaughter of the 2,000 civilians he found there.

3

In the censored press of Italy, Shelley read nothing of this. Freedom was indivisible and so those who supported the Ottoman, as did the British government, oppressed it. Russia's motives were malign, since she was not disinterested in the support of Greek freedom but hoped to make territorial gains from the exhaustion of both sides. Constantinople, if the Greeks triumphed, would not be a Greek city again, but a Russian. But look around! Spain was already free; Italy would be free one day. The cause of Greek freedom could not fail, since

> In the great morning of the world,
> The spirit of God with might unfurled
> The flag of Freedom over Chaos.[8]

For Shelley, the Ottomans had become the great enemy of freedom, even greater than the Metternichian Holy Alliance. *Hellas* is written in the form of a dream, nightmare rather, of the half-waking, half-sleeping Sultan Mahmud, in Constantinople. His vizier, Hassan, might have bad news but the Sultan was to take comfort from the fact that

> Four hundred thousand Moslems from the limits
> Of utmost Asia, irresistibly
> Throng like full clouds at the sirocco's cry ...
> They have destroying lightning and their step
> Wakes earthquake, to consume and overwhelm,
> And reign in ruin.[9]

The bad news was that the Tartar chivalry, 'its foaming cavalry, and blazing artillery' had provoked a baffling resistance from the rebellious Greeks, who made 'a bridge of safe and slow retreat with Moslem dead', and when finally overpowered refused to surrender, choosing death by their own hand. From the dead, one rose to deliver, before dying, a Shelleyan and macabre defiance of the 'weak conquerors', promising that the fragments of the battle dead which the vultures reject shall bring forth the Apocalyptic horsemen, famine, pestilence and panic, to wage war by the side of the rebels.

Hassan's reports grow more and more sombre. The vultures compete with dog-fish to feast on the dead of a great battle in which an Ottoman armada has been defeated by 'pirate bands', with losses of 9,000 men. So far Shelley reported correctly; Ottoman sea power was dependent on Greek sailors and without them could not resist the armed brigs, sometimes as large as frigates, that virtually closed the Aegean and the approaches of the Adriatic to them. Command of the sea, by which all parts of Greece could be independently supplied, had passed to the rebels, and the Ottomans were on the run. Shelley enjoyed himself piling disaster upon disaster on them, taking an intense personal delight in their fate:

> Nauplia, Tripolizza, Mothon, Athens,
> Navarin, Artan, Monembasia,
> Corinth and Thebes are carried by assault,
> And every Islamite who made his dogs
> Fat with the flesh of Galilean slaves
> Passed at the edge of the sword.[10]

That was true too. Pasha Ali of Yannina sits 'a crownless metaphor of Empire'; all the outposts of Ottoman rule are threatened: Aleppo, Damascus, even Medina besieged by Arabs, Sennar by Ethiopians, the Tigris valley by Persians, Georgia, Crete and Cyprus refuse their 'living tribute' of slaves for the seraglio. Worst of all, a dervish has prophesied that the sins of Islam would raise up a destroyer and that the Greeks expected a saviour from the West, not coming

> in clouds and glory
> But in the omnipresence of that spirit
> In which all live and are.[11]

Was a role for Byron already forming in his mind? It is more likely that he had in mind Prince Mavrocordato, then in Italy.

Mahmud summons, most improbably, a Jewish soothsayer, Ahasuerus, to tell him what is going to happen. One of the many semichoruses, playing the part of ancient Greek choruses, chimes in, having heard 'the crash as of an empire falling' and shrieks of people calling for mercy.[12] When Ahasuerus is unable to do more than utter gnomic prophecies about the future being in the past, Shelley has to admit that all is not going quite as well as hoped.

> Shout the jubilee of death! The Greeks
> Are as a brood of lions in the net
> Round which the kingly hunters of the earth
> Stand smiling.[13]

The Turks claim victory and

> Austria, Russia, England,
> And that tame serpent, that poor shadow France
> Cry peace, and that means death when monarchs speak.[14]

The final chorus, however, unites in a grand finale.

> A brighter Hellas rears its mountains
> From waves serener far

but ends with the lament

> must hate and death return?
> must men kill and die?
> The world is weary of the past,
> O might it die or rest at last.[15]

4

Not everyone shared Shelley's view of the Greeks. The man to whom Byron was carrying greetings from Captain Ball in Malta was Captain William Leake, and he had lived among them during the early years of the nineteenth century and observed the ebullition of revolt that erupted in 1821. He had originally come to Albania accompanying artillery and ammunition for Ali Pasha for use against the French, who had occupied the island of Corfu after the extinction of the Venetian Republic. He carried an official warrant to stay as resident at the court, such as it was, of the Pasha of Yannina. Leake was a 32-year-old artilleryman at the time, and had been in Ottoman parts on and off from 1799. He had arrived in Constantinople with instructions to train Turkish artillerymen in the arms being provided to their army, which was on its way to clear Egypt of the French. but as no one was in any sort of hurry for him to arrive, he had travelled incognito in Tartar costume to explore Cilicia and Cyprus on the way, and reached Egypt only in January 1800. As an artilleryman he was trained to scan the lie of the land for artillery placement and trajectories, but he also used the time to search for Greek remains in what he privately considered his real mission.

When he finally arrived in Egypt the peace of Amiens had suspended hostilities so back he went to Constantinople. He was still there when war broke out again, so he returned to Egypt, this time in a leisurely way by Athens, Smyrna, Cyprus and Jaffa, whence he diverted himself into Syria and Palestine on war business. He was in Egypt again in March 1801 when the French capitulation to General Abercrombie rendered his purpose there void. So he was sent to survey the upper Nile, about which very little was known apart from James Bruce's account, which had seemed, when it appeared in 1790, to have allowed fantasy to supersede truth. Leake travelled as far as the cataracts of the Nile with the secretary of the British ambassador to the Sublime Porte, and returned with him to Athens where the Ambassador, Lord Elgin, had just purchased the marbles that bear his name.

Leake being by now rather a connoisseur of things Attic, travelling and mapping the Athens hinterland, Elgin chose him to supervise one shipment of the Parthenon marbles back to London. He was to suffer an almost crippling blow when the ship sank in twelve fathoms entering Cerigo (Cythera) bay and with the marbles went down all his notes and drawings. Leake could not wait for the marbles to be recovered, though over two years at a cost to Elgin of £5,000 17 cases were eventually raised. He was under orders to return to London, which he did by Italy, and in 1804 he was sent back to the East to survey those Turkish provinces in Europe most vulnerable to French designs on the Adriatic. He had a special brief to learn what he could of the topography of northern Greece. This was work he loved, and he landed in Corfu in December 1804. Thence he pursued his way to the court of Ali Pasha slowly, taking time off to explore the Graeco-Roman sites and to speculate on whether he had landed where Julius Caesar went ashore on his way to defeat his rival Pompey in Illyria.

He quickly formed the view that there was not a great deal to be expected from the Greeks: 'The[ir] feasts, the[ir] fasts and the[ir] fears are a great impediment to the traveller. During their feasts they will not work, the fasts ... render them unequal to any great exertion while timidity is the necessary consequence of the Turkish yoke, following long ages of the debasing tyranny and superstition of the Byzantine empire.' 'The manners, lying and cowardice of the people' could, however, almost be excused as 'deceit was the only defence which their tyrants have left them.'[16] For knavery they were only outdone by the Armenians, who were a serious people, intent on money. The Greeks by contrast were 'flighty and inconstant'.[17] He was not long left in doubt that the Greeks were disappointed that the English did not seem ready to help them liberate themselves from the Turk. While he had to explain that Europe was convulsed in a cruel war, he did venture his opinion that Catherine the Great's earlier antics over setting up her son in Constantinople as the heir to Byzantium, and the behaviour of Russians during recent operations in that theatre, had not inclined the Greeks to put much faith in them. The French, for their part, if they took a hand in that area would quickly impoverish an already impoverished land.

That left Britain as the most likely to give the Greeks welcome support, but Leake's immediate purpose was to see what effective use could be made of Pasha Ali. He had quickly formed a very 'official' British view of the situation. Ottoman rule was abhorrent but effective, resistance to it was improbable and what he observed as a steady Mahommedanisation of Albania and the Epirus would render the country 'every day more savage and less capable of improvement'.[18] Leake, moreover, had a very negative view of Greek competence. 'So powerful is the effect of the Turkish system that all who dwell long in the country seem inevitably to feel the effects of this moral atmosphere by a want of energy, even indifference to everything but the vulgar pursuits of life.' Among these was concern for their personal safety, which Leake accepted as extenuation for the fact that even Greeks who had lived abroad made but 'the feeblest exertion for the improvement of the rising generation'.[19] If the Christian population continued to decline there would be no rising generation or a Greece to revive.

His mission took him on wide-ranging expeditions into Albania, the Epirus and Macedonia, which he spent methodically commenting on the inhabitants, the economy, the Ottoman administration, the Greek clergy, and Albanian colonists, all the time trying to match the modern topography to the historic sites of Greece and Rome. On his way he collected Greek and Roman coins which still circulated, less as money but, so extensively were they found when land was ploughed, as metal for melting down to make kettles and cooking pans. He became a self-taught numismatist and, by identifying the coins, established the sites of two ancient cities, Herakles Sintica and Cioricum in Thessaly.

For a time, when the Ottomans and Britain fell out in 1807, he was arrested in Salonika as a spy. To a Turk any foreigner searching for ancient cities or old coins could only be a spy, but Leake seemed inoffensive enough to be allowed to go back to Epirus, where he found Ali Pasha keen to mend the fences between the Porte and Britain, so that he could fulfil his ambition to annex Corfu. The peace with the Ottomans confirmed, Leake returned to London, only to be sent back in October 1808 with a consignment of artillery and ammunition for Ali, and instructions to take up residence at the Pasha's court. From there he took numerous exploratory trips into north Greece to replace his lost notes and was at Yannina when Byron arrived.

He only stayed in Greece for another year and then was recalled, so he never saw the Greeks at war with the Turks instead of with each other. For his services to Anglo-Ottoman relations, Leake was given a pension and promotion to Major, but his travels were over, apart from a mission in 1814 to map the defences of the borders of the Swiss Confederation to prevent the country falling as easily to an invader as it had to the French in 1798. He lived for another 46 years, accumulating fellowships of learned societies and writing up his notes and memoirs. His travels in the Morea and in Northern Greece appeared between 1830 and 1835, and his *Numismatica Hellenica* in 1854, six years before he died with the rank of Lieutenant Colonel. By that time the whole map of the Near East had changed, and Leake was the grand old man of Hellenic topography, honoured by the new Greek government with the presence of its ambassador at his funeral, and remembered for his collections, which he donated to the British Museum.

5

As Greeks enjoyed a privileged position in the Ottoman empire this led to much ambivalence in their struggle for independence. The Ottomans, like most imperial powers, depended heavily on others to discharge duties for which they were temperamentally or culturally unready. The knowledge of foreign languages was one, so that relations with foreign powers through embassies based in Constantinople were often discharged by Greeks. The common language of communication at the time of independence was Italian, a language accepted for centuries as a lingua franca throughout the eastern Mediterranean. Dragomans or interpreters translated everything into Italian and then into the language of their masters. The role of the interpreter was a highly prized one and often descended from father to son, and within the freemasonry of interpreters many of the inevitable mistranslations (as in the Treaty of Küchük Kaynarjar, where the Russian and Turkish texts differed substantially) could be sorted out. Not all Greeks, especially the Phanariot class that had served the Ottomans for centuries, were disposed to support an independent Greece, and many held on to important posts in Ottoman service after the declaration of the new kingdom. Indeed, a Phanariot Greek was appointed the first Ottoman ambassador to Athens.[20]

The Turks, not unlike the British in India, used the local aristocracy to do their ruling for them, like the despots in the Morea whose problems with dissident Greeks led to the slaughter at Corinth commemorated by Byron. Shelley had no real knowledge of the discordant greed and rivalry of the Greek *klephts* turned partisans, of the ambitions of petty chieftains, and of the airy but inept liberalism of their Phanariot leaders, who had no idea how to control the farmyard passions of peasants. He had no experience of the visceral hatred that existed between the faiths, whether Jewish, Christian or Muslim. His friend and principal informant on matters Greek was Prince Alexander Mavrocordato, born of a Phanariot family in Constantinople, but a stranger to events; for he had been resident in Wallachia since he was 21 and an exile in Russia and Italy since 1817.

For the Greek War of Independence was a contest of mutual extermination, Turk and Greek alike fed by a lust for blood and revenge. The Greek Patriarch of Constantinople was hanged for not keeping his co-religionists docile and, in revenge for the Greek massacre of Turks at Tripolitza, the Turks carried out an indiscriminate slaughter of the peaceful and prosperous inhabitants of the island of Chios (Scio), most of whom had not joined in the revolt. By one calculation 25,000 were killed and countless woman and children carried into slavery. The relieving party came too late; only 900 survivors were left on the island. Massacres were almost de rigueur in this frightful war but sadly Shelley's poem had few readers until Greece herself was safely free, and the massacring was over.[21] The prophecy of the last verse of Hellas: 'O cease! must hate and death return? / Cease! must men kill and die?' was partially fulfilled, but Europe's Romantic enthusiasm and indignation was shaken not by a poem but by a painting. The massacre at Chios was to inspire one of the great icons of the Romantic period.

6

Eugene Delacroix was 24; he had already made his mark with *Dante's Boat* in the 1822 Paris salon, but he was still poor, still reduced to pouring boiling water on last night's dregs to make his morning coffee. He had dabbled in Eastern subjects since he was 19 years old, copying Persian miniatures; he had already done a sepia portrait of a Turkish officer and an oil painting of *Turkish Horsemen in Battle*. Now he thought he had a big subject, big enough even for Rubens, whose mantle he believed he had assumed. There was a role, too, for his model and mistress, Emilie Roberts, as the naked captive being dragged off by a Turkish horseman; and to give her the requisite appearance of quiet despair and exhausted languor, he had his *chiavatura* with her each time she modelled for him, a fact he recorded in Italian in his diary. That may have been why he thought the figure lacked vigour.[22]

Delacroix did not think much of the finished painting, and found it 'depressing', lacking light. Not all the hanging committee liked it either, but they accepted it, and the painter, who had just seen his first Constables in Paris, was more than ever cast down by its lack of luminosity. He asked to be allowed to touch it up. Within four days he had transformed a picture which had taken him seven intensive months to paint. Baudelaire thought he was 'witnessing the gradual unfolding of some tragic mystery', for the scene of death and servitude was merely a preface to the achievement of glorious liberty. The dour and devastated background, with its greenish sea, so different from one's image of the Mediterranean, provided a kind of natural sympathy for the horror of what was depicted in the two main groups, despair at the imminence of slaughter on the left, at the imminence of rape on the right. Colour came from the dishevelled clothing, scattered jewellery and spattered blood. It was the *Guernica* painting of its day, exposing the horrors that were being carried out, not at a moment of past history but in the here and now.

FIGURE 8A   *Delacroix's* The Massacre of Chios. *He used his mistress as the model for the Greek girl being dragged off by her Turkish captor.*

Not everyone thought it good. Alexander Dumas remarked that he did not know they had the plague in Chios. Stendhal agreed; in fact he assumed that Delacroix had originally intended it for a plague scene, not a massacre. One critic found that the dying and wounded in what seemed an advanced state of putrefaction inspired not pity or terror, but horror and disgust. The artist Gros dubbed it *The Massacre of Painting.*[23] But one younger critic spoke

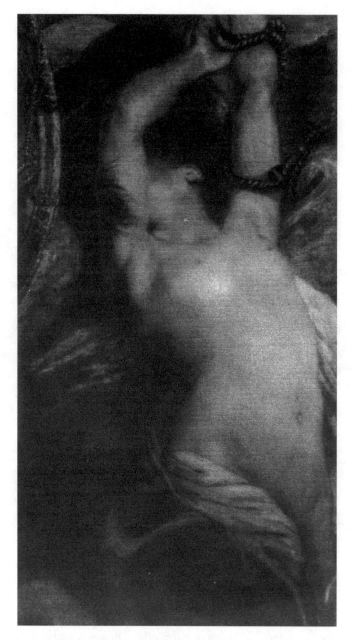

FIGURE 8B *After sexual intercourse, when she would be in post-coital lassitude as the helpless victim.*

for his age. Théophile Gautier dismissed the indignation of the classicists 'whose wigs quivered like Handel's' to salute the picture's 'extreme audacity and novelty'.[24] Delacroix was given his medal and the state bought the painting for the enormous sum of 6,000 francs. The colours faded but the picture still occupies a prime place in the Louvre. Like *Guernica*, it became a symbol of resistance to oppression and a call for help to the oppressed.

Delacroix was actually less interested in the Greek war than in the way he could produce the effect of disaster and death, in themselves the fruits of violence with which he was obsessed at the time. Two years later he produced *The Death of Sardanapalus*, a tableau of savage execution perpetrated by obvious orientals at the foot of the tyrant's deathbed. The nudes, fair skinned and Caucasian, were more obviously appetising than his mistress Emily in the *Massacre* – they were after all among Sardanapolis's most prized possessions, which were not to survive him, and vied for pride of place with a spirited stallion. Delacroix was still contesting with Ingres to be the true exponent of pure classicism, which he claimed for himself, to be the champion of the *Zeitgeist*, the Romantic sense of passion, action, and violence which spoke to him in the poetry of Byron.[25]

He found certain passages of Byron an unfailing spur to his imagination, and the death of Selim, in *The Bride of Abydos*, he thought sublime.[26] He fancied that he could summon up inspiration at will like Byron, and the Byronic swirl of drama in action reached its apotheosis in the paintings that he made from studies in the Paris Jardin des Plantes and on his visit in 1832 to both Morocco and Algeria. When he wanted to show man fighting man he took his subject from *The Giaour* and the fight between the Giaour and the Pasha, of which he made three versions; but in the version he made after his visit to Morocco the animals express the same sense of instinctive, aggressive ferocity as the riders on horseback. In his painting of Moors on a lion hunt Delacroix endowed his models, the beasts in the Paris zoo, with almost human qualities, as they were set against each other in the lurid russet red light in a struggle to the death.

North Africa was about to pass under European conquest or 'protection' and Delacroix captured the elemental courage, and savagery, with which the Moorish states had long been identified, and which reasserted itself in the Algerian struggle for independence in the 1950s. The savage energy of his Algerian scenes revived in the imagination the terrible energy of the Turks who had destroyed the Hungarians at Mohacs and who had nearly subjugated Vienna. The almost effete posturing of Sultans and Pashas in Constantinople and the lethargic terror personified in Ali Pasha of Yannina were in sharp contrast to the turbulent spirit of Algiers: all the more credit to post-Napoleonic France, still smarting from defeat, he implied, in subduing it.

FIGURE 9   *Delacroix's* Giaour and Pasha Fighting, *from the Louvre. The artist made three versions of this subject in a bid to catch the elemental ferocity of the encounter. Baudelaire said: 'His style is essentially literary. He has translated ... Byron, Dante, Ariosto, Scott and Shakespeare.' Baudelaire in 'The Life and Work of Eugene Delacroix', a letter to the Editor of the Opinion Nationale, Paris 1863, in 'The Painter of Modern Life & Other Essays', ed. J Mayne, London 1964, p. 45.*

Delacroix may have been recording not the future, or even the present, but history, in the belief that he was demonstrating what Rubens would have made of the same experience. But his painting was prophetic, for France was acquiring the exotic Empire for which she had unsuccessfully struggled in the eighteenth century. By bringing the North African coast under her control she was reviving the dream of a French sea and a Levantine dominion which had tantalised Napoleon. The empire that had succeeded Rome was crumbling and its African territories were ready for new masters. The Ottoman centre was reprieved by rivalry for control of its antipodes.

CHAPTER EIGHT

Look Upon My Works, Ye Mighty, and Despair

The Myth of Egypt

Nothing beside remains. Round the decay
Of that colossal wreck, boundless and bare
The lone and level sands stretch far away.
(Shelley, *Ozymandias*)[1]

I

IT WAS, IN fact, interest in ancient Greece and Rome that was to help raise the curtain on Islam. The Ottomans presided with almost sublime lack of interest over huge tracts of the Roman empire. They casually reduced the Graeco-Roman sites to rubble by using its buildings as quarries, and profaned the nursery of civilisation by a neglect that allowed the Sultan to reward the British for helping to liberate Egypt from Napoleon's armies by giving the British ambassador in Constantinople a licence to export what are now known as the Elgin marbles.

The door to understanding was opened a chink for the English by two Protestant clergymen, the first the 26-year-old chaplain to the English factory at Algiers, the second the future Bishop of Meath. Both had been inspired by their leisurely Oxford education to broaden their horizons of the classical world. Thomas Shaw (1694–1721) spent 13 years in Algiers, during which, his duties being light, he travelled extensively to Egypt and the Middle East as well as to the hinterland of Barbary. Despite instructions to remain in the far from safe embrace of a detachment of Turkish infantry he would wander off on his own among the ruins, risking life and freedom. The anarchy of the Holy Land he found more dangerous than anything he had experienced in the slave kingdoms of Barbary.

A Fellow of Queen's College, and elected to a Fellowship of the Royal Society for his paper on Tunis and Carthage in 1738, Shaw dedicated a lovingly illustrated, encyclopaedic account of Barbary to George II and his queen, who had helped to sponsor this cornucopia of fauna and floras, fossils, coins and inscriptions. He crossed literary swords with a fellow Oxonian, Richard Pococke (1704–65), ten years his junior, who set off to explore Egypt from 1735 and did in fact penetrate as far south as Philo, before returning to Cairo and then setting off for Baalbek in Syria, and for Turkey and Greece. In *A Description of the East and Other Countries*, which appeared in two volumes in 1743–45, Pococke took Shaw up sharply on certain points in his observations on Egypt. These inspired Shaw to respond, and the learned war in which the two men were engaged kept his book in print until 1808. Both books were widely translated, though Pococke found a new and less contentious interest in discovering wild Ireland, where he ended his clerical career as a bishop.

2

A greater traveller than either was to open the door wider. A traveller almost since birth, James Bruce (1730–94), dubbed 'The Abyssinian', was one of the many descendants of Robert the Bruce, and the son of a small Scottish landowner. His mother dying soon after his birth, he was sent at the age of eight to school at Harrow to escape 'Scottish troubles', and his father's second marriage. Showing a bent for foreign languages he went to Paris to perfect his French, returning when fluent to Edinburgh to study for the bar. But he was already caught up in the Scottish encyclopaedic movement and found, like Boswell, that the study of Roman and Scottish law was not to his taste. He toyed with becoming an East India merchant but could not raise the investment, so he accepted his mother-in-law's offer of a working partnership in the family wine business. As the vine grew mainly in the sun, in lands whose languages and culture he wished to study, he made for Portugal and Spain. In the usual eighteenth-century way, however, his future was determined not by his work, but by an acquaintance who became his patron.

Robert Wood (1717?–71) was not an Oxford clergyman, but he too had drunk of the ambrosial cup that had intoxicated both Shaw and Pococke and had set off to describe the glories of an imperial past buried in what seemed to be Islamic sand. His achievements as a traveller, however, 'disappointed the expectations of the public', meaning Edward Gibbon who – while applauding his desire to read *The Iliad* in the land where Achilles fought, Ulysses schemed and Homer sang – censured him for topographical errors. Gibbon, while praising his graphic description of the Hellespont, could not forgive his confounding Ilium with Alexandria Troad! Despite Gibbon's strictures he nonetheless gave the world two superbly illustrated books on Palmyra (1753) and Baalbek (1757), unveiling a Rome little known in the West.[2] Wood, whose lack of a clerical stipend had lured him into politics and who was now under-secretary of state for the southern region, saw in Bruce someone who might continue where he had left off, uncovering the ancient glories of Rome beyond the borders of continental Europe.

Bruce, meanwhile, had planned to accompany his studies of the Spanish grape with a ground-breaking work on the Moors in Andalucia and the fortunes of that province after their expulsion. Thwarted by his inability to get access to the Arabic manuscripts in the Escorial, he decided to move on to France to pursue his oenological studies there. With war brewing, and himself in trouble with the authorities over a duel, Bruce went on to Holland, collecting Arabic books on the way. In the meantime he had inherited his father's estate, on which was mined the coal vital for the growing Scottish iron-smelting industry, and was now a rich man. The under-secretary of state was glad to pull a few strings for the new laird of Kinnaird.

While in Spain Bruce had formulated an ingenious plan to attack the Spanish base at Ferrol, so Wood sent him to see William Pitt; but nothing came of it. Chatham's fall meant that the proposal just mouldered in the archives. But Bruce's cousin had been a former Chief Secretary to Ireland, and also wished to do something for his kinsman, so he brought him to the attention of the Earl of Halifax, the new Secretary of State, and former Lord Lieutenant of Ireland. The end of the Seven Years War had increased Britain's interest in the Mediterranean, while enthusiasts for the history of Greece and Rome, which was at the heart of the Grand Tour and of British education, now accepted that the horizon of the classical world, which Shaw, Pococke and Wood had already extended, needed exploring further. Its vast ruins, for so long off limits to Grand Tourists because they were under the control of alien powers, were to be brought into prominence as the legacy of an empire whose achievements the British were thinking to emulate.

Under-secretary Wood probably put the words into the mouth of his Secretary of State, who told Bruce that someone was needed to record and draw the unknown cities of North Africa, as Wood had done for the cities of the Levant. Bruce was the obvious man to do it. He had independent means, he knew Arabic, which he was keen to improve, and he had attended drawing school, so that he could look forward to making a significant discovery in some eastern land. He could perhaps measure the solar parallax when Venus transited the disk of the sun (thought to be the only way to measure the earth's distance from it) or, Lord Halifax suggested, he might travel deep into the heart of the unknown continent and discover the source of the Nile. By chance the post of Consul-General in Algiers was vacant. Would Bruce care to fill it?

Tempted by the sites of oracles and the birthplaces of Gods, by the remains of Carthage and the Roman garrison towns in the Algerian desert, by the Greek cities of Cyrenaica, and by the fora and amphitheatres dotting the countryside, most of whose masonry now formed the main structure of mosques, palaces and baths, Bruce quickly swallowed the bait. He did not think that the duties of British consul, usually held by a merchant, would interfere much with travelling deep into the interior; anyhow, he was promised an assistant to help discharge his official duties while he was on tour. Moreover, before he took up his post he was allowed to spend nine months travelling through Italy to his embarkation port at Naples, note and sketchbooks in hand, in order to study the relics of ancient Rome.

His duties on arrival in Algiers, however, proved more exacting than he expected and it was two and a quarter years before he could set off on what he considered his primary function. For shortly after arrival he was engaged in a battle to preserve British freedom from the attentions of Algerian corsairs. Treaty allowed British merchants to carry a licence giving them immunity from interference, but blank licences had fallen into the hands of the French, who were issuing them to shipping of nations at war with Algiers. As the corsair profits in booty and slaves were badly affected by this proliferation of immunities, Bruce was the subject of menaces, but being six foot four in height, a giant among the Arabs, he inspired physical respect.

His fearless demeanour impressed the Dey, Baba Ali, who had a notoriously brutal temper, which he only controlled during this dispute out of respect for British sea power. Bruce, without consulting anyone, threatened reprisals for any infringements of the freedom of British ships from molestation, but was not supported by his government, which was worried about essential supplies for its dependencies in the Mediterranean and was therefore more anxious to appease than confront the Dey.[3] He was held to have exceeded his powers, and as the promised assistant had not been appointed and he had now acquired more than serviceable Arabic, he decided to resign and devote himself, as a private citizen, to the mission he thought he had come to fulfil. That included, by his reckoning, discovering the source of the Nile.

After many adventures during which he was shipwrecked and washed up naked on an African shore without any of his clothes or instruments, he made his way to Robert Wood's old stamping ground of Palmyra and Baalbek. He early fell foul of the bastion of proper thought, Oxford University, when he wrote of a tribe of Arabs who hunted and ate lions; the correct procedure so the pundits pointed out was for lions to eat men. Bruce did not dispute the authority that gave the lions title to eat them but, since it was not founded upon patent, no consideration could deny the merit of the tribe who had turned the chase upon their enemy. 'The Arabs,' he wrote, 'a brutish and ignorant folk, will, I fear, not withstanding the disbelief of Oxford University, continue to eat lions as long as they exist.'[4] This was hardly the way to handle learned scholars, and it gave Bruce a reputation for a fanciful approach to the truth which dogged him throughout his declining years and beyond. Bruce was largely but not wholly vindicated by subsequent travellers but he certainly allowed the account of his travels, dictated in a great hurry from morning to night as they flashed on his inward eye in his Scottish home, to stray, now and then, from the strict truth.

Professional satirists chose to find in him a liar worthy of Baron Munchäusen; one traveller, purporting to have followed in his track (at least as far as Madeira), rhymed that 'not happy in a stomach framed of steel / On roaring lions have I made a meal'.[5] Bruce could shrug it all off, and notwithstanding the recovery of his astronomical instruments, thanks to French generosity, he now felt that observing the transit of Venus across the sun was not likely to give any positive evidence of 'the precise quantity of the sun's parallax'. It might be more profitable to make straight not for Tartary or Armenia, but Ethiopia. To get there he must traverse another part of the Ottoman empire, Egypt. His *Travels to Discover the Source of the Nile in 1768, 1769, 1770, 1772 & 1773* appeared in 1799; there were three editions in all and many abbreviated versions that tried to correct his prolixity and repetitiveness.[6]

Bruce entered Egypt with his scientific instruments, which gave the illusion that he was not an astronomer but an astrologer. As a *hakim*, prepared to practise his exiguous knowledge of herbal remedies picked up from his travels and from his insatiable curiosity, Bruce spent no more time than necessary in Egypt. He knew that the Nile rose somewhere in Abyssinia, and thither was he bound. He took time on the way to explore the ruins, the rock tombs and the pictography without understanding a word. He despised the Arab guides who were superstitiously afraid of the dead in the caves, though several millennia old, and was enraged by their contempt for the stupendous civilisation upon which they were squatting.

He was not a collector or an archaeologist so that the account of his *Travels* bristles with encounters with hostile tribes, with dilatory seamen and with grasping local officials, who were for another century at least to be the stuff of travellers' tales. Yet he moved with impunity from one area to the next, loosely protected by letters from the Pasha in Cairo and by his reputation, fraudulent though it was, as a doctor. He was to admire the loyalty of men who had pledged it and the rascality of those who had not. He shed little light on the civilisation of ancient Egypt and little on the Egyptians of his time, but much on himself, his resourcefulness and his sense of innate authority that partly stemmed from his size. Bruce's desert travels in North Africa and Egypt may, however, have impressed Rousseau with the belief that the Arab submission to Providence (i.e. Allah), in a world of permanent harshness and danger, had awakened 'the principles of first religion which Christianity had perverted through folly and superstition'.[7]

Bruce was a muscular Christian and held priests of whatever stripe in low regard, though he counted among his friends and helpers a Greek archimandrite whom he had got to know in Algiers. He had little time for the Jesuit priests who knew most about the land for which he was bound, despite the fact that their network remained in existence in Africa even after their dissolution as a Society. He paid scant attention to the Copts who had kept Christianity alive in Ethiopia or to the Franciscans who had preceded him, despite his friend from Algiers, now installed in the Patriarch's office in Cairo, who helped him with introductions. He found the Coptic church rituals tedious and its clergy suspicious, Ethiopians more likeable than Arabs and, made slightly dizzy by royal patronage, he felt that they appreciated and rewarded his worth by their attentions.

3

It was not to be Bruce who was to shed light on the Egypt through which he was passing like a meteor, but the community of Copts, monophysite Christians, in a sea of Islam. They had long attracted Biblical scholars and missionaries, for the intervening desert had become home to ascetics and anchorites, and monasteries had kept alive the communities which had once welcomed the infant Jesus on His flight from Herod. The winding tracts of the Nile had been the one direct land route to Prester John, and the Christian, if heretic, Abyssinians. A Jesuit made the journey in 1707 and reckoned in the Valley of the Kings that he had stumbled on the ancient city of Thebes. Thereafter travellers, like Pococke and Bruce, proceeded up the river beyond Luxor as far as Aswan, marvelling at the evidence of temples and palaces along the shore. But this civilisation remained a closed book, for its monuments were too monumental and stuck in the sand to excavate without tremendous resources and its writing could not be read. Only the chroniclers of other ancient and neighbouring civilisations gave any clue to Egypt's size, power, and wealth, or offered any ruler's name on which to hang history.

If a repressive and priest-laden religion were considered the despot's most potent elixir for rule, the ancient civilisation of Egypt, with its mighty monuments to the work of helots, seemed to hold the key to all those empires which had succeeded rulers whose dynasties had extended unbroken for thousands of years. Egypt for some centuries had been a part of the Ottoman empire, but was different in many degrees from the rest. It was ruled under very loose control from Constantinople by the Mamelukes, descendants of Caucasian slaves who had supported Sultans since the Middle Ages until the Ottoman conquest. They survived to glory in their status of Janissaries, bound together by the simple fact that they derived their authority from their origins in bondage. Soon after the Ottomans devolved power to local Janissary pashas and governors, they established themselves again as the virtual rulers of Egypt. Thereafter, like the Janissaries elsewhere in the Ottoman empire, they declined in power and efficiency and were a congeries of pashas who divided local provinces between them under a nominal chief Pasha in Grand Cairo.

They were servants of the Ottoman empire, but took their responsibilities lightly, and had little interest in the world beyond their restricted horizons, so that under their rule Egypt remained a land of mystery and romance. As Egypt lay across one of the routes to India, that mystery and romance became more than just a lure. It became a temptation. Those Company men who travelled to their posts by the land route through the Levant found the long haul across the intervening lands tedious and dangerous, whereas an overland journey from Alexandria to Suez on the Red Sea, with a short felucca trip to Jeddah where a Company boat was waiting to sail to Bombay, cut weeks off the journey. That way they spent less time in an *Arabia* that was not particularly *Felix*.

4

Egypt, moreover, was tantalisingly wrapped in a dense enigma which its blazing sun could not disperse. Most readers still relied on Herodotus's account of Egypt as their principal source of information, and travellers even today traverse the desert with him in their pocket, as if trying to link their experiences to his. In Ondaatje's novel *The English Patient*, made into a film, which demands all the patience of a patient Englishman, the hero had his pocket Herodotus well-thumbed. As travellers passed from Alexandria to Suez, or down to Grand Cairo, so they wondered who were the mighty potentates who figured so large in Biblical history, and who had once ruled an empire every bit as formidable as the Ottoman.

Their relics could be seen half buried in the centuries-old drift of sand, and their articulacy was muffled by a script no one could interpret. Homer was their authority on the heart of ancient Egypt, hellenised as Thebes, possibly a corruption of its Egyptian name. It was the birthplace of both No (No-Ammon) and of Zeus, so a city of the gods, and was reputed the oldest city in the world, which embraced 14 square miles of fertile land. Together with the sites of the ancient necropolis and of the temples of Karnak and Luxor and the river, about six miles wide at this point, Thebes was built on both banks so that at its greatest it may have covered something like this area. Later, known as Diospolis Magna, the great city on the Nile with a hundred gates and 200 chariots always ready to sally out and battle with an enemy crumbled into ruin from abandonment and neglect. Where was it now? Where was the greatness of yesteryear?

It was not difficult to buy in the *souks* relics of that dead civilisation. There was a lively and open commerce in mummified cadavers and papyrus scrolls in Alexandria, both genuinely old and counterfeit. In 1720 the

French consul in Cairo sent a mummy in answer to a request from the Grand Master in Malta, which was solemnly subjected to quarantine.[8] All that they did was to tantalise scholars by stubbornly remaining sealed texts. Some linguists familiar with oriental languages were beginning to accept that the key, if they could only turn it, might lie in the contemporary liturgical language of the Copts, but they had not yet been able to see how to crack the code. The enlightenment burned to overcome the challenge.

The antiquity of the Pharaonic civilisation suggested that the fundamental orthodoxies of the Bible story had put an age to the world pitifully short, and that Egyptian history might pre-date the Flood, providing one more stick with which to beat Christianity. Its hidden mysteries suggested a whole new theophany from those which had ruled the western world since the time of Constantine, and the eastern world from the time of Mahommed. Its mighty constructions suggested a race of architect giants who understood mathematics and the stars well before the Greeks, from whom the Greeks and Romans had derived their own architectural styles. A divine master mason was emerging from the ancient temples and burial sites to replace the God who had created man, as Michaelangelo had taught the world, by an electrical impulse from his extended fingers. In their impenetrable vaults was imprisoned a system that would give morality, peace and wisdom to the world, in which the rule of Sarastro would replace the otherwise only too human Queen of the Night. Isis, Horus and Osiris would be the new patrons of peace and mercy, in sacred halls 'Wo Mensch den Menschen liebt.'[9]

It was to be the romantic imagination of Napoleon Bonaparte that supplied the spark that began to illumine the Egyptian night. The idea that France could start a new imperial adventure after the disappointing result of wars in North America and India had been around since 1779, when Baron Tott had been sent on a mission to inspect French consular posts in the eastern Mediterranean. His hidden agenda was to assess whether the Ottoman empire was tottering into a similar decay as that which had overtaken the Mughals in India, and his conclusion was that an invasion of Egypt ostensibly on behalf of the Sultan to eliminate the corrupt and disobliging rule of the Mamelukes, would be comparatively simple and popular.[10]

Another French traveller, the Comte de Volney (1757–1820), fired by enthusiasm for Herodotus, learned Arabic to go to see for himself, and concluded that the whole Arab world was groaning under an Ottoman tyranny and was ripe for change. A ruined empire was presiding over ruins, and these ruins might contain keys to the true history of mankind. Volney did not believe that Christianity would be any great improvement on Islam as liberator of the Arabs, and opposed any military adventure there; but enlightenment, of which he was a true child, must achieve it. His *Voyage en Egypte et en Syrie*, published in 1787, was certainly read by Napoleon. Two years later Volney went on to elaborate his thesis: that ruins were the monuments of imperial decline and fall and that the Ottoman empire was in steep decline. His *Ruines ou Méditations sur les Révolutions des Empires* became required reading among the cultural classes that had launched the revolution in 1789, and were still awaiting its consummation. Egypt was the place where mighty ruins of mighty regimes as repressive as the *ancien régime*, against which they had rebelled, remained half-covered in sand and unexplored.[11] They were a perfect backdrop for Romanticism. Mary Shelley made Volney's work one of the principal sources for the mastery of language by the monster that Frankenstein had created. Listening to it being read aloud to the children of the cottager with whom he had sought asylum, he acquired proficiency as his imagination was fired when he heard 'of the slothful Asiatics, of the stupendous genius and mental activity of the Grecians and the wonderful virtue of the early Romans'.[12]

5

Almost as if on cue in 1786, the popular and prolific Gothic novelist Clara Reeve (1729–1807), a literary pundit and contemporary of Ann Radcliffe, wrote *The Progress of Romance*, which was in great demand in circulating libraries. The last story in this book was *The History of Charoba, Queen of Egypt*.[13] Reeve is a forgotten author who dared to criticise Horace Walpole's *The Castle of Otranto* as too violent, while acknowledging the influence of Walpole's style. She found the tale in a seventeenth-century French translation from the Arabic, and her rendering was enough to fire the enthusiasm of the 22-year-old poet Walter Savage Landor. He borrowed *The Progress of Romance* from his *inamorata*, Rose Aylmer, who had borrowed it in her turn from Swansea library.[14] Landor decided to write his story about Queen Charoba in Latin, just as William Beckford had written *Vathek* in French, in the forlorn hope that it might thus appear as an authentic tale of Old Egypt. But when he published his long poem as a sixpenny pamphlet in 1798, he completed it in classical English, only translating it back into classical Latin when he revised it six years later. Its appearance in the year of Napoleon's invasion of Egypt, while the young general was in the full flush of Romantic glory as a liberator, gave it an adventitious *réclame*.

Its heroic subject, Gebir, is a tyrant of Spanish origin – the etymology of his name was wrongly believed by Landor to be Gibraltarian – who invades Egypt to fulfil the wish of his father. Egypt at the epoch chosen by both Reeve and Landor existed in a limbo of history, between the end of the Nilotic dynasties and the onset of the Alexandrian line. Landor wanted to break with the Augustan pastoral themes of his time, but as Gebir has a brother who is a nomadic shepherd called Tamar he could not avoid a pastoral setting. Being among the finest Latinists of his day, he was too steeped in the pastoral tradition to escape its Virgilian echoes. The banks of the Nile thus bear a strong resemblance to those of the Thames, its 'pastures large and rich afford / Flowers to thy (Tamar's) bees and herbage to thy sheep'.[15] Flowering raspberry and the vine are not part of the Nilotic flora.[16]

In the tradition of the Italian epicists Tasso and Ariosto, Landor resorted frequently to the supernatural. Tamar has been worsted in a wrestling match with a sea nymph who wins by magical means. The contest is sexually explicit – surprisingly so, for the Augustan age – and Tamar is now firmly in love with the scantily clad maiden with whom he has lubriciously tangled. Gebir, meanwhile, is planning to build a new city for himself on the site, and with the remains, of an old one, but is meeting with supernatural obstacles to building. In his search for the solution to his problems he meets this nymph himself in similar combat – her vocation seems to be challenging strange men to a wrestling match – but as he is not destined to love her the contest is not so sensual, and Gebir subdues her by force.

In return for promising that his brother not he shall enjoy her, the nymph informs Gebir that Egypt is a land of incantation, that demons rule the waves and that it is they who were upsetting all attempts to build his city. In propitiating these demons, Gebir finds himself led through vaults as sinister and vast as those of Piranesi, to a hell of classical proportions where he meets his ancestors. This is not the abode of Eblis in *Vathek* but a sort of Tartarean Madame Tussaud's, where the dead stand wax-like, almost mummified, to regret their crimes. This is the high point of the poem. Such a fate befalls all tyrants, and if Gebir is to avoid ending up the same way he must now purge himself of the crime of invading a friendly country.

The final destiny of Gebir is to fall victim to the demons, headed by a sorceress who was once Charoba's nurse. She envelops him on his wedding day to the Queen of Egypt in a venomed cloak and, like Hercules before him, he dies in agony. In Clara Reeve's story Gebir is quite simply a brutal invader and Charoba his wily opponent determined to save her country. Landor turns it into a pseudo-oriental love story, in which the union of two kingdoms by love is successfully thwarted by a sorceress in league with the demons that inhabit the ancient land of Egypt. Tyrants, sorcerers, sorceresses and demons, in various forms, were commonly believed to inhabit the ancient lands that had fallen under the spell of Islam.

Like *Vathek*, *Gebir* is about as oriental as are the current epics of demons, malignant mummies, flying pyramids and pharaonic creatures from outer space who inhabit *diese heiligen hallen*, with apologies to Sarastro, in television soaps and cinematic horror films. Both books certainly implanted a taste for them. Southey was bowled over by the beauty of *Gebir*, and called it the miraculous work of a madman.[17] Like Landor he was an enthusiast for the French Revolution, which was engaged on the regeneration of the human race, and the more he read round George Sale's notes on the Koran, the more he became convinced that the East could contribute to this.

Having never lived there, Southey conceived the desert as a wonderful environment for creating a sense of moral rectitude.[18] His oriental poem *Thalaba the Destroyer*, started in 1799 and published in 1801, is oriental in that it is set in some faery world of evil demons in a waterproof capsule at the bottom of the sea near Tunis, engaged, like all tyrannous regimes, in adding to the miseries of the human race. It recounts the rescue of a sword, ringed by fire at the heart of the underground, by Thalaba, a youth dedicated to the destruction, over 12 rather tedious books, of the demons and their home, Domdaniel. It too has its origins in a French translation of an Arabic tale, *The History of Maugraby the Magician* (1792), and calls on Sale's notes to the Koran for authentic colour, as Tolkein called on Norse sagas for *The Lord of the Rings*.

Shelley at Oxford could not put *Thalaba* down, and when his friend Thomas Jefferson Hogg found he would not pay attention to what he was saying, he snatched it from him and threw it out of the window, whereupon Shelley calmly sent someone out to retrieve it and resumed his reading. Both *Gebir* and *Thalaba* were two youthful pastoral, tragical, classical Augustan romances which had as much orientalism about them as George

Sale's notes to his translation of the Koran persuaded Landor and Southey to include.

The real-life child of both books was another dedicated youth, Napoleon Bonaparte, who, when they were first written, was still a liberator and not a tyrant. In 1798 a fierce and radical light was thrown on the demon-ridden lands of fiction, and in Napoleon Landor's Gebir materialised as a flesh-and-blood tyrant in the making. And there was no Charoba to tame him, or sorceress nurse to despatch him. After his invasion of Egypt, Gebir/Napoleon returned to France, and seized power. Landor lived to regret that his poem had been read as a paeon to the renewable energy of the French Revolution, and in the 1805 edition he modified it. Southey, on the other hand, was still in his fine poetic and democratic rapture and Napoleon/Thalaba was wielding his sword to rout demons. It was not long before disillusion set in for him too, and the desert as the catalyst of moral integrity lost its charm. Soon, however, a real vision of Egypt was to displace these poems as imaginative sorties into the world of oriental fantasy, and change the world view.

CHAPTER NINE

Forty Centuries Look Down on You

The Myth of Bonaparte

Soldats, songez que, du haut de ces pyramides, quarante
siècles vous contemplent.
(Napoleon Bonaparte, 21 July 1798)[1]

I

THE FRENCH ATTACK on Egypt was ostensibly in support of the Ottoman empire, whose Mameluke viceroys were misgoverning the country, and it was the first frontal assault on one of the heartlands of the Islamic empire. Up till now the wars on the Ottoman European frontiers had been the reclamation of land formerly Christian. Despite its Coptic past, Egypt was only peripherally associated with the Holy Family, providing asylum when it fled from Herod, and could not be identified with the life and teaching of Jesus. If Napoleon's campaign was a crusade in the sense of being an attack on land largely inhabited by Muslims, its religious overtones were very strange indeed. Egypt in Pharaonic times had intervened many times in the history of Palestine, and the Egyptian chronicles, if they could ever be deciphered, might throw a new light on and add a new chronology to the Bible story, which was almost reason enough for the invasion.

The French scientific hope was that one of her citizens might be the first to crack the hieroglyphic code, even if it meant discarding theories and interpretations of world chronology that could very seriously undermine European confidence in the reliability of the Bible. What Napoleon himself hoped to gain from the expedition was far less certain. His ambition may have been to threaten India, perhaps even to invade her, though at no time did he make proper preparations for such a distant venture. At best the expedition was a filibuster, to catch the English wrong-footed, to escape the poisonous intrigues of the Directory and to gain new laurels for himself. Thwarted by Nelson's victory at Aboukir Bay, he may have thought of carving out an empire for himself in the Levant, where Baron Tott and Volney had foreseen imminent Ottoman dissolution and collapse. But far from shaping events he took advantage of them, and abandoned his oriental ambitions to pursue goals nearer home, leaving his army to face an Ottoman empire, stirred up to the reconquest of its territory, and an England determined to eliminate a French presence athwart her communications with India.

As an immediate result of the invasion, the centuries-old special status of France was replaced in Constantinople by the English, and the Ottoman empire was to remain a sometimes uncertain ally of her new benefactor. Any prospect of a French empire in Egypt or a protectorate in the Levant was thwarted, until revived at the end of the 1914–18 war. The principal effect of Napoleon's action, apart from helping him to power in France, was to lose that country any prospect of being a rival presence in India. His brilliant victories against the Mameluke satraps who ruled the country as virtually autonomous agents of the Grand Signor only revived Ottoman interest in Egypt, and paved the way for the rise to power of an Albanian Ottoman whose dynasty was to share the country with British overlords for over a century. The Ottomans had previously neglected Egypt, and their interest barely extended south beyond Cairo, but now they found that the entire country, which had once been ruled by 31 dynasties of Pharaohs, was of major interest to other powers, not always friendly to Constantinople, and certainly not disposed to solicit Ottoman help in understanding and profiting from it.

2

Napoleon arrived with a Commission for the Science and Arts of Egypt over 160 strong, accompanied by numerous students, with a brief to study, record and publish her natural and ancient history. The Commission consisted of 52 engineers, 11 surveyors, eight surgeons and seven chemists, with smaller numbers of interpreters, architects, designers printers, mineralogists, astronomers, economists, botanists, zoologists, pharmacists, painters, archaeologists, writers and musicians, and finally an engraver and a sculptor.[2] That so large a body of savants was ready to brave the perils of a sea voyage, pursued by the dreaded Royal Navy, to a land so little known was a tribute to the way Napoleon could capture the imagination, and to the awakening lust for knowledge about what was almost a lost civilisation. Napoleon had read his Plutarch and knew that Alexander of Macedon took philosophers and artists with him as he set out to conquer the East. It is a sign that Napoleon at 28 nourished hopes to rival the Macedonian, who was only 25 when he founded Alexandria and marched into the desert to consult the oracle of Ammon.

In addition to 'saving Egypt from barbarity' – he meant the Turks – Napoleon was going to give the world a whole new corpus of knowledge about the ancients; he would be philosopher king *and* liberator. The commissioners numbered some very eminent people, some who were less able, and surprisingly few Arabic interpreters, indicating that their interest lay not in contemporary Egypt, but in the Egypt of the Dynasties. The contemporary Egyptian Muslims had their uses as manual labour but it was their predecessors, the Copts, who attracted the learned attention, as their liturgical tongue might possibly contain the key to the hieroglyph. The choice of the Commission was ostensibly left to others but the young general, as a member of the Mathematical Section of the *Institut*, could not resist meddling.

Perhaps the most distinguished member of it was the associate of Lavoisier, Gaspard Monge, who is credited with the discovery that water was made up of two parts hydrogen to one of oxygen, and who secured the Mona Lisa for the Louvre as a spoil of war during Bonaparte's campaign in Italy. Monge was an ambitious Jacobin, nearly 30 years older than Napoleon, who consulted him about his Egyptian project from the very beginning. Its most important member, however, for the effect he was to have on the study of ancient Egypt, was the artist Baron Dominique Vivant Denon.[3]

Denon was a survivor of the *ancien régime*, having in his time served under Louis XV and XVI, and he was credited by some with being one of Pompadour's lovers. He escaped the Terror by residing in Venice and though his Bourbon barony aroused Napoleon's suspicion at first, Denon was ambitious for fame, with the talents to earn it, and soon the two men were close friends. Napoleon gave Denon his opportunity to record the lost civilisation in drawings, plans and architectural graphics of exquisite and accurate detail, as he travelled south of Cairo with Desaix in pursuit of the battered and tattered Mamelukes. Rushing as they were, the troops, without orders, at the sight of the temples of Luxor nevertheless formed rank and presented arms to a drum roll and martial music from their marching band. They were not the first temples they had seen but their magnificence on the edge of the vast river excited the sensibility of men who had been persuaded that they were at once rolling back as well as creating history.

A later visitor expressed best what they probably felt: 'It appeared to me like entering a city of giants, who after a long conflict were all destroyed, leaving the ruins of their temples as the only proof of their former existence.'[4] Denon recorded the majestic ruins and fortunately he could draw what he saw at great speed. He needed all his skill not to fall behind the rapid march of the soldiers, but when they were resting they willingly allowed their knees to form a drawing table. His supply of pencils could hardly keep up with his fingers and to improvise replacements when they were worn to a stub, the men melted down precious lead bullets. His prodigious output was crammed into the year between landing in Egypt and leaving with Napoleon in 1799. His *Voyage dans la Basse et la Haute Egypte* appeared in 1802, some of the drawings in which are the only record of antiquities since destroyed.[5] Egyptology was 'a science created with a pencil in one hand and a musket in the other'.[6]

3

The French were at least methodical about Egypt. Their archaeological collection formed the basis of the Cairo museum; the public lectures and the library of the *Institut*, which was collecting books on Arab language and civilisation, attracted ordinary solders and some Arabs. But the speculative spirit that had made the courts of Cordoba, Granada and Palermo rare centres of scientific and religious enquiry had long since died under Ottoman incuriosity. What was the point of looking for new plants, fish, insects or mammals when the Prophet, peace be upon him, had already enumerated the species God had created? Outside and beyond Cairo researches were supported by military logistics and funds from the *Institut* as far as they were able to go, and this meant, in the last analysis, the French government.

With the extinction of the expedition and the treaty of Alexandria which followed soon after in 1801, the British and French agreed to share some of the discoveries. The French savants could keep their field notes, plans and specimens of the fauna and flora, but what they had found of Egyptian antiquities went to Britain. With the obelisks, sarcophagi, statues and pieces of statuary also went the most significant discovery of all, the Rosetta Stone. What was believed to be the key to Egyptian hieroglyphs was faithfully copied, and copies were circulated in both England and France for linguists to pore and theorise over. But it remained an exasperation for another 21 years until Jean-François Champollion found the first combination of the lock. Having identified the names of the Greek Ptolomies in the script, he was able to decode the names of Egyptian rulers, known to classical authors, in transcriptions of carved hieroglyphics much older than the trilingual text of the Rosetta Stone. But while Champollion struggled with his discovery, the war with Napoleon had ended and Egypt was no longer the single preserve of the English.

4

By then the de facto ruler of Egypt was the Albanian Mehemet Ali (1769–1849). Like Byron's Pasha Ali of Yannina, he was an Albanian, born at Kavala, a small seaport on the frontier of Thrace and Macedonia. Trading in Egypt in tobacco, he joined a regiment of Albanians when Napoleon invaded, and at the Battle of Aboukir he and the Albanians were driven into the sea. He owed his life to a British sailor who fished him out of the water. At the peace in 1801 he was back in Egypt, this time in command of Albanians, whom he used skilfully, if unscrupulously, to make himself indispensable, first to the Mamelukes, who tried to reassert their control of the country, then to the Ottomans, who were determined to stop them. In 1806, the sheiks in Cairo, wanting a strong man to restore peace and order, elected him the Pasha of Egypt. Two years later, he saw off an incompetent British expeditionary force, which wished to replace his French advisers by British. The only use he made of the British was to show his ruthlessness by marking their defeat by a ceremonial avenue of posts with the heads of the British slain displayed in all their gory splendour.

Mehemet Ali at least understood what the French had tried to do in Egypt, which was to reanimate a civilisation, even revive an ancient, seemingly dead, one. If he did not share their encyclopaedic quest for information, he did their lust for change and development. He recognised that economic prosperity would strengthen his ambition to become not just the Ottoman governor of Egypt, but its independent, undisputed ruler, even perhaps successor to the Caliphate at Constantinople. He eliminated the surviving Mamelukes and, using paid-off mercenaries from both French and British armies, he and his formidable son Ibrahim established Egypt as a broker in the struggle for supremacy in the East, with a fleet and an army of formidable strength.

Mehemet Ali had no interest in the ancient world, seeing it as a hindrance to modernity, and he did not resent the competitive passion of European museums to acquire ancient Egyptian treasures. He saw that indulging, even encouraging, it was useful in securing support for his modernisation plans in the form of influence and cash. As a result there existed a free-for-all in the market. Greedy governors, inscrutable pashas, contracted fellahin, all saw the possibilities for enrichment and, while they could personally see no sense in competing for and carting off derelict bits of carved stone, they were all determined to profit from the new craze.

In this scene of antiquarian anarchy strode a giant, reputed seven feet tall, of prodigious strength and indomitable energy. Born in Padua in 1778, Giovanni Belzoni was a refugee from the French recruiting sergeants in Italy, and arrived in England penniless. His height, strength and shaggy leonine looks soon secured him a job in what was in effect a circus, exploiting his strength as the base of a human pyramid. Belzoni, however, had no desire to be a circus act for the rest of his life and, after making a study of hydraulics, passed himself off as an engineer, setting off at the end of the war with a diminutive English (or possibly Irish) wife to see what he could make of post-bellum Europe. He found his way to Malta, now in British hands and a stepping-off post for the Orient, where water was held in special regard. There he met an agent of Mehemet Ali, instructed to recruit engineers to use the annual flooding of the Nile to make the agriculture in its fertile valley more productive. An opportunity now offered an opportunity for a saltimbanque, even a charlatan, to make himself into an inspired Egyptologist.

Belzoni's special invention – designed to lift more water more quickly than the traditional Persian water pump, which was a wheel of buckets driven by a donkey or a camel – did not impress the Egyptian satrap. Mehemet Ali's courtiers saw in it a device to put men out of time-honoured jobs. But Belzoni's eye had, from his hydraulic studies, become used to reading the contours of land for what they might hide. What they hid from time to time was a buried tomb or, better, a buried temple site, and buried temple sites had statues and tombs and, if not already looted over the centuries, might also have artefacts of gold. He found a sponsor and paymaster in the British consul, Henry Salt. He thought he was engaged to find objects for the British Museum but soon realised that Salt was not in the business for national honour. Very few collectors were, despite the apparent support of government officials.

The chief French agent was another Italian, Bernardino Drovetti, who was unscrupulous about appropriating objects for his special clients, his henchmen even on one occasion making an attempt on Belzoni's life. Drovetti, being a Piedmontese, did not have Belzoni's visceral dislike of the French, and as he held a commission in the French army, and was originally engaged to help modernise Mehemet Ali's army, he had official authority as well as both more money and more clout with the local administrators than his rival. He used his money and his influence to corner the labour required to excavate and transport finds, frustrating the Paduan at every turn. Successful though he was at making finds, he lacked Belzoni's 'nose', his strength and his stamina. In the end he had to acknowledge that Belzoni's 'finds' were more significant than his own. Belzoni's greatest coup was to find the temple that Rameses II had built to himself behind the colossal figures of Abu Simnel, virtually buried in sand, which Belzoni helped to clear away with his bare hands.

He had an almost religious passion for his work, willing to sacrifice his health and marriage to a lust for exploration, and this in itself was almost mystical, inspired to travel south as he was by the Swiss explorer Burckhardt, who himself had a streak of religious frenzy about him. Burckhardt span Romantic dreams about what he had observed as he travelled on his lonely quest for enlightenment down the Nile. It was he who had spotted the heads of the colossal statues of Abu Simnel emerging like condemned prisoners from a sea of sand, and who had excited interest in them by falling in love with their youthful countenances, almost Greek in their beauty. One of them, but for his beard, 'might well pass for a head of Pallas'.[7] Their presence seemed to the lonely Swiss to suggest a vast temple if only anyone could shift the sand.

Belzoni, reading this, felt he must be the man to do it. The lure of Egyptian discovery was no longer a quest for the quasi-Masonic wisdom of the ancients and knowledge of a better world. The stupendous buildings being uncovered were revealing themselves to have been the symbols of a militaristic quest for conquest, to ensure slave labour to help preserve a hieratic and priestly order based on the divinity of one man, the Pharaoh. Sarastro paled before Rameses. An antiquarian love for a knowledge that seemed penetrable at last, as the hieroglyphics revealed their secrets, replaced the search for a new vision of life, especially as the texts seemed predominantly concerned with inducting the souls of the dead into an after-world remarkably similar to its forerunner. Modern Egyptians hardly counted in the scheme of things, except as authorities to be bribed or browbeaten and workers to be exploited. Egypt was no longer perceived as an outpost of the Orient but a series of holes in the rock slowly revealing their contents.

It was the revelation of a civilisation that predated Islam, predated Greece, predated Rome, and had disputed the known world with the Mesopotamian world powers that had tried to overwhelm them. All were now with Nineveh and Tyre. Egypt was no longer Pharaonic, Hellenic, Roman. How much longer would it be Islamic as the new world empires were no longer Asiatic? Mehemet Ali had ambitions to rule his state like another Sultan, another Shah. 'In the golden prime of good Haroun Alraschid'[8] the Islamic commonwealth embraced Grand Cairo, Baghdad and Tabriz, where every night was an Arabian Night. Would Cairo now emerge from the Ottoman Night as a rival to Constantinople? But a more intense question was to engage Europe. It was to be the fate of Greece that determined it would not be Cairo. But before Greece's fate could be decided, Byron's meteor had turned the spotlight upon Constantinople.

CHAPTER TEN

Barbering and Shaving

The Myth of Persia

Truth-loving Persians do not dwell upon
the trivial skirmish fought near Marathon.
(Graves, *The Persian Version*)[1]

I

UNTIL THE EAST India Companies of England and France became interested in the Persian empire, almost as little was known of the court of Isfahan as of the Pasha at Grand Cairo. Its institutions might mirror those of the Ottoman, but the reviver of its greatness had in the sixteenth century decreed that the country would espouse not the Sunni version of Islam but the Shi-ite, and the Ottoman empire was halted on its eastern borders. To the watchers both in the West and in the East, Persia remained an enigma. She had succumbed to Arab, Mongol and Turk, her ancient script and religion had suffered the fate of Egypt's, her old Imperial capital of Persepolis mouldered in the desert, but Isfahan had risen in tiled and carpeted splendour as the cultural lodestar of its Shi-ite, Aryan people.

While the model of Islamic monarchy remained the Grand Signor at the Sublime Porte in Constantinople, the Shah's was an older monarchy. Europeans knew about King Ahasuerus and the Jewess, Esther, while everyone learned at school that at Marathon the Greeks had stopped the armies of Xerxes from spilling over into Europe. Most of the information about the contemporary Safavid empire came from the French-born, naturalised Briton Jean Chardin (1643–1713), who trafficked in jewellery and became accredited merchant in the trade of jewels, clocks and other desirable goods to Shah Abbas II. It was almost a country of fantasy.

Chardin spent four years at the Persian court in Isfahan but, as a Protestant, he decided after the revocation of the Edict of Nantes in his mother country to make his home in England. There he became adviser to the East India Company and was knighted by Charles II. His account of the Persian culture that stretched from north India to western Iran[2] made him a useful ally in the increasingly aggressive and competitive policy of the Company to expand its newly acquired foothold in western India at Bombay (Mumbai) in competition with both the Portuguese and the French. Portugal only wanted to keep her factories in the east, but France under Colbert and the young Louis XIV were more ambitious and wanted to build in both the Safavid and Mughal empires something like her most favoured nation position in the Ottoman empire.

To outsiders the Ottomans and Safavids seemed to be identical. They were obviously no different in their attitudes towards women. When in 1809 James Morier told his interlocutors in Persia that 'in company we (English) pay more civility to any female than to the greatest man, they have remained astonished, wondering that any creature ... born only for their pleasure and convenience should at all partake of those attentions which they deem to be due to themselves exclusively'.[3] Morier then fictionalised this conversation in one between the Persian and British ambassadors to the Porte: 'Women here are counted as nothing. We put no trust in them. We look upon them as entirely devoted to the use of man; and you might as well expect the tiger to do homage to the lion, as to see a Persian submit to be ruled by a woman;' Chardin added the bearing of children to pure pleasure as the sole purposes of women.[4]

It was true that, with certain national differences, the Shah of Persia ruled over a society similar to that of the Ottomans: it too was autocratic, self-indulgent and fearsome by turns. It was also heavily reliant on foreigners, often Georgians and other Caucasians, who formed the heart of the administration, but these were not kidnapped slaves but free adventurers. Chardin picked out Georgians as the most loyal servants of the Shah of Persia.[5] Corruption, enlightened by bursts of benevolence, infected a court, ruled over by a Shah who was often pitiably unprepared for his position. Ill-trained for the exercise of supreme power he could be capricious and violent. One Shah ordered a wrestler to be disembowelled for breaking into a brothel, an action viewed as unworthy of anyone who performed at his court.[6]

As a breeding machine, the Shah was effective. In 1809 the secretary to the British mission in Tehran (capital of the country and residence of the court since 1788) reported that the Shah had 65 sons and no one knew how many daughters – possibly about the same number. On one night alone, six women were brought to bed, of four boys and two girls. One of the women, being a wife not a concubine, received as a reward four muleloads of rich clothing from Isfahan, no doubt the city from which she hailed. The harem was jealously ordered by a household of women and eunuchs who fulfilled, for the women, the counterparts of the male servants who serviced the men of the court itself. The Persian harem was not entirely closed to uncastrated men, for an Armenian was ordered to teach the bored king's women how to play *kamouncha* (an Islamically forbidden Turkish game of chance played with shells, at which Armenians were legendarily adroit). But this was a rare privilege.[7] To that nursery of intrigue and self-indulgence the education of the chosen heir was entrusted, and based more on pleasure than duty, so that a strong succession was unlikely. Whoever it was dropped into the throne, as Chardin noted in a remarkably contemporary idiom, 'from outer space', was usually an incompetent, surrounded by sycophants. To add to his incompetence, his mother often intrigued with harem eunuchs against a powerful grand vizier who was usually the effective head of government, and this compounded the sense of indecision and confusion that often afflicted the Persian court.[8]

The succession was also bedevilled by male infanticide. If not killed outright, an inconvenient son who might be a threat to his sibling, whom influence or faction had chosen to succeed his father, would be blinded. Blindness rendered anyone unfit to rule and a blind man could, as a result, not be a competitor for the throne.[9] After the first four Mughal emperors of India similar uncertainties, amounting to civil war, surrounded the succession in the house of Timur. Whoever became ruler of Morocco usually did so as the result of a power struggle between rival siblings. Succession was seldom assured in the empires of Islam.

2

When the rival East India Companies of France and England began to vie for power in India, interest in what really went on in Iran assumed a greater urgency. France's long alliance with the Porte did not, as she hoped and expected, give the French any advantage in India. Relations between the Mughal and Ottoman empires had long been reduced to ceremonial

exchanges to remind each other of their existence – and of course greatness
– divided as they were by the sprawling and often hostile power of Persia.
For all the menace the Ottomans posed for Europe, there was always the
great distraction and rival, Persia, which drew their attention away from the
West. The Persian empire was religiously schismatic and economically
aggressive, and the Sultan in Constantinople and the Shah in Tehran were
engaged, like the French and English, in a series of hundred years wars from
century to century as their fortunes changed.

The Mughals in India drew their inspiration and language from the
Persian court, but their culture was more eclectic than Persian since they
ruled a people as intensely artistic and literary as they. North Indian rulers
lived in the shadow of a Persia that ruled also in Afghanistan and they
initially judged the European efficacy as allies in various power struggles
between rival houses, but shattered by the invasions of Nadir Shah, a Turkic
adventurer who had seized the throne of Persia, the Mughals helplessly
watched the end of French power in India, and the virtual reduction of the
Grand Mughal to a pensioner of the East India Company. The French
Revolution for a short time revived English fears of a revival of French
ambitions to be the protector of Islam in India. French envoys of dubious
authenticity appeared in certain Muslim courts and French adventurers
were seen, drilling troops of Tipu Sultan, wearing Phrygian caps and
saluting a 'liberty tree' in honour of the revolution. With Napoleon's
Egyptian campaign, the fear that Bonaparte might march with an
overwhelming force over land, following Alexander of Macedon's route to
India, haunted the dreams of men in both London and Calcutta, who
followed his putative route through Persian lands.

The Ottomans, being England's allies for the most part in the
reconquest of Egypt, had no ambitions in India. The danger to them came
from Russia's ambitions to found a third Rome in Constantinople, and to
keep that at bay they needed English support. But there was not much that
England in Europe could do to keep a *cordon sanitaire* round the two weaker
and volatile states in the East peculiarly open to Russian influence:
Afghanistan and Persia. The English in India, however, could. A revitalised
Persian state, moreover, might resist Russia's expansion into South Asia
more effectively than the Ottomans had been able to do.

Both Afghanistan and Persia were penetrable from Turkestan to the
north, so that the Russians redoubled their efforts to subjugate the Turkomans
in and beyond the Caucasus. The East India Company, which had trading

residents in the coastal towns of the Gulf and agents in the Persian royal cities, kept a careful watch on both Russian and French agents. The revitalisation of Persia was soon bedevilled by intrigue and rivalry so that the Persian empire appeared as ramshackle as the Mughal, and much less secure than the Ottoman. It was believed to be open to influence by bribes on an international scale, so that if a combined Franco-Russian army were to march overland to India, it could buy its passage through Persia. The Persians, according to Company reports, would be in no condition to resist it.

3

In 1800, with the French army still in Egypt, the Company sent one of its notable paladins, John Malcolm, to Tehran on a mission to secure a declaration of Persian friendship. The mission was successful in that it obtained both political and economic advantage on paper, but the scraps of paper were little more than expressions of politeness. French bribes and influence, and the reputation of France's military might, were too powerful to secure any promises for the future. Seven years later, France and Russia signed a treaty at Tilsit. The British saw in its terms a clear threat to Iran, so the Company sent Malcolm off once more to Tehran. At the Gulf port of Bushire (Bushehr), he learned that his mission was superseded by one sent from London – not the first or last time that the governments of the East India Company and Britain acted independently and at cross-purposes. A letter from the King of England took precedence over one from the Governor-General of India, and the Persian government accepted that it needed the support of a strong power to resist any combined Franco-Russian infringement of its sovereignty. Britain was about to engage seriously with Iran.

The secretary to this mission – who played a central role in the proceedings, taking divine services on the march and acting as personal factotum to the Envoy, as courier and latterly companion to the Persian ambassador sent in return to London – was to be one of the principal informants on Persia and the Persians. For a public, reliant hitherto on John Chardin's *Travels* and on Scheherezade's *Entertainments* of a thousand and one Arabian Nights, he provided not only an account of the mission in much topographical and personal detail, but also the 'memoirs' of a Persian Gil Blas, the barber Hajji Baba of Ispahan.

James Justinian Morier (1780?–1849) had been born into the cosmopolitan world of trade in the Levant. He was of Graeco-Jewish stock: his father Isaac was a successful Smyrniot merchant, and his mother was the daughter of the consul-general of the Dutch company. Isaac Morier was first the consul-general of the Levant Company in Smyrna but transferred in 1803 to be its consul-general in Constantinople. When the Levant Company was wound up in 1806, he remained in the city as agent of the East India Company.

James Justinian, therefore, was born with a diplomatic spoon in his mouth, and went to Harrow and shared schooldays with Byron. He was back in Constantinople before 1807, however, when his Levantine languages recommended him to Sir Harford Jones, who was to lead the British government's mission to Tehran and who employed him as his private secretary. The mission took its time to get to Tehran, travelling there by way of Bombay, and Morier kept a diary of it, recording not only its progress but the ancient sites and curiosities on the way. Sir Harford had been a servant of the East India Company but was a very correct diplomat. He shared with the Persians an obsessive regard for punctilio and ceremony, all of which demanded a considerable expenditure of time. Most of his entourage were servants of the East India Company, and the residents he visited on the way from Bushire to Tehran were Company appointments. It was important that Sir Harford should understand all ceremonies and courtesies required of a mission to the Shah, so that his mission should not be taken for just another from John Company.

The dignity of the King of England had to be recognised as paramount. When one provincial governor tried to indicate that the more than adequately expensive gift of cloths and chintzes was beneath his gubernatorial worth, he snatched back one piece of chintz and gave the rest to his servants, in the hope that the mission would be shamed into being more generous. Sir Harford merely congratulated the servants on their good fortune and refused to offer anything more. 'The governor, to the laugh of everyone, remained with the single piece.'[10]

Morier's *A Journey through Persia* exhibits the Romantic traveller's preoccupation with topography and tells us little about the people of the country through which he passed. Anecdote is rare. At one point he describes the fate of a crew of a Company sloop that fell prey to Trucial pirates, who took it as their religious duty to slaughter their infidel prisoners to cries of 'Allah-il-Allah'. He remarks on the antagonism that existed between Arabs and Persians at the marches of the state, 'much greater than between Christian and Mahomedan, or Sheyah and Sunni'.[11] His view of the religious divide was expressed four years later by Thomas Moore, pretending to be Abdallah, in London writing to Mohassan in Ispahan:

> You know our Sunnites, hateful dogs!
> Whom every pious Shiite flogs.
> Or longs to flog! – 'tis true they pray
> To God, but in an ill-bred way...[12]

Bastinadoes, screws and nippers had failed to convince Sunnis to wear the green slippers of the Shi-ite faithful, as they constituted an abomination.

Of the mission itself, Morier tells us more. He describes at length the ambassador's encounter with the Shah and his court. Sir Harford's insistence that King George's letter should be first read in English and then translated annoyed the Shah, but when he addressed the Monarch of the Universe in fluent Persian, which he had made his study as a servant of the East India Company, he won his point. The English for their part did not find the Shah very knowledgeable about the universe of which he was the monarch. He wondered whether America was underground, and was genuinely puzzled that the English had imposed restraints on their king in the way of a parliament. But the Persians were anxious that the Jones mission should be successful. The negotiations were tedious; at one time the Persian principal negotiator fell asleep and Sir Harford and Morier 'stretched themselves along', as the so-called Prime Minister started first on a history of the world and later, to fill in while they waited to see the Shah, on the history of Russia. The result, however, was what the English wanted. The French in the capital were sent packing, the mule drivers hired to take their baggage dumped it all on the ground once outside the city walls, and they were not allowed to withdraw through Russia.

The entertainments were squalid among splendour: dancers, funambulists, bear-dancing and horse-riding, and the Shah, to emphasise his greatness, was bedecked head to foot in pearls. To show his appreciation he presented Morier with a sword that had once adorned his person. The delegation ate mountains of candied fruit and sugared almonds, and Sir Harford insisted that straight faces were kept throughout. Finally Morier was designated to escort the return embassy to London, led by a man,

Mirza Abdul Hassan, who had once bared his neck to the executioner's sword, only to be reprieved at the last moment. Thinking it prudent to go to Mecca and from there to India, where he stayed until he learned that his family had been restored to the Shah's favour, Hassan was entrusted with the embassy because he spoke some English and had lived among them in India.[13]

Time seemed of very little importance in those leisurely days and Morier took his time over the journey, joining his family in the Ottoman capital, and leaving the ambassador there while he visited Armenia and dropped in on his elder brother who was consul-general in Albania. The fruits of that journey were, in 1812, an account that was to command interest as a first eye-witness account of a whole region, which Byron was bringing into the public eye in *Childe Harold*.

Morier was soon back in Persia, as part of a mission to bolster the Shah's resolve to stand firm against Russo-French designs on the area. He stayed in charge of the embassy in Tehran until the war was over and in 1817, at the age of 37, was superannuated. His diplomatic career was not to end there, however, as he was sent as a special commissioner to Mexico in 1824 following the ill-fated Empire of Iturbide I after the declaration of Mexican independence of Spain, and he was a signatory to the Anglo-Mexican treaty of 1826, which formally recognised the federal constitution.

4

Morier had by this time embarked on a third career, devoting himself to writing. In 1818 a second account of his travels to Persia established him as an authority on the area, and in 1824 he capped it with *The Adventures of Hajji Baba of Ispahan*, dubbed by Sir Walter Scott in 1826 his 'oriental Gil Blas'. The sense of the absurd that had been hidden in the sober prose of his *Journey* now was free of all constraint. This was to be the Persian novel extraordinary. Morier wrote it in the first person, lending reality to Hajji Baba's picaresque exploits: barber, turned domestic servant, turned trader, turned dervish, turned assistant to the public executioner, turned assistant to the Shah's official doctor, and finally secretary to an ambassador bound for London.

Hajji falls in love with a Georgian slave in his employer's harem and mocks the system by making his assignations with her in the forbidden area itself. As assistant to the Shah's doctor he sees the corrupt, megalomaniac face of oriental despotism, as Morier wished to present it. Otherwise, it is in the eighteenth-century style of Smollet and Fielding, an engaging account of the ups and downs of life in a land where fortune and misfortune were accepted as the normal pattern of existence. The tone is facetious, sometimes sardonic, but seldom fearsome. The Persian monarchy is shown as more absurd than frightful, its solipsistic preoccupation with ritual and ostentation hiding the incompetence and weakness that will make it a plaything of rival powers in the nineteenth century.

The novel ends with Hajji's appointment as learned assistant to the man who is to lead a special mission to London, and this provides the setting for the sequel, *The Adventures of Hajji Baba in England* (1828). It was just what Morier's readers expected. To add to the sense of authenticity Morier paraded the usual Muslim opinion of Europeans as 'an unclean race, for that they treated the Prophet as a cheat, and eat pork and drank wine without any scruple; that they were women in looks, and in manners bears, that they ought to be held in the greatest suspicion, for their ultimate object (see what they had done to India) was to take kingdoms and to make shahs and nabobs their humble servants'.[14] Morier may have privately agreed that the portrait was not too far from the truth, but it underlined what Europeans had suspected all along: that the cultural divide was too great to bridge.

He peppered his narrative with Persian terms to reveal his close observation of Persian society at the time of his visits, but sympathy and understanding were not characteristics he chose to display. Court officials were consumed by greed, vanity and love of gifts, the Shah remained a shadowy figure, wielder of capricious life and death sentences, but inept and basically helpless. The 'Franks' had real power, the result of scientific examination and experiment. Even Hajji recognised that nostrums and charms were ineffectual when compared to the western use in medicine of mercury and the knife but, ever opportunistic, he saw advantage in being benighted.

He is, however, the personification of the Persian problem, as Morier saw it. Quackery passed for medicine, flattery for advice, selfishness for philanthropy, indulgence for abstinence, superficiality for wisdom and bluster for courage. Hajji Baba's adventures are one man's *Arabian Nights Entertainment*, as he exercises the ingenuity, imagination and fatalistic philosophy of Sinbad, Aladdin and Ali Baba. Morier did not wish this society ill. He had lived most of his life in it before he wrote *Hajji Baba*, whom one is forced to like despite his deception, betrayal and abandonment of friends and benefactors, but he was convinced of its corrosion and helplessness before the influence of the West.

Morier did not claim that western ways were any better. His books have the usual gallery of rogues and pickthanks which studded most English novels of the eighteenth century, and the villainy or stupidity of Hajji's associates contrive to spin Fortune's wheel against him at the end of every episode. They all accept Islam's doctrine of predestination, which taught that success and reverse were the will of Allah, fixed for all time, about which it was both pointless and heretical to complain.

Morier believed, a little like Byron, that both western and oriental cultures embraced love of show, rank, and sexual power, and had been infiltrated by cheats and robbers. He had a particularly mordant view of the religious establishment, and his sardonic mockery of the clergy in both faiths is relentless. Hajji is unimpressed by the service he attends in church, though he likes the unveiled beauties who distracted the male congregation from the young, unbearded 'mullah'.[15] There are no Vicars of Wakefield or Parsons Adams in Hajji's Islamic Iranian world. It had become, to Morier's mind, too self-regarding, too incurious, too ignorant to be more than a tiresome buffer between the English and the Russians in the Near East, and a space between their Levantine interests and India that needed filling. However, he was not convinced that the Europeans would fill it any better. Hajji's *History of the Franks*, prepared for the Shah about to receive an English diplomatic mission, was no worse than the ignorant, prejudiced and superficial Western accounts of Persia at their worst.

5

Hajji's account of life in England is a series of tableaux presenting the profound ignorance but resilience of the Persian delegation, and the chasm that separated the customs of Muslim society from those of post-Napoleonic England. Resentment at the patronising influence of the West touched a sympathetic chord in Morier, who put that resentment into the mouth of the Persian ambassador:

> they think, because they have looking glasses in their houses which we have not; because they make clocks and penknives, and cloth, which

we do not; and because they have got possession of Hind, which was once ours, that we are men to sit behind them, and that they may lead as they would a *yedek* (a led horse).[16]

As an outsider, Morier saw that many of the customs of the West were not without their absurdity too: the grand formal meals, the rituals of receptions, the fussiness of dress, the pointlessness of going for walks (to nowhere in particular). Above all, he saw not the despotism of a ruler, but the despotism of money, and enjoyed contrasting both societies with an almost affectionate nonchalance.

What Morier could not accept was the Muslim treatment of women (in which he could see no merit whatever). While gently satirising the trivial social ambitions of English society women, even so cynical an observer as James Morier/Hajji Baba is shocked that the Persian ambassador kept his comfort woman shut up in a cupboard in his embassy. Dilferib is a Circassian, of course, transferred from someone else's harem to be the ambassador's erotic plaything. Yet, despite her virtual imprisonment, she manages to become a subject of general and embarrassing curiosity. The apparent authenticity of Morier's story merely seemed to confirm one more myth of the time that every travelling Muslim of consequence would have a Circassian girl in his baggage.

Morier repeats, almost ad nauseam, Hajji's opinion that a man is an undisputed despot in his own home and that the Shah, being the Asylum of the World, is a despot in his own realm. In this he was reflecting the received wisdom about a country which had come late to western knowledge. But behind the mockery there was an underlying warning contained in *Hajji Baba in Ispahan*, and it is repeated in *Hajji Baba in England*. It is no less relevant today than it was in the 1820s: any society that thinks it is at the acme of civilisation and power will have a long way to fall.

Morier knew more about Persia and the Persians than most, but one who knew them as well, Sir John Chardin, had not found Persia the benighted land of Hajji Baba, and had enjoyed the friendship and courtesy of prominent Persians. But he too had described the despotic caprices of an untutored Shah, the intrigues and jealousies of officials and the corruption of a society based on self-preservation when not self-advancement, and so helped to form the image of a country in which being a barber, while not entirely safe, was safer than being a vizier.

6

In 1855 another barber appeared this time from the pen of a 27-year-old would-be best-selling novelist, who had just fathered his third child, and was bursting to emulate his rather cantankerous and ageing father-in-law, Thomas Love Peacock. *The Shaving of Shagpat*, subtitled *An Arabian Entertainment*, was George Meredith's first novel. Was this James Morier *redivivus*? Shibli Bagarag, Meredith's barber, comes not from Isfahan, but Shiraz. He is also a poet, and he bursts into verse at every turn; if Meredith's readers would not buy his poetry, then they would read it in his novels. Shibli Bagarag talks very like Morier's barber – he hails, after all, from the same country – but Morier knew more about Persians than Meredith, whose story falls as a result into the pure realm of fantasy.

Things are not going well with Shibli. 'A curse had fallen on barbercraft' and he is reduced to sitting in a desert bemoaning his fate when he meets an old woman. She listens to his story and promises him great things if he shaves Shagpat, a notoriously hirsute tailor, who has a pathological aversion to the razor and scissors. Meredith is vague as to who Shagpat is or where he is to be found, but he is to be found in a land whither 'caravans came (with) the people of Oolb and the people of Damascus, and the people of Vatz and they of Bagdad, and the Ringheez, great traders', and which had a King, the usual capricious tyrant of the East. When Shibli presents himself before him and reveals that he came from 'that reptiles nest', Shiraz, the monarch orders him to be given fifty stripes.

Unknown to Shibli, Shagpat is a powerful and malicious sorcerer, the secret of whose power lies in one of his hairs, which is why there is this interest in shaving him. Unsuccessful in getting a commission from the King and smarting from his whipping, Shibli meets the old woman again and, feeling truly despondent, promises, if she can truly change his fortunes, to marry her. Like Papageno when solaced in the masonic dungeon by an old crone, Shibli feels that nothing is to be lost, and at her urging returns to the vizier who had the stripes administered. They exchange verses, at which the vizier, satisfied of his poetic genius, introduces him to his young, beautiful and desirable daughter. With a shock Shibli recognises in her the old woman he has contracted to marry. At this point Meredith introduces the story within the story. To secure the good graces of the vizier, whose daughter he appears to have been tricked into marrying, he launches himself on the story of Bhanavar the Beautiful.[17]

Peacock did not care much for *The Shaving of Shagpat*. It did not seem likely to make the fortune of his indigent, philoprogenitive son-in-law, who produced brats to disturb his calm, and who neglected his wife. Perhaps he thought the fantasy was a poor imitation of his own light-hearted and mocking style, which had secured him the fame and fortune that being secretary to the East India Company had not bestowed on him. Meredith, in his view, did not do it as well. Perhaps he disliked the strong erotic undertone of Bhanavar, the longest and most substantial of the entertainments Shibli was offering the vizier. Perhaps he read in the wiles of Queen Rabesqurat, who tried to seduce Shibli while in a state of magical bemusement, a foreboding of the author's infidelity to his daughter, who could not lay claim to the beauty ascribed to the various sorceresses in Meredith's tale.

Still, George Eliot, then Mary Ann Evans, thought *The Story of Bhanavar the Beautiful* a work of genius to be explored for deep meaning.[18] If it is set in Morier-land, it is not a Morier tale. Its parentage is the *Thousand and One Nights*; and if the eroticism is not so explicit, it lingers in Meredith's language of opulence, his description of physical beauty and the protracted kisses (no more) of love. Bhanavar, almost divinely beautiful, longs for the jewel that shines from the head of a serpent in a Caucasian lake. When her first lover – Bhanavar manages in 80 or so pages to spend many months in a passionate embrace with three lovers without benefit of mullah – secures it for her, her beauty becomes almost supernatural, but she is transformed very subtly into a serpent queen, whose ravishing beauty depends on her securing a feast of blood for her attendant serpents.

Bhanavar the Beautiful is set in some cool and fragrant land not Arabian, not Persian, more Turcoman, like Lermontov's Caucasus (the English translation of *A Hero of Our Time* had appeared a year earlier in 1854). Its rich language and quicksilver pace, its handsome men, fast horses, heroic action, wanton cruelty, ambivalent sorceresses and settings of chrysolite and chrysoberyl, all recommended it for separate publication in pocket editions that would slip undetected into a reticule. It is Romantic rubbish but was surprisingly popular, except with Peacock, but it was this kind of bewitched Scheherezaddery that was attractive to readers who wanted an erotic thrill that required no displacement of clothing.

The preliminaries over, Shibli Bagarag sets about the shaving of Shagpat with the help of the vizier's daughter, who turns out also to be a sorceress of formidable power. called Noorna bin Noorka. Though Noorna is not as powerful as Shagpat, she controls a truculent genie and various magical helpmates, and with their help Shibli shaves Shagpat and releases the world from his thrall. Meredith caught the taste for oriental extravaganza which was starting to fill the pantomime stage, similarly imprecise as to location, where Turkoman princesses mix freely with Arabian slaves, Indian rajahs, Chinese laundrymen, and the Widow Twanky, born within the sound of Bow Bells.

His fantasy confirmed the strength of the oriental myth. The lands indeterminately between Turkey, Persia and Russia were still largely unknown to the West and were still lands of make-believe. There Allah ruled, but though All-Powerful and All-Merciful, he seemed powerless before sorceresses and sorcerers who could control fire and water, peris and djinns. Having a supernatural power behind you was an essential for survival. Magic rather than predestination ruled; when Shagpat is finally shaved, Shibli has been through a succession of magical encounters with all the stock personalities of *The Arabian Nights*, from which no ordinary mortal could have passed unscathed. Beside them, the trials undertaken by Tamino and Pamina in Mozart's semi-oriental opera are trivial, and the Queen of the Night, who was supposed to be a powerful thaumaturge, is pathetically under-powered beside Bharnava and Noorna bin Noorka. Today, in Romantic fiction, supernatural powers have revived to stand at least equal to and more sinister than the peris and djinns of orientalia, but they have emerged not in oriental never-never land, but in the cold northern climates of *The Lord of the Rings* and in the gothic mansions and woods of Harry Potterland. Meredith's Romantic imagination sent orientalism into the sky, like a fire rocket, and befuddled the senses.

These senses were being orientalised by poetry, which had a larger readership among the impressionable than the accounts of diplomatic or mercantile missions to the East, of Beckford's sorcerers, or of James Bruce's man-eaten lions. As Landor's and Southey's Orient proved spurious, compared to the raw and bleeding pungency of Byron, it was to be an Irish poet, anxious to give the world a fairy tale, who presented orientalists with the sugar and water version of Islam that was to hold the Romantic generation in thrall, until it curdled with the Indian Mutiny.

CHAPTER ELEVEN

Lalla Rookh and the Lyre of the Oriental Minstrel

The Myth of the Romantic Dream

Who has not heard of the Vale of Cashmere
With its roses the brightest that earth ever gave,
Its temples and grottos, and fountains as clear
As the love-lighted eyes that hang over their wave?
(Moore, *Lalla Rookh*)[1]

I

The tortured Greeks, the corpses on the beach, the slender young limbs in the sack, the slavery of the *serail*, the shabby finery of power flowed like indelible ink from the pens of Byron and Shelley, planted an image of the East as barbarism cloaked in cloth of gold. Where the heavy hand of John Company had not yet fallen in India, the land was full of capricious tyrants who trampled enemies beneath the feet of elephants, of war and mayhem under ruthless and despotic adventurers, worst of all the ferocious house of Haidar Ali. The Romantic nightmare was that the cruel ideologies of the Middle Ages and Wars of Religion, which had devastated Europe, were to return from the East, where they still survived. The nubile young bosoms might throb to the enchantment of love forbidden and the despair of heroes of their favourite poet, but for the moment the threatening scimitar was held far from their own swanlike necks. The East, however, smelled of greed and danger. But for one poet, who never went there, it might be a land of ruthless monotheism but it was a monotheism fragranced by love.

There had for centuries been a vision of an enchanted land, somewhere in Asia, where beautiful women embroidered intricate patterns on the clothes of sultans, but few had found it. Now, at the end of the eighteenth century, John Company's scouts in pursuit of bandits had penetrated the passes into the foothills of the Hindu Kush and discovered Cashmere. They did not find the roses, temples, grottos or clear fountains they had been led to expect, but were confronted by a miraculous combination of mountain and water, pink with lotus and green with floating gardens, a land of kingfishers and golden orioles. The Mughals had built their pleasances at the edge of lakes there, fringed with the stately *chenar*, to which later tourists were to tether their houseboats. It was a land of magical beauty, an oasis of liquid calm after the torrid Gangetic plain where the Mughals had their capital. It was a land of escape, of palpable Romance.

In May 1817, Thomas Moore, in the mellifluous voice of Ireland, inscribed a long poem to the crusty *breakfasteur* Samuel Rogers, whose table he had entranced time after time with his Irish brogue. 'We may roam through this world, like a child at a feast,' he had written, and he was now wafting himself East where the pleasures were new and far from dull.[2] India was the defining influence as Company servants returned from a fabled land with tales of pagodas, fakirs, snakes, elephants and carbuncles as big as plovers' eggs. Moore had learned from Byron that the East was beguiling, and seen how it had profited Landor and Southey. Moore specialised not in virgins soft as roses, but in Irish beauties, and Lalla Rookh was an Irish belle in a palanquin rather than a donkey cart.

He had also learned that political points could be made more safely by pretending that they applied to *Erewhon* or Nowhere. Swift knew this when he sent Gulliver off on his travels, for Swift's Nowhere was really nowhere. There are no lands of tiny midgets, giants or talking horses. Beckford and Southey had pretended that Nowhere was Somewhere, though alien, barely explored land. Byron on the other hand had no use for Nowhere; he would only write of lands he had personally 'discovered', filled, not with fantastic but real people. All three, however, were not anthropologists but poets passing a moral judgement on their times. The seven-year trial of Warren Hastings, which ended in 1797, had presented Somewhere to an enthralled public in the trappings of Bengal and the Carnatic. These lands were, like Byron's Albania, the real Orient. Moore, who had never been anywhere east of London, knew that he was writing about Nowhere, but struggled to make it sound as if it really existed. Nowhere was to be Erewhon, clothed in the gaudy apparel of Cashmere.

Moore needed little encouragement to unleash his romantic imagination on Erewhon. Work on *Lalla Rookh* took over ten years and he was dismayed when Byron published his *Turkish Tales* before him. He feared they would scoop the market by their stunning success. But Byron, who knew that Moore was working slowly and methodically on his oriental romance, encouraged him to go on. He considered his own oriental poems had been strangely overrated, and hinted that from now on he would leave the way clear for Moore's: 'The North, South and West have all been exhausted; but from the East, we have nothing but S***'s unsaleables.'[3] He believed that Southey's lucubrations, his outrageous fictions and fantasy people, did not interest anyone, whereas Moore's invented world would.[4] Frissons of chaste but erotic excitement already clung to the name of Thomas Moore so that his readers were ready for the saga of *Lalla Rookh*. His publishers gave him 3,000 guineas for the finished poem and it ran to several editions. There were seven editions in the first year, and 22 of its songs set to music, and it was one of the publishing triumphs of the century, riding on the back of Byronic enthusiasm for narrative verse.[5]

In his *Turkish Tales* Byron had been careful to get his facts and locale right, as he constantly asserted in his footnotes. The setting of Moore's poem was Kashmir/Cashmere, but the land, though real enough, was only a shadow away from the Romantic fiction of Peristan, the Persian fairyland, home of fair sprites and luscious maidens. Moore, however, was very anxious to give it a realistic eastern flavour and the poem sometimes groans under the effect of many hours with the oriental books he could find in the library of his patron. Lord Moira had sailed for India in 1813 to be governor-general of India; but despite the number of accounts of India Moore found there, most of his oriental references were to Persian sources, and gave some of his readers the impression that the author was, if not a Persian, at least an oriental.

They made the poem, however, no more orientally authentic than the Prince Regent's Pavilion in Brighton, neither Mughal, nor Saracen, nor Turkish, nor Chinese but a confection of all of them. Moore luxuriated in the exoticism of his images: 'the oloriferous woods of Comorin', the 'gay sparkling looris, such as gleam between the crimson blossom of the coral tree', 'Mecca's blue sacred pigeons', the 'golden birds in the spice time drunk with that sweet food', 'the green birds that dwelt in Eden's radiant fields of asphodel'.[6] His poem was backed by references to the older authorities on the Orient, to d'Herbelot, Bruce, Thévenot and Savary, and he punctiliously gave chapter and verse for each image in his carefully selected footnotes. Their authenticity earned tributes from such seasoned living travellers as John Carne (1789–1844), who travelled extensively in the Arab and Persian East and dedicated his letters from those parts to Walter Scott; as Sir William Ousely (1769–1842), a Persian specialist who was secretary to his brother Sir Gore Ouseley's embassy to Persia in 1810; and as Colonel Wilks, the author of a History of Mysore at the time of Haidar Ali and Tipu Sahib. Colonel Wilks offered his opinion, on learning that Moore had never been east, that 'reading over D'Herbelot is as good as riding on the back of a camel'.[7]

The Romantic imagination swooned over *Lalla Rookh*, but moralists found it all too pretty and sugary. One who followed the same route to Cashmere as the heroine of the poem did not see a tree on the way, and called Moore a liar.[8] His description of life in India was not how it was, 'where man tramples upon man in a series of cruel oppressions down to the drooping wretchedness of the squalid population, who have neither the reason nor the rights of men'.[9] But to describe life thus was not Moore's purpose, for *Lalla Rookh* is a sequence of love stories at which Moore was an acknowledged master. It has a superficial resemblance to *The Arabian Nights Entertainments*, told by a raconteur who is masquerading under the name of Feramorz. He has been selected to accompany Lalla Rookh, daughter of the Mughal emperor Aurangzeb, to her betrothal to the prince of Bucharia, a descendant of Genghis Khan and the heir to a fragment of his former empire. He is to entertain her on her journey through Cashmere and to while away the tedium, like Scheherezade, he spins out his tales from camp to camp until the all-enveloping love story is revealed: Lalla Rookh has fallen in love with the story-teller, who is no other than the prince she is on her way to marry.

2

The first tale is in the spirit of *Vathek*. Though readers were not daunted by a poem nearly 150 pages in length, of some five and a half thousand lines, Moore had to capture his readers from the start. *The Veiled Prophet of Khorassan* is a sinister tale of evil overcome, at a price, by lovers. The East had to be sinister as well as Romantic, for that is what Europeans had been led over the years to expect. When the story opens the lovers, Azim and

Zelica, both think the other dead. Azim is reported to have perished in battle and Zelica, in her grief, has been inveigled into a marriage, sanctified by infernal rites, to a religious impostor called Mokanna. Though styling himself a prophet, professing nothing but good for his followers, Mokanna is in fact driven by hatred of mankind whom he is resolved to subjugate and abuse. Concealing features that are hideous to look upon by a veil, he is resolved on establishing a Satanic tyranny by artifice and deceit, in revenge for not being like other men. His unwitting agent will be Zelica, once her innocence has been corrupted by thraldom to his hellish will. Mokanna has none of the angelic nobility of Milton's Satan, for his hate and envy of the vile human race, 'for hell's amusement given' drive him to avenge his shame and wallow in hate.[10] The scene is set for the two lovers to thwart him. They are reunited when Azim, far from being dead, comes to enlist in the service of the false prophet.

True to Romantic convention, this tale has no happy ending. Azim, an avatar of El Cid, a puissant champion of the faithful, has been recruited under false pretences by Mokanna to lead his army of deluded fanatics against the rightful Caliph. When he finds his former beloved in his new employer's camp and learns from her that, believing he had been killed in battle, she has become enslaved to Mokanna by sinister arts and cannot leave him, Azim changes sides. He vows to save the army of the Caliph, the true representative of the Prophet, from defeat at the hands of a false one. Mokanna, besieged and outnumbered by the true believers, reveals his hideous countenance to his surviving followers and then uses his demonic influence to force them to drink a venom which consigns them all to hell rather than Paradise, for which destination they thought they were intended. He insists that Zelica consumes the last drop and then immolates himself in a cistern full of burning acid to leave not a trace behind. His last words are a prophecy, revealing what sort of prophet he was: 'Where knaves shall minister and fools shall kneel … so shall my banner … be the rallying sign of fraud and anarchy … my spirit … shall walk abroad in all the stormy strife and guilt and blood, that were its bliss in life.'[11]

Zelica knows that the venom she has drunk can only kill her and decides to die at the hands of her lover. She puts on Mokanna's silver veil which concealed his hideous features, and goes out alone to face the besieging army. Azim, mistaking her for Mokanna insists that it is he who must kill the hellish tyrant for what he has done to his beloved, and transfixes her with his spear. When he learns of his mistake the champion assumes the robes of a mendicant and spends his remaining years praying at her grave, being vouchsafed a vision on his death bed that she is awaiting him in Paradise.

So far so Byronic. This preposterous tale has the statutory Romantic icons, a virgin soft as a rose and an ambivalent hero; it is suitably oriental, a tapestry of allusive learning, buttressed by footnotes in the Byronic style. Moore harnesses Sale's Koran and d'Herbelot's encyclopaedia to Islamise his theme. There is no Christian note, and Greeks are mentioned only because Azim had overcome them as part of his military career. To deChristianise his theme Moore's Satan, or Eblis, on whom Mokanna is modelled, is not a Miltonic figure in rebellion against God but a Koranic one, envious of Man, predestined to be superior to the angels. He is closer to the Satan of the book of Job, permitted by God to go 'to and fro in the earth, and (go) up and down in it',[12] tempting man, a fallen angel with divine attributes, not a serpentine figure of unmitigated evil. Despite his specious splendour and winning ways, the Koran is emphatic that those who follow him will be consigned to hell. That is their choice as it is also, in a predestinarian oriental world, their fate.

Mokanna has, like Satan a 'deep-felt, long nurs't loathing of man's name' and is determined to lure them all to destruction.[13] To secure his victory over mankind he must, like Satan, bribe those who will follow him with immediate rewards. All the attractions of Paradise, which Islam appears to forbid in life and promises only after death, will be available in the here and now. Prominent among them will be the pure wine which 'the Dark-ey'd Maids above / Keep seal'd with precious musk, for those they love.' (Moore insists that he is quoting the Koran.[14])

Mokanna is not Satan but he apes Satan in his attitudes, for the purpose of his tyranny is wholly malicious. It is based on fraudulent prophecy and selfish aims supported by a faithful hoodwinked by false dogma. The tale follows the then current myth in the West about Islamic tyranny, but Moore makes a larger point. Political tyranny is fed by ideological fanaticism and Moore saw, as in a glass darkly, the ideological likes of Stalin and Hitler, Pol Pot and Chairman Mao. For Mokanna's message is that of many a supposed liberator; he rallies his followers with the cry that earth's shrines and thrones will fall before his banner and 'the glad Slave shall at these feet lay down / His broken chain, the tyrant Lord his crown, / The Priest his book, the Conqueror his wreath.'[15] All tyrannies start in this way, especially Napoleon's. He became a tyrant, for when 'the darkling-house of Mankind (was) burst' by the exercise of that Satanic energy that is the tyrant's, then tyranny takes over.

This was perfectly acceptable theorising, as most of the British population had subscribed to it for the long years between 1793 and 1815. Why then cloak it in oriental mumbo-jumbo and in a plot about as fusty as any that Southey had thought up? In the prose passages that link the tales in the poem, Moore submits *The Veiled Prophet* to the mockery of the princess's chamberlain, a crusty old scholar who sees all revealed knowledge in the Koran, and not in any Koran, but in *his* Koran, whose authenticity, being contemporaneous with the Prophet himself, cannot be denied. Therein lay the myth of an unalterable society, embalmed in amber. Moore treats the Koran with the same light respect with which he treats the Old Testament, less as a holy book than as a repository of information about the East of which he is writing, a well of inspiration from which to draw elixirs. As a lyric poet he luxuriates in the verbal imagery to which the Koran has introduced him. As a key to India, it is more accessible than the conflated and confused imagery of Hinduism, and he sets his poem in a land which had been Muslim since at least the invasions of Mohammed of Ghazni in the twelfth century.

3

In the third of the stories, *The Fire Worshippers*, Moore was to insert a hidden message. The story of the last resistance of the autochthon Zoroastrians in defence of the old religion of Iran against the proselytising Arab conquerors was a very opaque allegory of the condition of Ireland. If Moore was writing an oblique critique of British policies in Ireland he kept it well hidden. The light laments of his *Irish Melodies* had said all he really wanted to say about Ireland.[16] The love between the Iranian resistance leader, Hafed, and Hinda, the daughter of the invading Arab emir, has, like all good love stories, an unhappy end. Hinda is being evacuated from the war zone when her boat is stormed by Zoroastrians. On being taken to their final Megiddo-like stronghold, where they will resist to the end, she realises that those resisting her father are not benighted savages or crazed arsonists but ordinary human beings with just another view of the divine. Of course Hafed and Hinda fall in love and, when the citadel is threatened by the emir's army, Hinda tries to persuade her lover to escape with her to a neutral land far away. This is too great a strain on Hafed's loyalty to his cause and to his followers so, like her father before him, he ships her out of danger. She is not out of earshot when she hears the triumphant roar of the conquering army and, realising that Hafed has immolated himself as promised, she jumps overboard to a watery death.

4

Moore set his fantasy in the glamorous and exotic hinterland between India and Persia, so that few understood that one of the tales was an allegory of England's subjugated sister, Ireland. Moore was encouraged to take an eastern subject because everyone knew that governance in the eastern world was the operation of a despotic tyranny, bolstered by an army of privileged warriors and protected by an *ulema* of privileged holy men. Two of the tales are about resistance to a would-be tyrant, and most people in England held as an article of faith that tyrants were commonly to be found in the East. But not only in the East. For an Irishman the tyranny of the English in Ireland was positively oriental. It was not until the 1841 edition of *Lalla Rookh* that Moore admitted cautiously that reading of the fierce resistance of the Iranian fire worshippers had roused his sympathy for oppressed people: 'The cause of tolerance was again my inspiring theme, and the spirit that had spoken in the melodies of Ireland soon found itself at home in the east.'[17] Moore's attitude to the faith of both his heroine, Lalla Rookh, and of the story-teller, Ferramorz, was ambivalent and in the mouth of the latter he puts sentiments that resonate loudly today. The Emir is 'One of the saintly murderous brood / To carnage and the Koran given, / Who thinks through unbelievers' blood / Lies their directest path to heaven.'[18]

Some recognised that Moore's Orient, suffering from oriental oppression, was not too different from Ireland, and that Hafed had a walking resemblance to Moore's student friend, the Irish insurrectionary leader Robert Emmet. But for illness Moore might have joined him in the ill-fated 1798 rebellion which led to Emmet's self-imposed exile. Among those who thought they had divined Moore's purpose in writing the poem was Francis Jeffrey of the *Edinburgh Review* and, perhaps less percipiently, if not maliciously, Lady Holland, who informed Moore that she had read *Larry O'Rourke* and did not like Irish stories.

5

In the concluding part of the poem, Moore pulls out all stops. It is scarcely a tale at all, but a hymn to the imaginary Kashmir/Cashmere, the land beloved of Lalla Rookh's grandfather, the son of Akbar and third Mughal ruler of India, Jehangir. It tells of the love of that emperor for the pride of his harem, the young Nourmahal, a girl of astonishing beauty with a fine singing voice. Moore introduces his stories with a question, which, in fact, few of his readers may have been able to answer in the affirmative: 'Who has not heard of the Vale of Cashmere?' For his Cashmere is a land of make-believe, of roses, nightingales, and fountains where a lover could glide across the lake with his beloved. 'If woman can make the worst wilderness dear, / Think what a Heaven she must make of Cashmere.'[19]

Despite her peerless charms Nourmahal must have recourse to an Enchantress to help her harness the natural beauties, the flowers of the Vale, to enhance her beauty, an Enchantress who knew 'The Great Mantra which around the Air's sublimer spirits drew'.[20] This Enchantress, however, is no Carathis, the witch mother of Vathek, but one who can appreciate true love and weaves her spells accordingly. True love must have its way for 'Tomorrow the dreams and flowers will fade.'[21] Jehangir, assembling the Valley's loveliest, 'all the bright creatures that, like dreams, / Glide through its foliage, and drink beams / Of beauty from its founts and streams,'[22] holds his feast in the Shalimar palace (beside which a later poetaster loved pale hands). Moore gives us the menu: grapes of gold, pomegranates full of melting sweetness, pears and sunniest apples of Caubul, Malaya's nectared mangusteen, prunes of Bokhara, sweet nuts from Samarcand, Basra dates, apricots from Iran, Visna cherries, all washed down by Shiraz wine blushing red as the ruby for which Kublai Khan offered a city's wealth. Despite his virtual reversion to John Keats's food hall,[23] Moore weaves as magic a spell as Nourmahal's enchantress when Jehangir's beloved, disguised as a lowly slave accompanying a 'lovely Georgian maid' on the lute, sings that 'if there be an Elysium on earth, it is this, it is this', a paraphrase of lines carved on the Diwan-i-Khas, the pavilion in the Red Fort in New Delhi, which served as the pleasance for the emperor, from which he appeared to his people. The couplet is attributed to a minister of the emperor Shahjahan: 'If on earth there be a place of bliss, it is this, it is this, oh it is this.' It was also used in the gardens of Shalimar in Kashmir.[24]

Lalla Rookh is hardly a political poem, despite what is read into it, for Moore was intoxicated by the voluptuousness of his imagination. The Vale of Kashmir evoked the simple rusticity that should attend perfect love and which so often did not. A beautiful East, exotic, languorous, charged with suppressed or delayed orgasm, contrasted with the busy, mechanical, soot-laden West, breathing inhibitions and falsity. Late Georgian society was insincere and promiscuous. Lalla Rookh might have her head turned by an eloquent poet but infidelity to her promised husband never crossed her mind. She was lucky that they proved to be the same person.

Moore, however, could not pretend that love conquers all. In *The Fire-worshippers* Moore's sympathies were with the Zoroastrians. Ali Hassan was a man of blood, driven by religious zeal, resolved to reduce Iran to a land of 'carcases and of slaves'[25] but like Byron's men of blood he loved his daughter. There was no way, however, that their daughters could be allowed to side with the Infidel. That could only lead to death, for there was an ineluctable Romantic decree that the loves of Selim and Zuleika, and of Leila and the Giaour, were as doomed as that of Zelica for Selim and Hinda for Hafed. Despite Moore's rhapsodies, culture and belief were stronger than love.

6

Given this tragic sentiment, *Lalla Rookh* was an international success. Widely translated it was hailed, except in the *British Review*, which thought it was 'mellifluous nonsense', as the perfection of orientalism. The future Tsar, Nicholas I, and his Tsarina, dressed up as Ferramorz and Lalla Rookh at a masquerade in Berlin; as his armies absorbed the Caucasus he savoured his future as an Islamic potentate. Byron's approval was unreserved: 'the tone of the east has been perfectly preserved'.[26] But *Lalla Rookh* did not make Moore an orientalist. Though he manfully researched his locale, he could only write in his style of 'mellifluous' Romanticism. The virtual disappearance of the poem from the libraries of literate men confirms that poets should write about what they know. Islam and the East were pegs on which Moore hung his poetic garments and, fearing that a later, bantering, faintly satiric poem on the *The Loves of the Angels* was attracting hostile criticism as impious, he suggested that he might disarm it by setting future editions of the poem in an Islamic not Christian heaven.[27] Sale and d'Herbelot were forgotten.

CHAPTER TWELVE

Scott and the Quest for Chivalry

The Myth of the Crusades

> May heaven forgive it be a sin but I can see little save folly in these
> crusades that the priesthood have preached up so successfully.
> (Wilkin Flammock in Scott, *The Betrothed*) [1]

I

*G*IBBON IN HIS quest for the historical truth of the crusades had banished
fancy, making of the great poems of Tasso and Ariosto so much trash
for burning. For him there were no heroes, no villains, no magi, no
sorceresses, but the clash of economic forces, themselves not always
rational. Over them hovered the angel of religious division which justified,
though it did not explain, the loss of life and happiness, the real object of
mankind, over many centuries. Walter Scott accepted Gibbon's rationalism,
without his cynicism. The crusades had seen the high and the low water of
chivalry. Was chivalry itself burned out, did the centuries old religious
conflict burn it out, and could it be revived?

Scott never visited the East but could be said to have written four
crusader novels. The first was *Ivanhoe*, in 1819, the second and third, *The
Betrothed* and *The Talisman*, were twin novels he published as *Tales of the
Crusaders* in 1825, and his fourth and last novel, *The Siege of Malta*, was left
almost completed at his death in 1832 but never published. Scott visited
Malta on his way, not in his case to the Levant, though he wanted to visit
the Ionian islands, but to Italy. It was to be his last journey. His interest in
Malta was fired by the Great Siege of 1565; his preliminary reading had
disclosed what to him was a new clash of ideologies, new in the sense that

they owed less to chivalry but more to modern warfare, to a new psychology of rivalry in dedication to hopeless causes and to historical causality. Scott was always able to see both sides of every debate and the crusades were to provide him with a frame in which to explore the irrationality of wilful incomprehension.

Historically the crusades were defensive not offensive wars. They may have coincided with a time of population explosion in the West and the need to harness the aggressive energies of a superficially civilised people, but they were in defence of what was considered the heartland of Christianity. The first crusade aimed to defend the Holy Land from conquest by an alien faith. Subsequent crusades, in which the participants took the Cross to indicate their intention, were launched to defend the Christian inheritance (seen as virtually the boundaries of the Roman empire), from a challenging and expansionist Islam. That both sides called the other Infidels meant that the two proselytising religions were bound to clash at all the points of contact.

National epics formed round crusaders, real and fictitious, round Roland (Orlando), Godfrey of Bouillon, Tancred, Rinaldo, Rodrigo Diaz de Bivar (El Cid), the Mameluke Sultan of Egypt Baibars (Rukn ad-Din), Saladin (Salah-ed-Din Yusuf), Richard Coeur de Lion. They peopled the formative legends of the Mediterranean world and despite subsequent conflicts between nation states, and even total war, their memory lingers on in both sides of what became known as the Great Debate. Active crusades continued until the Napoleonic wars when, with the ejection from Malta of the last of the crusading orders, the Knights Hospitaller of St John of Jerusalem, who had a remit for perpetual war with Islam, the religious sanction for conflict on the Christian side ceased.

The eight-pointed cross disappeared into heraldry, the knights who took their professions seriously returned to the hospitals where they properly belonged, and those who adopted the title and the cross did so mainly for reasons of charity, prestige and social advantage. The Hospitallers never disappeared like the Templars. They survived in Russia to sanctify the Tsar's acquisition of a largely Roman Catholic population in Poland and Lithuania, and as the last survivors of the crusades and of knightly endeavour they inspired the creation of an almost secular prototype in Protestant countries of the north. There the notion of chivalric behaviour was invoked to give a moral lead to a people who saw their mission to lead 'lesser breeds without the law'.

It was a lead that had to be exorcised of those undesirable features that had led to episodes of great courage and endurance but also of great cruelty and crime. Accusations of heresy, sexual deviance, necromancy and ambition had engineered the suppression of the Templars in 1312, and the behaviour of the Teutonic Knights (of the Hospital of St Mary of the Teutons in Jerusalem) in Eastern Europe had identified them so closely with Germanic penetration into Eastern Europe that the most Catholic Poles saw them not as Christian defenders but as oppressors. They suffered a crushing defeat by the forces of the King of Poland at Tannenberg in 1410 but they limped on as a sovereign order until 1809. Shorn of lands by the French revolutionary wars, and riven by Protestantism, the Order was quietly suppressed by the Pope. The crusading leaders had not always upheld the high principles of chivalry that they espoused.

Even that Christian paladin Richard the Lion-Hearted had no unblemished record. His coronation had been marked by a pogrom against the Jews of London who had inadvertently allowed themselves to be within persecution distance of the ceremony. On his way to the Holy Land, at Messina, he had been told by the mystic saint, Joachim of Flora, that Saladin was the sixth head of the Apocalyptic dragon, and that Richard would slay him. Richard then enquired about the seventh head, which was that of Antichrist. The saint told him that here Richard was powerless, for the Antichrist was already living in Rome and would occupy the apostolic throne. Richard assumed he meant Pope Clement I, whom he disliked, but had to accept that he must be content with Saladin's head.[2] Richard may have been a doughty fighter, not afraid to fight with Antichrist himself, but he could also be an unthinking, arrogant, and hot-headed bully.

Sir Walter Scott entered the crusader canon, looking for the real Richard against this backdrop of fantasy. As a child of the Scottish renaissance he was intrigued by the characteristics of a period when Islam, Christianity and Jewry were mired in hostility and prejudices which even in his time (and ours) had not disappeared. His so-called crusader novels were written to cast a humane view on what for him was basically the irrational behaviour of people with strong convictions. Though he was dependent for his background on chroniclers whose devotion to truth was subordinate to that of their religion, he hoped he would be fair to all sides and represent the times not so much as they were but as they might have been.

2

The most famous of his oriental romances never got as far as the Holy Land, but *Ivanhoe* touches it tangentially. All the principal characters, Brian de Bois-Guilbert (a paladin of the Templar order), Ivanhoe himself (a Saxon knight in a society in which Norman held Saxon in contempt), and the Black Knight (actually Richard Coeur de Lion), had fought in the Holy Land. Scott in all his work showed an Olympian detachment towards his characters and his view of the crusaders and all those with a religious calling showed this most of all. Human behaviour may have improved since the fourteenth century, and society may have been governed by good manners, but it was not yet governed by reason.

Ivanhoe is an oriental novel despite its being set in England and despite the fact that only two Muslims actually feature in the novel – they are the Saracen servants of Bois-Guilbert, and play an insignificant part in the plot. Its orientalism lies in Scott's interest in the treatment of Jews in King Richard's time, which epitomised for him irrational behaviour based on prejudice. The heroine, or more properly the principal female in the book, is a young, beautiful and amazingly articulate Jewess, Rebecca, daughter of the stereotype of a cringing usurer, Isaac of York.

The villain is a Christian paladin, a Templar knight; indeed, the members of the order of Knights Templar are the personification of harsh Christian racialism. Their Grand Master, on a visit to the English chapter of the Order, expounds the view of religious enthusiasts of all convictions, that there must be intolerance of breaches of those laws which are of God. Scott contrasts the rigid and austere discipline of the Templars with that of the secular clergy. The Prior of Jorvaulx is shamelessly self-centred in the practice of his religion and cowardly with it, and it is the hard-drinking, hard-fighting Friar Tuck who provided Scott's preferred model of medieval priestly behaviour. At least Tuck was true to his nature and honest in his vocation. All the gentiles, even those for whom Scott feels the strongest sympathy, subscribe to distrust, even hatred, of Jews, who can only buy temporary exemption from the arrogant prejudice and cruelty of the Christians whose treatment of them at best oscillates between tolerance and exploitation.

Rebecca, whose beauty has aroused the dark and illicit passions of the Templar Bois-Guilbert, defies the accusation that she had used witchcraft to do it, and should be burned as a witch. When she demands a champion to decide her case before God, she opposes one irrational conviction, that she practises black arts, by another, that there will be found a champion to fight her cause. Her eloquence stirs even the flinty Templar Grand Master, Lucas Beaumanoir, who is her judge. Scott's portrait of Beaumanoir disturbingly evokes the future image of that perverted Romantic, Heinrich Himmler, whose crazy, Templar-like order was dedicated to the pitiless purification of the world from the Jewish race. Scott believed that unreason is never entirely purged by enlightenment. In the speeches he puts in the mouths of his Gentile characters we find arguments used, a hundred years later, by Nazi propaganda, demonstrating that the irrationality of Christian, indeed of any, prejudice is wicked, for prejudice is ultimately self-seeking.

The Templars are the supreme proof of this. Lucas Beaumanoir is convinced that survival in the Holy Land is dependent on their existence, not as a religious order, but as brokers between the Christians who will tire of the never ending war in strange lands, and the Muslims who will not. The military power of the Templars will alone rescue something for Christianity from the grand debacle. Beaumanoir knows that the danger to his Order comes not so much from its enemy, Islam, as from the Templars' dabbling in 'the accursed cabalistical secret of the Jews, and the magic of the Paynim Saracens'. As late as the 1840s Alexander Kinglake wrote that the Jews of Jerusalem had such a strong faith in the power of magic that they believed that the miracles of Jesus could only have been wrought with the help of the powers of darkness; more understanding Jews referred to Jesus as the Good Magician – but magician for all that. Kinglake's contempt for Egyptian magicians was total when one of their practitioners was unable to raise the image of the flogging headmaster at Eton, John Keate.[3]

As part of Beaumanoir's campaign against that secret corruption, Rebecca, who has bewitched Bois-Guilbert, must be purged as a sorceress. The machinations of sorceresses in the Holy Land formed a large part of the crusader myth, for how otherwise could the 'Muslim paynims' have prevailed against God's army? They figure in all the crusader stories, most notably in Tasso's *La Gerusalemme Liberata* (Armida) and Ariosto's *Orlando Furioso* (Alcina). Scott saw the irony of this. Belief in sorceresses was a major irrationality which had until recently prevailed among his own countrymen. Its effects on human behaviour could be calamitous, and when Beaumanoir accuses his Order of dabbling in the black arts, he foretells the historical case against it at its demise, when its principals were condemned to death in an injustice as gross as that he was about to wreak on the helpless

Jewish girl. The Templars as an order were deemed by Philip IV of France to have become too rich and awkward, and they succumbed to heavily orchestrated accusations of sins against the Holy Ghost, such as sodomy and witchcraft, and of heresies, notably that of seeking after forbidden knowledge. Scott knew that the Order perished not because of its pursuit of supernatural secrets, but because of its independence, defiance, wealth and pride.[4] The supposed supernatural secrets of the Templars still receive periodical airing in contemporary films such as *The Raiders of the Lost Ark* and books such as *Holy Blood, Holy Grail* and *The Da Vinci Code*.

Ivanhoe becomes positively operatic towards its end. Designated by the Grand Master as the Order's champion against any whom Rebecca can find to defend her, Bois-Guilbert believes that there is no champion, apart from Richard Coeur de Lion himself, or Ivanhoe then grievously wounded, who has any chance of overcoming him in single combat. 'Proud, inflexible and unchanging', his honour demands that he must triumph in any challenge and Rebecca must burn. But he cannot lose her without one last effort and proposes terms to her. They are, of course, Romantic rather than real: if she will accept his love and his religion, he will take her from the tyranny of western prejudice, and enrol as a mercenary in one of the Christian enclaves of the Near East, whose rulers are not too fastidious about who fights their battles. 'Rather with Saladin will we league ourselves and endure the scorn of the bigots whom we condemn.'[5] Bois-Guilbert gives the girl no real alternative; rejection means inevitable death. Rebecca's firmness in rejecting this offer inevitably means that he must stand his ground, watch her burn and subsequently scheme to succeed the bigoted old dotard, Beaumanoir, as Grand Master, after which the Templars, 'who think and feel as men free from such silly and fantastic prejudices' would, Scott suggests, become a very different and possibly even more dangerous enterprise.

Such a dénouement being unacceptable in a Romantic novel, Bois-Guilbert is felled by a divinely delivered heart attack, as he unhorses the hapless Ivanhoe, who has hastened to Rebecca's rescue. As Bois-Guilbert has fallen in mortal combat, God has spoken; Rebecca is innocent by divine fiat and is freed. Richard the Lion-Hearted is revealed as a prime actor in the drama throughout and virtue triumphs. The sudden reappearance in rude health of a Saxon thane after he had been presumed dead and about to be buried and the supernatural death of Bois-Guilbert were both mocked at the time as being melodramatic, but *Ivanhoe* established the Jews as being both separate from and identified with western civilisation, and contributed to the climate of sympathy in which Disraeli could become Prime Minister at a time when George Eliot was writing *Daniel Deronda*.

3

Scott pursued his crusader interests over the next five years and in 1825 *The Betrothed* and *The Talisman* both appeared. The first is barely a crusader tale. None of the action takes place in the Holy Land, nor do any of the principal characters, save one, ever go there. Set in the reign of Henry II when the Third Crusade was in the making, the plot hinges on a vow which an Anglo-Norman baron has made to go on the crusade, but he then puts off his departure to marry the heroine. He is persuaded by the successor to Thomas Becket to fulfil his vow, and the crusader goes off two-thirds of the way through the book, his broad pennant streaming from the prow of his vessel and 'a more gallant band ... never went to avenge on the Saracens the evils endured by the Latins of Palestine'.[6] They leave the remaining characters to pursue their lives on the turbid Welsh border for the rest of the novel.

The crusader returns at the end, like a character from one of Handel's operas, to make all things right and behave, as Scott was at pains to stress, like an honourable man, renouncing the bride who does not love him. The commentary on this novel is spoken by one of Scott's plain-spoken minor characters, the Flemish weaver Wilkin Flammock, who represents the views of common sense: 'Let those who lost the Holy Sepulchre regain it ... If those Latins and Greeks, as they call them, are no better men than I have heard, it signifies very little whether they or the heathen have the country that has cost Europe so much blood and treasure.'[7]

Scott's best-known crusader novel, *The Talisman* is the only one of the four set in the Holy Land during the crusade of which Richard Coeur de Lion was the dynamic head. Despite being set in the reign of the same monarch it takes place in a world quite different from that of *Ivanhoe*, and that not just because it is set in a Holy Land which Scott had never seen. Indeed, Scott admitted in his preface that he had great difficulty of giving a vivid picture of a part of the world with which his only acquaintance had been through *The Arabian Nights Entertainments*. Richard is also a different person from the Black Knight of *Ivanhoe*, for Scott had in the meantime formed a different idea of the crusade which provided only the backdrop to the former work. What the two novels have in common is their exploration of relations between races, between two schools of prejudice, in the hope that they might find a personality able to rise, like Scott himself, above them.

This is also one of the sub-themes of *The Betrothed*, where relations between Norman, Saxon, British (Welsh) and Flemish intrigued Scott. Norman and Saxon are opposed in *Ivanhoe*; Christian and Muslim in *The Talisman*; and Scott's predilections are for the one which seemed the greater victim of prejudice. Ivanhoe, the despised and defeated Saxon, and Saladin, the paynim Soldan, are the true knights. Prejudice, however understandable its causes, is essentially an irrational activity, and Scott fills *The Talisman* with descriptions of irrational behaviour, starting with crusading itself. He contrasts the character of the diplomatic and cautious King of France, Philip IV, with that of the impetuous Richard; and concludes that in the crusade 'sound reason was the quality, of all other, least estimated, and the chivalric valour which both the age and the enterprise demanded was considered as debased if mingled with the least touch of discretion'.[8]

To the characters in the novel the fate of the Holy Sepulchre seems almost as indifferent as it was for Wilkin Flammock in *The Betrothed*. All, except a slightly crazed hermit, are interested in themselves and their personal ambitions, of which fulfilling the great object of the crusade itself is not one. The presence and folly of Queen Berengaria and her women – what are the Queen of England and a cohort of high-born ladies doing in the no man's land between Christian and Muslim even during a period of truce? – only underline the irrationality of the myth of knighthood, that knights are faithful to their cause and to their ladies, however common, like Don Quixote's Dulcinea, or light-headed, like Queen Berengaria.

Scott's instinct was to place himself somewhere in the middle of extreme positions. King Richard in *Ivanhoe* is a reasonable man, hoping to unite Norman and Saxon into one nation. In *The Talisman* Richard is the flawed leader of the crusade, constantly threatening to destroy it by his hot-headed behaviour. He is the embodiment of certain leadership qualities – extreme courage; fearsome physical strength; certainty, even blindness, of purpose; and broad generosity – but he is also their victim. He cannot, like his opposing leader, Saladin, conquer his arrogance, impetuousness and total absence of self-criticism. His southern blood, tinged with the spirit of the irrational troubadour, makes his devotion to the spirit of knighthood stronger than his devotion to the Christian faith.

Among the myths of chivalry, which Richard had imbibed, was that all problems can be settled by conflict, in which the better man will prevail, because God will so decide. Richard wishes to put the arbitrament of Jerusalem to the test of a single combat between himself and Saladin, not because he despises Saladin but because he respects him as his equal, and the decision on who wins will be God's. Saladin himself has, of course, no intention of throwing away his advantages on a combat so irrational. He has the numbers and the local strongholds while the crusading armies – in the face of starvation, sickness, desertion and internecine rivalry – will soon be too weak to continue. Scott leaves the rest of this very doubtful tale to history.

Saladin already had the reputation of being the 'good paynim', and Scott gives him the exemplary characteristics of such a hero. His behaviour throughout is chivalrous to the point of being foolish. The novel opens with an encounter the Saracen leader has with a Scottish chevalier *sans peur et sans reproche*, Sir Kenneth of the Leopard, in which they both behave politely to each other, quite a demand on the prejudiced Scottish knight. Saladin reappears then disguised as a *hakim* within the crusading camp, treating Richard himself for a debilitating fever which has deprived the crusading armies of leadership. Saladin behaves, in fact, as irrationally as Richard himself, infected in his turn with the spirit of chivalry: Richard's demise from a local ailment would deprive Saladin and the Saracens of the chivalric glory of defeating the crusader army. The idealisation of Saladin was, however, part of Scott's desire to dismantle a view of Islam which the crusading myth had perpetuated, to show that Muslims had been and could be again more rational and generally better conducted than Christians. At one point it seems that Vathek is intruding on the story in the person of two dwarves who play a curious role around the supremely irrational hermit Theodoric, but they are not sinister Gothic apparitions but players in a silly game Queen Berengaria wants to play on one of her maids in waiting. Scott was illustrating his belief that odd Gothic things were usually susceptible of a plain and rational explanation.[9]

Villains, if villains there are, belong to the Christian camp. Templars again are cast in this role, as Scott seems to accept that their historical suppression could not have been without some basis. In his novel their object is survival in the Holy Land after what the Grand Master of the Order is sure will be an ultimate Saracen victory. Prince John, the would-be king in *Ivanhoe*, has his counterpart in Conrade of Montserrat, Richard's nefarious ally in *The Talisman*, who wants to be king of Jerusalem. He knows that this will not happen if Richard is successful in liberating Palestine. Heroes, in the sense that they are the opposites of villains, are the hapless Sir Kenneth and Richard's principal aide, the Baron de Vaux, a border warrior of the kind that Scott loved to imagine; brave, pig-headed, loyal and true. But the principals, Richard and Saladin, represent the two poles of leadership: one bold and intemperate, the other subtle and wise, both generous and romantic, but ultimately foolish.

Scott almost created in Richard Coeur de Lion a hero in the image of Godfrey de Bouillon in Tasso's *La Gerusalemme Liberata*. But the English national hero remained King Arthur, for Richard, with or without Scott, could not have created the fellowship of the Round Table and, if Richard had seen and nearly 'liberated' Jerusalem, it was not to be his Holy Grail. He too, from a fundamental defect of character, is not destined to achieve his mission. His Sir Galahad, Sir Kenneth of the Leopard, achieves his, and Richard's Merlin proves to have been a Saracen, and an enemy. But in a century that created heroes, and looked for them in Horatio Nelson and the Duke of Wellington, Richard Coeur de Lion nearly made it to the Protestant pantheon, resembling as the film critic Graham Greene put it in a lapidary phrase, 'those honest simple young rowing-men who feel there is something wrong about sex'.[10]

4

Scott was to return to the crusades in a last, unpublished work which he plucked from the then standard and authorised history of the Knights of Malta by the Abbé René d'Aubert de Vertot (1655–1735). The abbé's detailed and stirring story of the Siege of Malta by the might of Suleiman the Magnificent in 1565 caught his imagination as he prepared for his visit to Italy, via Malta, in his sixtieth year. A novel about the great siege would, he felt, be a certain success and help to pay off his debts by selling widely. In the event he was to die within the year and his matchless fluency was marred by cloudy language and an undue reliance on Vertot with fictional interpolations by himself.

The general opinion of the British who then ruled Malta was that the Knights had cravenly surrendered to Napoleon in 1798, and shown none of the valour of the great siege two hundred years earlier. Scott could hardly have thought otherwise but, then, what were the Knights doing in an age so far removed from the golden years of chivalry? What interested him was to discover how far the Knights of the Great Siege in 1565 had lived up to the example set by Melec-Ric, Richard Coeur de Lion, four hundred years before. 'The interest', he wrote to the man who had sent him off with Vertot's History of Malta, 'turns on the changed manners of the European nations which about that time began to renounce the Doctrines of Chivalry whilst they made great changes both in manners and morals.'[11]

He poses the question of those changes in the draft of his novel in a debate between two of the Turkish commanders outside the besieged cities of Malta. One cites the 'most honoured tongues' on the Turkish council which aver repeatedly that 'our enemies are changed in their manners, and no longer hold themselves bound to fight to the last extremity as they did in the ancient days of Melec-Ric'. The other commander is less certain. If there has been a change it has not reached the superiors of the Order. Immense efforts and sums of money had been spent to raise the fortifications which were defying the might of Turkey against fearful odds and he challenges them to 'say if the Christians, who have defended themselves desperately against such extreme odds are in [any] respect changed from the countrymen of Melec- Ric'.[12]

Inside those fortifications there is a rumour that there has been 'treachery never heard of in the annals of the Order, the very thought of which called for tears from the old Knights'.[13] When St Elmo, the bastion of the tongue of land that controlled the entry into what became Grand Harbour, was being most heavily pressed, the younger knights were saying that the struggle was hopeless, the fort must fall, and they would not risk their lives in a hopeless struggle. For Scott, the Grand Master, Jean de la Valette, has the same rigid certainties as Beaumanoir, the Grand Master of the Templars in *Ivanhoe*, but he is a historical hero and must be shown to lead from the front.

He tells the assembled knights that he cannot allow the young men – who nursed, of course, no personal reluctance or consideration of danger – to bear all the brunt of the action. He himself and the older knights will make up the relief force which was to ship across the water into St Elmo under cover of darkness to replace its losses. It was only right that the veterans should share the perils of 'high-born gentlemen ... and Christian Knights'.[14] Of course, the murmurings are suppressed in the general shame, and La Valette is left in safety to conduct the general defence of Malta.

Chivalry may have faltered, but the Siege of Malta was to be chivalry's finest hour. 'For the Knights had the usual pride which annexes itself to high birth, great resolution and long practice in arms ... Death, however painful, (was) preferable a hundred times to the least slur on reputation.'[15]

This may be irrational but it is one of the virtues that can transform an ordinary, even mediocre person into someone great, heroic, Romantic. Fighting a hopeless war for a cause which cannot triumph was a human activity which fascinated Scott. His Knights of Malta had little hope that succour would arrive before they had all perished, but by holding out they ensured that, if it did arrive, they would still be there. The cause was the saving of Europe from the ever onward encroachment of Islam, so not only history would reward them but also their God. Scott was content that he had found 'the Spirit of Chivalry blazing in its ashes'.[16] In 1798 when Napoleon arrived outside the island there had been no prospect of succour and the Knights' cause was not just hopeless, it was dead. The fateful six-day siege of Malta was mounted by fellow Christians, and there had been treason in the ranks. Scott was a distinguished citizen of the only possible saviour for the Order, a Protestant power which valued Malta as a bulwark to its growing territorial empire in India. If Scott saw the irony his draft novel does not reveal it.

Chivalry, moreover, was wearing a little thin. Scott was delighted to find La Valette in the crypt of the conventual church provided 'with a superb sepulchre of Bronze, on which he reclines in the full armour of a Knight of chivalrie', but there was little about the Siege of Malta, the closer he got to it, that was chivalric.[17] It was fought with singular brutality, no quarter given. Knights captured by the Turks were slaughtered, bloodied with the Maltese cross on their bodies and sent to drift back to the besieged. Turks captured by the knights were decapitated and their heads fired into the Turkish lines. The spirit of 'defend and die' belonged more to the age of total war than to that of chivalry.

Neither side could take the honours for knightly endeavour or charity. The siege was too important for that, and Scott tries to be as fair to the Muslim as he is to the Christian. He intended to give the Algerian corsair Dragut, who was the most feared and implacable enemy to the knights, a heroic death but he never wrote it. A younger Scott could have woven round the personality of Dragut a myth as fascinating as the one he wove round Saladin in *The Talisman*. The older Scott was too dependent on Vertot.

He did not invent the divisions in the Turkish command he described any more than he invented the character of Richard Coeur de Lion, nor did he invent the impatience of the younger knights in Malta with the resolve of the elder to resist to the end. He was not, by this time, concerned imaginatively to analyse the reactions of two ideologies in combat. As he explored the island he was fascinated more by the technical wizardry of the builders of fortifications that withstood so violent a siege, and by the sheer ingenuity and courage of both attackers and defenders. It was the fate of the citadel of St Elmo, which fell at last to sheer numbers and the attrition of bombardment, which roused Scott's liveliest interest in *The Siege of Malta*.

Was chivalry dead? At one point Scott makes a knight tell La Valette that he had tried to persuade Cervantes to come with him to defend Malta. Cervantes is, in fact, the key to the riddle of *The Siege of Malta*. Cervantes mocked the excesses of chivalry but not chivalry itself. Chivalry was not insane, only Don Quixote. No man in Spain, the knight assures the Grand Master of Cervantes, 'is more capable of impelling his countrymen' to the call of patriotism or of honour.[18] Cervantes was only 18 in 1565 and Don Quixote first appeared in 1608, so Scott was making an unhistorical statement he might well have felt he must remove had the book ever approached publication in his lifetime. The defence of Malta, however, was a matter of serious war, quite unlike the posturing of King Richard and his allies before Jerusalem in *The Talisman*. Malta was saved by the same devotion to patriotism and honour that had been the pride of chivalry in its prime. The final relief of the island by the *Gran Soccorso* or Great Relief from Sicily, written hastily between Malta and Naples to meet Scott's deadline to get the manuscript to his publisher, is almost an anticlimax. He was writing a lament for the passing of an age of great causes, a kind of requiem for the greatness of Ottoman and Christian arms. The Turks had been beaten off, not beaten.

By the time of both Scott and Byron, the Ottomans were there to be defeated. In *The Betrothed* the hard-headed Wilkin Flammock may have seen 'little save folly in these Crusades', but Scott could not resist them as providing an allegory on chivalry.[19] However fine its ideals, in the end they would be betrayed. The Knights of the Round Table ended in squalor and hope betrayed, as did the crusading orders – Templars, Teutonic Knights and Hospitallers – all of them worsted not by Muslims but by Christians. All they left behind was a wistful nostalgia which took shape in the famous Eglinton tournament of 1839. The accession of Queen Victoria, 'a virgin soft as roses' brought to the throne of England not a Zuleika or a Leila, more an Eveline de Beranger (*The Betrothed*) with the spirit of a Rebecca (*Ivanhoe*).

After her two disreputable uncles, a virgin queen coincided with a 'strange medieval fever sweeping over the European continent'. Women were, as in the high days of Chivalrie, once again a protected species, their role to be passionate, patient and quiescent, sensible like Eveline and Lady Rowena (*Ivanhoe*) not foolish like Queen Berengaria (*The Talisman*). Chivalry was a male preserve, and 'the days of chivalry obsessed the minds of everybody and Knights in armour stirred a thousand dreams', epitomised in a tournament devised with all its chivalric trappings at Eglinton.[20] Scott was largely responsible for this for when *Ivanhoe* appeared in 1819 Lord Eglinton succeeded his father, and the author of *Waverley* had become the very champion of chivalric behaviour. The Royal Academy acted as host to painters of crusader subjects, more than one from *Ivanhoe*, and Joseph Severn, who had been present at the death of John Keats and had now married Eglinton's half-sister, was exhibiting his canvas of *The First Crusaders in Sight of Jerusalem*.

Scott may have unwittingly become a propagandist for crusader imperialism, but that had never been his intention. In *The Talisman*, the sympathetic portrayal of Saladin showed that Muslims, like Christians, had their ideals and sense of chivalry and were not unworthy of acceptance as brothers under the skin. It was a view of them, however, that was not to survive the Greek War of Independence. The image of the abominable Turk was revived to haunt the imagination of Mr Gladstone.

CHAPTER THIRTEEN

Tancred and Eva

The Myth of Religious Unity

> 'Sensible men are all of the same religion.'
> 'And pray what is that?'
> 'Sensible men never tell.'
> (Disraeli, *Endymion*)[1]

I

*B*ENJAMIN DISRAELI WROTE *Tancred*, as the third of his political trilogy that began with Coningsby. If it was the apotheosis of a political trilogy, it was also the last novel Disraeli wrote before his political career took him over and after he had contributed to the fall of the ministry of Sir Robert Peel. Its theme was the sacredness of faith, any faith, in a world being taken over by Gradgrindism and greed, but it ends on a note that is anything but triumphant. Its trail is marked from the outset, for the young Tancred Montacute, cherished only child of a Duke and Duchess, has completed his time at Oxford, and should now announce at his coming of age party, before all the ducal tenants and future constituents, that he will enter Parliament for the family seat. This will be obediently vacated for him by the sitting member, whose function had been to keep it warm for him for the years of Tancred's minority. But he has other plans, which shock and confuse his parents and most of his relatives. He will not enter Parliament but go to Jerusalem to seek an answer to 'the Asian mystery'. Parliamentarians and primates cannot dissuade him and finally he sets off with his military, medical and diplomatic entourage, wished upon him by his doting parents, in a custom-built yacht, with untold wealth at his disposal through the agency of a rich and influential Jewish banker.

So far Disraeli has written his wish-fulfilment autobiography. It may have opened with suggestions of a satire on the privileged aristocracy but it soon revealed its serious purpose. As a dutiful but not wholly devoted Anglican, Disraeli believed that his semitic birth tapped him into the civilisation and culture of the race that had produced Moses, David and St Paul, as well as the founder and most of the Biblical fathers of the religion he now professed. The Asian mystery, the key to which Tancred engages himself to find, is never defined in the book but Disraeli suggests that it is the spiritual elixir that inspired the creators of the Abrahamic faiths, which now covered the world. Disraeli's chief Muslim character, Fakredeen, is the dispossessed son of a mountain emir, and foster son of a Jewish banker. Not surprisingly he is ambivalent about his real faith, any one of which – Muslim, Christian, Jew – he espouses when it suits him. His ambition is to secure European money to buy guns in order to carve out for himself a mountain principality in what is later (historically) to become the state of Lebanon. There the explosive mix of Jews, Muslims, Christians and Druses will act as midwife to a kingdom, mixed in religion, but fired by a common nationalism and ethic. That is also to be Tancred's solution to the Asian mystery.

The early Victorians were discovering the Holy Land. Pilgrimages were easily arranged by Thomas Cook & Son, open to all the family. Christianity had returned to the land of its founders, not in the cacophonous cackle of the religious who wrestled for places at the Church of the Holy Sepulchre, but in the persons of its local (Protestant) bishop and the Consuls of Christian nations, who through their ambassadors to the Sublime Porte, could secure Ottoman protection and neutrality between faiths. Walter Scott's novels had opened the Holy Land to the imagination, and Kinglake had extended it to tourists. Disraeli was enraptured by it. Of Jerusalem he writes to his sister in 1831: 'Except Athens I never saw anything more essentially striking, no city except that whose sight (from the Mount of Olives) was so pre-eminently impressive ... Athens and Jerusalem in their glory must have been the first representatives of the beautiful and sublime.'[2]

2

It was an invitation to add the Holy Land to the now mandatory visit to Greece. Rome was seen as perverted by Romanism and brutalised by the modern Turk, the Austrians. Athens, the home of true democracy, and Jerusalem, the home of true religion, were now safe to visit. Regenerated religion and regenerated democracy – which Disraeli believed was safe in the hands of a regenerated aristocracy, – would regenerate a world grown coarse and crass in its devotion to science and materialism. Europe had forgotten that it worshipped a Jew and venerated a Jewess. Tancred/Disraeli does not believe that humans are more animal than angel. It needed a regenerative philosophy to prove that those who believed that this was so were wrong.

Disraeli had returned from his Levantine tour an Abrahamite, but gave the impression that he had not wholly decided which Abrahamic avatar he followed. He was more impressed by what the faiths had in common than by what divided them. The future Protestant Jewish protector of the Islamic Ottomans, purchaser of the shares in the Suez canal, and founder of the Indian empire – whose Queen would rule pacifically over Muslims, Christians, Jews and Gentiles in a new Caliphate – was born as he wrote *Tancred*.

The novelist in Disraeli, when he arrived in the Holy Land, was, like Byron, entranced by colours, polychromatic stones, and gorgeous stuffs, and gave his characters clothing to contrast that of foggy London. More than by the peacock luxuries of his London society hostesses, presiding over elaborate table settings, Disraeli was fascinated by the allure of eastern women, in the shaded seclusion of garden kiosks and fountains. It worked as a kind of intoxication. Did he actually meet any, like Lady Mary Wortley Montagu, who had found the Ottoman ladies in their naked causeries amusing and intelligent? Both Disraeli's eastern beauties in *Tancred* are lovely by any criterion as well as philosophically profound. First there is Eva, the granddaughter of a desert sheik and daughter of a Jewish broker, who speaks with the oracular wisdom of many years – she is not yet twenty. She has the key to Tancred's mission. Her 'face presented the perfection of oriental beauty, such as it existed in Eden … Her skin was so transparent that you occasionally caught the … splendour of some vein like the dappled shades in the fine peel of beautiful fruit.' And so he goes on: in her eyes the Orient spoke and you could hear in them the starry vaults of Araby and the splendour of Chaldean skies; her small mouth, her teeth like the neighbouring pearls of Ormuz, the round chin, polished as a statue, the hands with nails shaped like almonds, all contrive to give Eva the allure both of a *femme fatale* and of a heroine.[3]

Eva is no milk and water heroine, nor a practical paragon, but a masterful spirit with cosmic ambitions. To her the Asian mystery is why the semitic peoples of the book, Jews, Christians and Muslims, do not unite to throw off the yoke of the alien central Asian Turks and forge a new empire from the Caucasus to the Atlas Mountains, based on justice and moral integrity. She wants more than Fakredeen, and distrusts his limited ambition and his shady deal for guns for which Tancred must somehow be persuaded to pay. For her, great ideals are not achieved by intrigue.

Then there is the teenage Astarte, queen of the mountain Ansareys, who worship not the God of Jesus or Mahommed but the ancient deities of Antioch, Zeus and the pantheon of ancient Greece. Hers are 'features very Greek, her complexion radiant, hair dark as night, and eyes of the colour of the violet'.[4] The Ansarey are a tribe that keeps itself to itself, envies no one their prosperity, and shares none of their ambitions. They only wish to preserve their own customs and beliefs. Tancred is admitted to the reclusive presence of Astarte because his classical education has given him a knowledge of the Gods of Mount Olympus, 'who loved the people and whom the people loved'.[5] Tancred tries to interest her in his project: Asia, as the only portion of the world the Creator visited in person, should reassert its spiritual supremacy. The men of the desert and the men of the mountains must exercise the virgin vigour of their intelligence, untainted by the superstitions and vices of towns and cities, and become the natural and united conquerors of the world, in which Tancred hopes to establish the happiness of man by a divine dominion, crushing political atheism and extinguishing 'the grovelling tyranny of self government'.

Disraeli knew that by and large human ambitions are met by a mixture of intrigue, conspiracy and combination, and his analysis of the Levantine political scene was embroidered with exotic fancies bred of tourism. Eva and Astarte might have noble ambitions, but those of lesser men amount to little more than the pursuit of wealth and power. Fakredeen, for example, wearied of the glittering cage in which he has been born, thirsts for action, and 'wishes to astonish Europe ... and to baffle and control the thrones and dominations of the world'.[6] The Syria of Disraeli, incorporating the whole geographical area of the Levant, had recently experienced European meddling when it forced Mehemet Ali, Pasha of Egypt, to leave the Damascus he had occupied with his trained levies in an ambitious move to extend his control to Constantinople and perhaps his occupation of the Sultanate.

His departure left Syria and the Holy Land prey to the turbid ebullition of rival tribes and religions. The ambitions of Tancred and of Eva were to forge a nation out of its indigenous peoples, establishing a moral authority by their common religious inheritance. Tancred for all his blue ducal blood is Disraeli, and Disraeli is a semite. Eva is also a semite, whose intellect and beauty raise her to the gentile Tancred's equal. Eva belongs to the race of Moses, whom 'God had recognised as a human instrument too rare to be entrusted with the redemption of an Arabian tribe from a state of fellaheen (in Egypt) to Bedouin existence.'[7] Her foster brother Fakredeen is, despite all his noble and quixotic qualities, a Bedouin with all the limited vision of a Bedouin. He believes that if he captures Tancred's party while on its way to Mount Sinai, where Moses had heard the still small voice of God, he will be able to demand a ransom which will pay for the guns he needs to raise the revolt which will give him his mountain kingdom.

3

Tancred is captured, and an intense affection develops between the two men.[8] Tancred pays Fakredeen spontaneously for his guns, is treated as an honoured guest and almost converts the Emir to his eirenic vision of a revived Arab world. At this point the shade of William Beckford stands at one shoulder of Disraeli, Thomas Moore at the other. A visit to the forbidden community of the Ansareys, worshippers of the ancient Gods, ruled by a lovely and passionate queen, lifts the novel from a commentary of Middle Eastern life to a foray into an imaginary world, and leads to a rapid and fanciful dénouement. The queen falls in love with Tancred, 'because he resembles a marble statue older than the time of the pre-Adamite Sultans'.[9] Eva is taken by the Ansareys in a caravan raid. Fakredeen contemplates a union of his bedouin and the Ansareys in a marriage to Astarte and, in an attempt to turn Astarte from her infatuated love of Tancred, informs her that the 'foreign prince' is actually in love with Eva. In a jealous rage Astarte orders Eva's death and Fakredeen, appalled by what his intrigues seem to have achieved, helps Eva to escape.

Astarte's kingdom is invaded by Ottoman troops sent to rescue Eva, Astarte is disabused of the idea that he has any affection for Eva by Tancred himself, and in a fit of chivalric enthusiasm he agrees to lead the defence of her kingdom. His tactics win, the Osmanlis are repulsed but Tancred's party is cut off and he has to make his own escape into the desert, providentially released from Astarte's thrall. On reaching Jerusalem, where Eva has returned to her father's home, he has to declare his part, innocent though it was, in the imbroglio. He still nurses his ambitions for the Middle East, and tries to persuade Eva to join her hand to his, when in the last sentence of the book, his parents, the Duke and Duchess, unexpectedly arrive in Jerusalem.

The sudden ending requires no explanation. The Duchess has always feared that Tancred would get involved in the East with someone who was not a true blue Protestant English lady. She had no knowledge of or interest in his religious beliefs or in his ambition to revive the land where his Saviour was born into his Abrahamic religion. It was now time for him to return to his seat in Parliament and devote his energies, like Disraeli himself, to the Corn Laws and the reconciliation of Ireland. The Eastern Question continued unsettled and unsettlable, and despite Tancred/Disraeli's general dislike of the Ottomans, he was to dedicate much of his foreign policy when in power to shoring up their empire.

4

Disraeli's parade of knowledge of the Holy Land and Syria was more authentic than that of most novelists of the time. He was clearly fascinated by the religious mix; if he did not entirely understand the complexities of the Lebanon, Lebanon had always formed part of the Biblical greater Palestine, and its beauties were the stuff of Hebrew poets. The Mountain, an area of high mountains and impenetrable gorges, had provided a refuge for dissenters of many creeds, particularly those who professed an incarnationist creed: Monothelites, Nestorians, Maronites and, most peculiar of all, Druses. The Druses were Unitarians, believing in one God who has taken many incarnations, the most significant of which was the sixth Fatimid caliph, who believed he was the incarnation of the Divine Intelligence. Unfortunately, he was also a classic oriental tyrant, excessively cruel and almost certainly insane, so that despite all attempts in the grand mosque of Cairo to convince his Islamic subjects that he was the Logos, his only adherents were a tribe of mountain people in Lebanon who, it is said, took their name of Druse from Ishmael Darazi, the first missionary from Egypt.

Though the deluded Caliph was assassinated in 1020, the Druse people developed a theophany that was secret and relied on a final revelation when the murdered Caliph will reappear, conquer the world and unite it to his faith. Tancred's naive faith in the unity of different faiths found support in the Mountain, but Astarte, named after the Syrian goddess sometimes equated with the Roman Venus, was not of an Abrahamic faith. The Ansareys were devotees of one of the Incarnationist faiths, but Disraeli makes them devotees of the Olympian gods. Whatever their merits they were not going to unite the followers of Abraham. Disraeli ends his novel suddenly. Parents arrive to end the nonsense of union with a Jewess, and a joint campaign to create a new world order. If *Tancred* had a message for its readers in 1847, the year before that of revolutions round Europe, it was that the affairs of men were complicated by men who could not be relied on to act either sensibly or in their own interests. Fakredeen surrenders his high ideal to tribal politics; Tancred risks life and fortune in a conflict as far removed as could be from what really interested him. They had to learn that politics was the art of the possible, not the impossible. It is a lesson that still needs to be learned.

Isabella, Hester and Jane

The Myth of the Amiable Turk

There was a solemn concert in honour of the Sublime
Ahmed Vassif, whose musicians, seated like dogs on a
carpet, piping and drumming and howling a doleful ditty.
(William Beckford, 29 December 1788)[1]

I

LONG BEFORE THE bashi-bazooks moved into Bulgaria in 1876
prompting Gladstone's rhetoric that the abominable Turk should
'carry themselves off … bag and baggage'[2] from Europe, the Ottomans had
rather unexpectedly (given their historic animosity to Russia) found
themselves on the side of the Ancient Order in the conflict stirred up by the
French Revolution and its avatar, Napoleon. Turkish troops were allies of
the English in the expedition to free her Egyptian dominion from the
French and, despite the fact that using Turks' heads as targets was a
favourite sport of the *lazzaroni*, they were unlikely allies of Christian Naples
in the 1799 push to expel the French from the Vesuvian city. Naples, under
its Spanish kings had been in the forefront of the perpetual war with Islam
but with the accession of Charles III, king from 1759 to 1788, Spain had a
moderniser who decided that Turkey was too important to ignore
diplomatically. An ambassador from Constantinople arrived in Madrid and
William Beckford was delighted to meet a stereotype that he had created
some years earlier in Vathek. 'My dear ambassador takes no exercise and is
for ever lolling in his sofa, fumigating himself with the vapour of wood of
aloes.' His suite entertained him with 'a sort of pantomimic dance with the
strangest leapings, wrigglings and scrambling … The music played doleful,
piteous strains that grated my ears most cruelly and two old fellows with

black rusty beards sung.'[3] Almost forgotten were the days when Turkish armies threatened the greatest citadels of Europe.

The Ottoman had always ruled over a divided people. The rulers might be Asiatic Turks, but its capital was set in Europe, and the richest and fairest of its lands had once been Christian. Christians, 'Mahommedanised', formed its élite; Christians, Orthodox and Armenian, provided the administrative and financial sinews that held it together. Its strength which depended on the efficient management of its divisions, was, however, dissolving. The Grand Turk had already become a costumier's model. In 1743 George II, king of England and Elector of Hanover, threw a great assembly in the electoral opera house, and 'appeared in Turkish dress, his turban was ornamented with a magnificent *agrafe* of diamond, and his mistress Lady Yarmouth was dressed as a Sultana'. Thackeray, in 1855, found it contemptuously amusing. 'For twenty years more, that little old Bajazet – he was then aged 60 – went on in this Turkish fashion ... O naughty little Mahomet! In what Turkish paradise are you now, and where are your painted houris?'[4]

By 1808, the empire needed a firm hand, and when Mahmud II became Sultan in that year he embarked on a fierce programme of modernisation. He delivered a blow against the fissiparous ambitions of viziers and governors by eliminating Pasha Ali of Yannina, whose severed head he received with glee. In 1826 he destroyed the Janissaries, who had deposed his cousin and blocked every attempt at reform and to whom he attributed the empire's fatal weakness in the face of modern Europe. He put his army into 'tight trousers and epaulettes' on the French model (despite the mockery of the Egyptian pasha Mehemet Ali) and conferred military rank on a new, professional cadre trained by Germans. He also abolished the cumbersome and top-heavy turbans that symbolised the ponderousness, even immobility, of society, and replaced them with frock coats and trousers, topped by a fez. The European uniform and the fez may have seemed ludicrous to the old guard – as much a fancy dress as that worn by good King George – but it was no more than a recognition that the world was changing, that the tremendous power and majesty of the sultanic office was fading.

Already, in 1804, in the hands of Maria Edgeworth the redoubtable Suleiman the Magnificent had become a wise and moderate monarch, prowling the streets of Constantinople with his vizier in disguise, not checking up like a secret inspector to find malpractice and to punish offenders summarily, but, as Haroun al Raschid was reputed to have done in Baghdad, to find out what the people were thinking. *Murad the Unlucky* is a morality tale for children, written in the style of *The Arabian Nights Entertainments* to show that prudence and imprudence govern our lives, not the fatalism that accepts that it is either blind fortune or bad luck. Murad is unlucky because he is imprudent; Saladin, his brother, is successful because he is not.

Suleiman and his vizier have had a difference about the part chance plays in man's fortunes but, after overhearing the two brothers' stories, Suleiman recognises that he was wrong and his vizier right. Prudence pays after all. And the Caliph 'could bear to find himself in the wrong and could discover his vizier to be in the right without cutting off his head'.[5] In her slight tale Maria Edgeworth accepts the fabled ruthlessness of Oriental monarchs, for viziers come and go with lightning rapidity, but this time the terrible Sultan sees reason. His image was not used to frighten children any more. She recognised that the terrible Turk was not always a creature of fantasy, living in the world of a thousand and one nights' entertainment. He could be sensible and ordinary enough to behave like her father, with whom Maria had collaborated in a book on practical education.

Neither the Sultan in Constantinople nor the emperor of Morocco were converts to Edgeworthian political economy. When Sidi Muhammad, one of the many sons of the frightful Moulay Ismā'īl, recognised that trade was more important than booty, he released his female captive, Elizabeth Marsh, from immurement in his seraglio. There was one condition: that her countrymen should appoint a commercial consul. He understood that amiability could be more fruitful than hostility.[6] It was not long before the Barbary Regencies were also looking to transform the tributes they received from states that wanted immunity from their pirates into some form of diplomatic recognition. In 1788 the Coggias led a palace revolution in Tripoli to throw off nominal Turkish suzerainty, and sent an ambassador to Madrid to negotiate an end to permanent hostilities. Part of his mission was to endure sitting, at a reception, amiably if uncomfortably sandwiched on a sofa between several of the 'potent females' of Madrid.[7] By the middle of the eighteenth century Turkish male society was already pleasingly open to western contact; by its end the Turk in European imagination had become, when not a figure of fun, positively amiable.

2

Amiable, but not without reservation when it came to his women. Lady Mary Wortley Montagu, fifty years earlier, may have been convinced that Turkish women were not oppressed, sexual automata, scheming dynasts or empty-headed sybarites. They dressed and undressed with taste, were good company, and they were emancipated from the social tyrannies that afflicted women in the West. In her view they enjoyed in the anonymity of the veil, and household seclusion, immunity from the indignities of gossip, rumour-mongering and backbiting that constituted society in Europe. Casanova may have hoped he could share Lady Mary's experience of agreeable encounters with women, but he was defeated by the jealous convention that excluded a woman from the company of a strange male. He could engage his Turkish friends in conversation about tobacco, religion and sex, and was tantalised by the offer of a rich bride and dowry but only if he turned Muslim. Casanova's insatiable quest for female company was frustrated all the time he was in Constantinople.[8]

Byron in the East trod warily on the hem of the skirts of womanhood. He recognised that Turkish women were off bounds. Greeks were not, and he could rescue, if only in his imagination, one on her way to being drowned 'in the sack'. He had abandoned the stern vision of Turkish morality in his *Turkish Tales* when he came to write *Don Juan*, ten years later. The hundreds who had read Lady Mary Wortley Montagu were now the thousands who read Byron. The constraints that bound Turkish women seemed not so different from those that bound the majority of Byron's readers, and Byron in *Don Juan* made fun of both. The Sultan is an uxorious husband, dutifully fulfilling his marital duties; Baba, the chief eunuch of the harem, a cynical time-server in charge of passionate women. The Sultana herself is starved of romance, bored and frustrated by life in the seraglio. Bored housewives could be found in both East and West. Was the harem so very different?

There seemed, too, a certain ambiguous amiability about the women. Lady Mary Wortley Montagu found it perfectly amiable to join a nude coffee or sherbet party in the *bagno* at Adrianople, but women were still jealously protected from social gaze. The *bagno*, however, was no longer threatening. When Ingres painted *Le Bain Turc* (in 1859) he depicted it as a fleshly waiting room in which he was ready to portray his buxom young wife. It was hardly what Edmond de Goncourt was to call 'a group of savages from Tierra del Fuego',[9] for he intended it to be viewed, as Lady Mary had described it, as

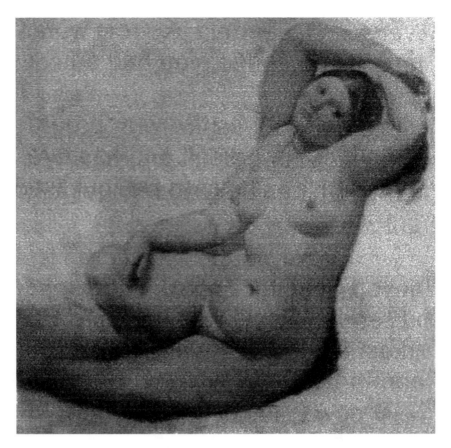

FIGURE 10   *Study for an odalisque at the baths. In 1859 Dominique Ingres painted* Le Bain Turc *as a fleshy waiting room in which he was ready to portray his buxom young wife, in an attitude suggestive of erotic expectation.*

a normal gathering for the pursuit of chat and cleanliness. Some of the lascivious gestures of the crowded women, however, the fondling and squeezing of breasts, the air of post-orgasmic lassitude, endowed it with the eroticism which was still how western eyes viewed the bath.

3

There was one artist who was immune from the Romantic sense of elemental angst and thus able to see what Turkish society was really like. He was the Maltese Amadeo, Count Preziosi, a water-colourist from a race of people who had much inside knowledge of society in Islamic lands, most of it gained from the experience of slavery. Preziosi was born in 1816, years after he was in any danger from Turkish or Moorish pirates. His family had been ennobled by the king of Sardinia a hundred years earlier, and he was named after that munificent monarch. The Preziosis were actually of corsair stock but had changed their role to that of discreet but critical aristocrats under the Knights Hospitaller, who only reluctantly recognised their titles. Amadeo's father had represented the indigenous nobility in the talks which presaged the adherence of Malta to the British Empire. Amadeo was born two years after the *de jure* transfer of sovereignty to Great Britain and had grown up used to the fact that Islamic lands were no longer the perpetual enemy. He was not enthusiastic about his father's intention to article him to the law and enrolled in the studio of a painter who had formed part of the Nazarene movement in Rome. From there he managed to get himself in the 1830s to the Ecole des Beaux Arts in Paris where Daumier and others were adding to the ebullient social froth of the time with sketches of life in the raw. Unable to overcome his father's hostility to a career in art, and fired by the views of Constantinople by two Maltese artists who had travelled to the city, he decided to go to see for himself what he could do.[10]

Land or seascapes were not quite what the increasing number of tourists visiting the Porte wanted. They mostly came, when not for business, to savour the frightening and forbidding world that had menaced them for so long and was now as quiet as a sedated lion. In their discontent with increasingly monochrome societies, they longed for the glamour and glitter of a wholly alien society. Unless they could prevent it, Constantinople was running headlong from its past. It was as if the picture postcards that should have been available of palaces, mosques and gardens were to be replaced by those, on the Soviet model, of practical utilities like factories, office blocks and railway stations. Preziosi, who had experienced the English passion for sketches of Old Malta, saw a market for the presentation of a society that was passing, in all its colourful quaintness and splendour, into western modernity. He set it fairly and squarely, as earlier artists had not, in the context of an everyday life he was able to experience at first hand before it died.

They were not just sketches of dress or uniform that had so seduced Byron but vignettes of real life. Somehow he gained admission to a harem to sketch an odalisque drinking coffee and smoking her *çubuk*, or water pipe, attended by a Nubian slave, and a possibly Circassian girl playing a mandolin. As a non-Muslim he was privileged to sketch so many Muslims who had a religious dislike and a mordant suspicion of portraiture. His rambles took him to all parts of the Great City, and his rapid and unobtrusive sketching made him a familiar sight in its picturesque and steadily disappearing streets. He had come originally to see what Turkey was like and to stay for a couple of years. He lived there until 1882, marrying a Greek woman, and becoming for a time dragoman at the British embassy, and possibly court painter to the Sultan, until he died in a hunting accident at the age of 66. His studio was itself one of the tourist attractions of Constantinople, and by the time he died the Turkish capital had ceased to be 'a sojourn of unwearied and exciting delight', except through the medium of his prolific work.[11]

4

In the theatre, too, the Turk was becoming less tyrant, more pantaloon. In 1813 the Italian Girl went to Algiers. Rossini had already, at the age of 21, written two operas and this, the third, was an *opera buffa*, commissioned by the Teatro di San Benedetto in Venice. He took his plot from a libretto that had already been once set to music. He had only 18 days in which to write the opera and he could not fuss about libretti. It contained just the right ingredients for comedy: a ridiculous suitor, a sparky young woman, a frustrated lover and a wronged wife. What was unusual was that the ridiculous lover was Mustafa, Bey of the fearsome pirate state of Algiers.

Mustafa was tired of his wife, Elvira, and thought it would be nice to have a change, for example one of those Italian girls, who, he had heard, were charming. He would settle his wife on his personal slave, Lindoro, a Christian and the captive lover of a real Italian girl. This was the sparky Isabella, the Italian girl of the title. Captive stories in which the tables are turned on the captor were the staple of contemporary entertainment, an eighteenth-century soap opera in which the tables, having been turned upside down by cultural differences, are downside upped again, proving the ingenuity of the enterprising characters, the Figaros, the Pedrillos, the Blondes, the Isabellas. That, in relation to the Turk, was what Europeans were popularly held to be – enterprising.

Mustafa in Rossini's hands is no Pasha Selim; he is the standard figure of fun, vainglorious, silly and easily gulled. Isabella has been shipwrecked on the Algerian shore in her quest for Lindoro, and as the Bey has instructed his corsair captain to capture him an Italian girl, she is quickly earmarked for the Bey. The humiliation of the fatuous Mustafa, easy meat for a sparky Italian girl, is only part of the story; the rest is the misunderstanding between and the reconciliation of the true lovers. Mustafa's prowess in taming women as if they were racehorses is extolled by a chorus of eunuchs, the least likely of men to understand women, and in fact he is no match for Isabella, who recognises a puffed-up egoist when she sees one. She might agree to have coffee with the Bey, but not sex.

Indeed, the Bey must himself join her secret society of the *pappataci*, the most select society in Italy, whose members must swear not to enquire about what their wives are up to while they enjoy food and drink. Rossini's librettist invented the word from *pappata*, which signified a more than square meal and, in the argot of the time, a fraud. As a *pappatacio* Mustafa will become irresistible to Italian girls. When he has passed through the initiatory ceremony and been stupefied by the food and drink provided, the Italian girl and her lover creep off and sail away to freedom. Mustafa in his infatuation has done what a good Muslim would never do: remove his turban and drink to intoxication. He regrets that he ever meddled with an Italian girl and is reconciled to his wife Elvira, so a happy ending is secured all round.

Algiers was, however, far from being the tamed terrain for Romantic encounters. In 1819, Walter Scott was able to compare the surrounding of a traveller on the high road of Scotland to that 'of a stately merchantman in the Gut of Gibraltar … by three Algerines'.[12] The enslavement of a foolish lover by a soubrette might be a standard enough entertainment for Venetians, but it was an improbability in Algiers. In Rossini's hands, however, it sounded more like a blow for women, and Italian women at that, against male hegemony, typified by the ridiculous Turk and his harem. Rossini was not tilting against Turks but against all men. After all in the final chorus of *L'Italiana in Algeri*, sung by eunuchs, pretty disinterested witnesses:

> La bella Italiana
> Venuta in Algeri,
> Insegna agli amanti
> Gelosi ed alteri,
> Che a tutti, se vuole,
> La donna la fa.

(The Italian beauty when she came to Algiers gives jealous and self important lovers a lesson that a woman, when she wants to, can outdo them all.)

Outwitting a Turk, and reminding him of the faith he owed a wife, mocked and minimised the whole apparatus of terror with which the North African pirates had menaced Europe. The Venetians had enough experience of the Abominable Turk to know that jokes are far from reality but, safely ensconced within the Austrian empire by 1798, they were confident that he was now on the retreat. Yet the Massacre of Chios was only eight years off.

The Italians were delighted with the 21-year-old Rossini's trivialisation of the dreadful, and he was persuaded to write another Turkish tale for Milan in 1814. When *Il Turco* came *in Italia*, he was already a stock character for *opera buffa*. Rossini hoped by reversing the destinations of the principals to repeat the success of *L'Italiana in Algeri*, but the Milanese were not impressed, probably because they thought they were being cheated of a new and original plot. The ambivalent Turk, Prince Selim (no relation to Mozart's Pasha Selim), is not sure whether he wants to be taken for a prince or just an amorous tourist, but when he comes ashore near Naples – just dropped off without bag or baggage – he has already, on an earlier visit, met one of the characters. She is in this case a wronged lover, not a wife. Zaida, the gipsy girl, having loved and supposed herself to be loved by the Prince, has been cast off as amorously unfaithful, as well as an infidel.

Where this earlier liaison had taken place is not important, for the cosmopolitan character of Naples had rendered Turks, and Moors, a regular sight. Selim, in the words of the perennial tourist, greets Italy, where 'l'aria, il suolo, i fiori e l'onde / Tutto ride e parla al cor' ('The air the land, the flowers, the sea, all laugh in wooing the heart'). And as if to prove his words true he meets a lonely beauty on the seashore. The amiable prince has come for a good time, and since he is so amiable he and the lonely beauty (Fiorilla, a bored housewife) hit it off at once. Keeping pace with the Rossini score that never draws breath, they go off immediately to have coffee when Fiorilla asks Selim how many women he has in his harem. Can it be true that the amiable Turk has really only loved one woman before he met Fiorilla? She is cautious:

> Siete Turchi, non vi credo:
> Cento donne intorno avete:
> Le comprate e le vendete,
> Quando spento è in voi l'ardor.

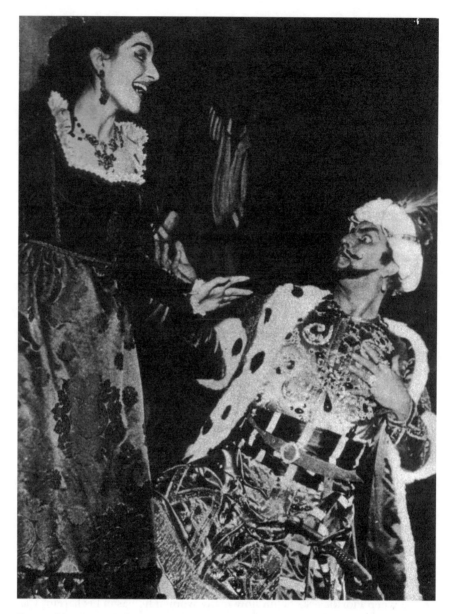

FIGURE 11   *Maria Callas as Fiorilla and Nicolai Rossi-Lemeni as Selim in the 1955 revival of Rossini's* Il Turco in Italia *at La Scala, 150 years after its disappointing first night.*

(You're a Turk and I don't believe you. You have a hundred women round you, and when your ardour dims, you sell them and buy others.)

From that moment the opera descends into farce. The Turk, going to the beach for a rendezvous with Fiorilla — he seems well able to wander round unnoticed – meets his former gipsy love and with the arrival of Fiorilla, and the other characters of the opera, the first act ends in a jealous spat.

The librettist then makes play with the supposedly different marital customs of Turks and Italians. When Turkish husbands get tired of their wives they sell them. If Fiorilla has been married six years already, her jealous husband should be ready to enter into negotiations. The Turk will pay for Fiorilla enough to buy three more wives. If her husband won't sell her, then the amiable Turk will kidnap her. Needless to say the kidnap fails and Selim finds himself partnered with his former love and, after an eventful day, sails off contentedly with her to wherever he originally came from. The matrimonial tangle – Fiorilla has another, non-Turkish, admirer – could have been set anywhere from John o'Groats to Gibraltar, but Rossini, as in *L'Italiana in Algeri*, was mocking the random affections of men. He pairs off the man, who had a legal right to enjoy many women, and the husband, who has a right to only one, with the proper women at the end. Both Zaida and Fiorilla will no doubt live unfaithfully ever after, and the abominable Turk had been revealed as, if amatory, also amiable.

5

So too, according to Pierre Loti, had the enslaved Turkish woman. In 1876, Pierre Loti was part of the international fleet that tied up at Salonika, then part of the Ottoman empire, to exact reparations from the Porte for the incautious assassination by a hothead of two consuls. Going ashore, disguised, as far as possible, with the help of two Jewesses as an Albanian, he sallied forth to try the nightlife. This was the genesis of a Turkish love story that appeared, under suitable disguise, as a novel in 1877. *Aziyadé* was a *Così fan Tutte* in reverse. As an Albanian Loti has attracted the attentions of a harem wife, who watches him through the bars, not lattice, of her window. With the help of go-betweens he is able to enjoy a short but passionate idyll with the Circassian, legal fourth wife of an elderly effendi.

In his own words he seemed to confirm all the legends of the Orient. Sophisticated Turkish women held fidelity to their husbands pretty cheap. If anything deterred them from liaisons it was the fear of savage punishment. So it was hardly surprising that these warm-blooded, sexually aroused women, bored by monotony and solitude, were ready for an adventure and none too choosy about with whom they enjoyed it.[13] Loti, however, was a true Romantic. At the end of this, his first novel, Aziyade is denounced and punished by the fate which attended all who broke harem rule, and Loti in his novelettish disguise prostrates himself upon her grave. No one is quite sure whether the novel was strictly autobiographical. To disarm Turkish anger at the violation of the harem, Loti considered depicting the love affair as between a man and boy – but if Turkish taste may have accepted this, French would not. That Loti had a passionate affair with a woman is borne out by the prominent appearance of one Hakidjé in his journal.[14]

The Ottoman government was not unduly worried by Loti's impertinence about established customs, for the number of his books about and love for Turkey, as well as his being admitted to the *Académie Française*, made him a prominent cultural ambassador, worthy of a select, male-only dinner, offered in the Topkapi seraglio, and hosted in one of his favourite kiosks by the Sultan himself. In 1894 Loti took extended leave from the French navy to return to the Islamic world, which was the source of most of his fantasies. He went to Constantinople from Cairo via Jerusalem and Damascus, first as a pilgrim to the holy city, then as a *dévot* to the city which still radiated the cultural riches of the medieval caliphs. Unlike Byron, who wanted to but did not, Loti did become a tent dweller for a time as he journeyed over a desert covered with small blue flowers which reminded him of the pilgrimage the Queen of Sheba made to Solomon. But the further he travelled the more he became aware that he was not a man of the tents, tormented by djinns and winds, as he turned towards Mecca five times a day in simple faith. The faith to which he was so strongly attracted was more easily imagined in stone houses, as he contemplated the trees and streams and the products of the rich soil that made Arabic pastoral poetry so seductive. Back in France again, Loti set about creating a Turkish asylum near Rochefort on his native soil, in the manner of Lord Leighton.

Loti confirmed European opinions about Turkish women: they may have become sophisticated, musical, well-read and fashionable young women but they were still prisoners, first of the '1320' or traditionally conservative older generation brought up in more restricted times, then imprisoned by the fear of replacement by a younger, more nubile wife. Life in the harem might be comfortable, tasteful and femininely sociable, but it was monocular. Loti's *Désenchantées* was a timeless yet contemporary tale of assignations and frustrated ambition, in which 'the despotism of our masters' could change life unilaterally by a decision on marriage. 'The matter was settled in family council. The executioner is chosen, … a handsome man with hard eyes, whom they condescended to point out to me one day below my window, so there will be no delay.'[15] Loti's heroine decides to die rather then be forced 'into the embracing arms of the master'. Loti acknowledges that she has been 'killed by the West who would not leave her ignorant, primitive, if lovely', but regrets that death is the price of liberation.[16] The Turk needed to become more amiable yet.

6

If joining a harem seemed ignominious to most western women, ruling as undisputed queen of a Muslim household was not an unattractive prospect. Was this because women began to be more openly aware of their sexual needs or because the Abominable Turk was evolving from Amiable to Adorable? Though Lady Mary Wortley Montagu met one western woman who lived happily in the Turk's embrace, she noted that that particular bride had driven a hard bargain. She alone would be wife. There would be no other wives, no concubines. Such a choice was not open to most women who found themselves victims, enslaved in war or sold into captivity. Elizabeth Marsh, who refused the advances of the ruler of Morocco, did so on the grounds – actually spurious – that she was married already and she could not share her affections with another man. However attractive the prince might be, he already had a household of women bedfellows and this was culturally unacceptable. Western women who read the account of her captivity expected wives not to have to live in a state of polygamy.

Western women felt most strongly about polygamy. Lady Hester Stanhope – niece, companion and both private and social secretary to her uncle, first chancellor and then first lord of the treasury, the unmarried younger William Pitt – nearly married but in the end decided that she preferred the independence of the single state. Deprived after Pitt's death in 1806 of her central position in the high politics of Torydom, she deserted the otherwise vapid social scene of London, which she had amused by her wit and annoyed by her satire, and buried herself in Wales. Not having the earthy interests of a George Borrow, she decided to indulge a 'longing for the East, very commonly felt by proud people when goaded by sorrow'.[17] Her brother was going to Gibraltar to join his regiment, and she would go with him and, if the fancy took her, on to beyond.

On her arrival in Constantinople her independent and unconventional manners aroused consternation in the British ambassador, the 24-year-old Stratford Canning. She was travelling in the company of a younger man, clearly her lover, and a personal physician who, if not already her lover, was clearly in love with her. This made her socially unacceptable but Lady Hester quickly decided that, as Canning had no social connections among the Turks, she would establish them, and not just with the women of the harem, but with men of affairs. What she discovered, contrary to polite belief, was that Turkish men were courteous and interesting and the women, far from feeling like prisoners in their own houses, enjoyed life in the harem and were tolerably contented. Lady Mary Wortley Montagu was right after all.

Lady Hester's habit of dressing like a Turkish man upset the European community, if it spared her undue attention as she rode round the city astride her horse. It also caused a host of naked women to flee like chattering magpies at her entrance into the women's baths. But she managed to carry out an inspection, admittedly in male costume, of an Ottoman man of war, and was politely ignored when she failed to dismount and grovel as the Sultan's cortège proceeded to the mosque.[18] It was not surprising that someone who so clearly enjoyed the protection of the highest authorities in both London and Constantinople should be unmolested, but in her turn she did not affront Turkish custom. Her proud indifference to it evoked a public respect. Lady Hester, so agreeably surprised at the charm and beauty of the women of the harem, found it hard to understand why so many of those men who could enjoy their company seemed to profess a preference for dancing boys. Her very manliness may have evoked dreams among them of pederasty.

By this time she was tiring of her lover, Michael Bruce, son of a successful East India Company merchant who indulged his son's aristocratic tastes in women generously, and they set off as a semi-attached couple in search of the sun and amorous adventure, first in Egypt, where Lady Hester captivated the *arriviste* Mehemet Ali, and then to the Holy Land. Her dress grew exaggeratedly Arab but she allowed no one to take advantage of her. The roving Bedouin and skirmishing Arab clans knew that she travelled with firmans from authorities who could, if they chose, have taken savage measures to expunge any offence. She set up house in Damascus, just as Bruce's father was in financial straits and was uncomfortable with his son's failure to get married, and as the couple grew further apart Lady Hester felt the attraction of being a solitary and powerful woman in a male society.

Her power lay rather in her intrepid nerve and her proud bearing, as well as the mystique of her powerful, perhaps royal, connections. She moved as if protected by an aura of invulnerability, and though she placed herself in positions that invited insult, she was never insulted. Her horsewomanship woke the admiration and envy of the legendary Bedouin horsemen, and when she decided to go as the first woman to explore the deserted city of Palmyra, whose Graeco-Arab queen had defied Rome, the untamed inhabitants turned out to applaud her and provide a costume welcome, which included a mock attack and repulse, that would have satisfied Hollywood. By now, the lure of a society where she could shine as a queen without responsibility had become irresistible. She released Bruce to go to see his dying father and to philander thereafter through a very undistinguished life, while she wrapped herself in a vague and solipsistic mantle of pretended magic and religious seclusion. Her tent was finally pitched among the Druses of Lebanon, and she established her command of a motley gang of Muslims by her courage in breaking unruly horses for the Bedouin. Alexander Kinglake wondered how much the exploits of Sir Sidney Smith in thwarting Napoleon, the universal conqueror, at Acre had contributed to the local belief that she might be a royal princess preparing for an English take-over of the area.

7

The Queen of the Desert lived in a former fortified convent, protected from intruders of all kinds including western travellers by a female companion, by an orientalised Italian physician, who believed strongly in her supernatural powers, and by a company of Albanians who ensured local respect for their self-appointed monarch by the exercise of their national ferocity. Mehemet Ali had reputedly ordered Ibrahim Pasha to get rid of the Albanians, but on being invited by Lady Hester to 'come and take them' he had decided not to risk being worsted by a woman. She was said to have caused the Pasha of Egypt more trouble than all the insurgent people of Syria and Palestine.

Lady Hester's neutrality or indifference was important to the virtual viceroy of the Levant and son of her former admirer Mehemet Ali, Ibrahim Pasha, who was planning in 1832 to wrest Syria from Ottoman control. She acquired the sobriquet of a prophet, as she dabbled in astrology and syncretic religion behind an imperious independence. The Messiah was yet to come, and though she never claimed that heavenly role for herself, she was not above insinuating that she had a special relationship with the Divine. Kinglake, by claiming the prophetess's previous acquaintance with his mother, secured admission to her house at Djoun, a few miles from Sidon, and found her 'a good business-like, practical Prophetess, long used to the exercise of her sacred calling', wearing a very large turban and a mass of white linen more like a surplice than anything else resembling female attire. After the exchange of memories, Lady Hester launched into her prophetic discourse for several hours, ending by promising to induct Kinglake into occult science. 'Vain and false', she held, 'is the pretended knowledge of the Europeans' and, eschewing newspapers and books, she passed the nights in communion with the stars. She claimed, in the spirit of Vathek's mother, to command the arts of the sorceress, but any demonstrations of magic would be 'derogatory to her high rank in the heavenly kingdom'. Her protector and ally, Ibrahim Pasha, she claimed, was a fellow adept who had secured immunity from sword and bullets by magical arts!

Lady Hester was a figure of Romance but not a Romantic. She despised Lord Byron who gave 'orders to his Greek servant in *un ton d'apameibomenos* [*sic*]' and in a 'curious coxcombical lisp'. She hated dandyism in all its forms so that the French poet Lamartine, like Byron, incurred her ferocious contempt, and she displayed in all her conversation 'a sober, patient and minute attention to the details of vituperation' which no doubt contributed to her solipsistic manner of life. Eccentric, even slightly mad, Lady Hester may have been, but Kinglake accepted that the intellectual regime of the Levant was much conditioned by belief in the power of magic, from which even the western mind is not immune. Magicians, even today, wear oriental headgear to demonstrate that their powers of legerdemain and trickery are oriental, and the careers of Madame Blavatsky and Annie Besant in India are witness to 'the powers of self delusion over an otherwise sane and practical mind'.

8

Lady Hester made it possible for others to follow and for another lioness of Georgian society, Jane Digby, to make the progression from society wife to Sheikly paramour. Jane Digby, like Elizabeth Marsh, even Lady Hester herself, had no intention of becoming one woman in any, Christian or Muslim, household. Her notorious career encompassed all the ambiguities of an occidental woman accepting an oriental man used to different marriage arrangements. She could cohabit, even marry in a legally, binding, almost Christian manner, but she could not share a man. Altogether she enjoyed the sexual favours of at least seven lovers, in what she imagined were monogamous conditions, four of whom became husbands. From only one did she secure conjugal fidelity, but fidelity, though temporarily important to her while the romantic passion was mutual, was dispensable. When, however, she married her last lover when he was about 30 and she was approaching 50, she insisted on his divorcing his wife, so that there would be no rival in the household. Was this Christian acculturation or the exercise of feminine independence? For Jane had become by inheritance and legal settlements a very rich woman, with the complete disposal of her wealth. Though she lavished this on husbands and lovers while they were husbands and lovers, she guarded her rights tenaciously. When one of her Greek lovers, a bandit turned condottiere, purloined her jewellery she was indefatigable in retrieving it.

Jane Digby kept a journal and filled sketchbooks, and she kept a record as she progressed from young wife of a serial adulterer (Lord Ellenborough), to lover of an Austrian prince and diplomat (Felix Schwarzenberg), to putative mistress of a King (Ludwig I of Bavaria), to wife of a German and indisputably faithful baron, to wife of a Greek adventurer, to lover of a Greek bandit leader 'turned' patriot, to mistress of the leader of a Syrian caravan and, finally, to wife of a Bedouin sheikh, in which state she lived and died. Was Jane Digby predator or the predator's victim? Her beauty, which kept her sexually attractive and active until late in life, and her generosity both of spirit and of wealth made her, even in the sexually closing world of Victorian England, almost forgivable. The men she chose, with one exception, were undoubtedly sexual predators, but the only woman who seemed actively to turn against her was the wife of King Ludwig's son, King Otho, First of the Hellenes, and she was jealous of Jane Digby's social rather than her sexual glamour.

The enduring appeal of Jane today, in a world sated, almost bored by sexual licence, is the manner in which she bridged the cultural gap between West and East. Her family and religious roots – she was the daughter of an Admiral and scion of a hereditarily noble family – required monogamy not polygamy for reasons of pride rather than preference. In making herself at home voluntarily and happily in what Lesley Blanch has called *The Wilder Shores of Love*, she satisfied the Romantic longing for space and freedom that had tormented Byron. She had no missionary inclinations as had so many women at the time, and she never became a Muslim. She was not a coloniser for she always moved on. She chose the desert life of discomfort and danger when it had a destination, Palmyra or Jerusalem, but the houses she built in different places were notable for their taste and comfort. They provided suitable havens in her quest for travel and stimulation. Not for her the seclusion of the harem. Indeed, she had total contempt for this institution. 'What a melancholy sight are these harems, and the poor wives. ... What a total waste of the mind. Every thought concerned on dress or the means of pleasing – not a husband, or even a lover – but a cold selfish master at most.'[19] In that respect she was neither an orientalist nor a cultural synthesiser, but a perpetual tourist.

There were many valiant and powerful women in Islamic society, the despotism of the man in his world being matched by the woman's despotism in hers, but few if any could at once be obedient wife and free spirit in the way that Jane Digby was. Both Hester Stanhope and she reconciled the questing, intelligent freedom of the European female with the acceptance of a culture of protection and a society in which things were managed under different rules. They did not seek to change either; they just did not accept that the rules applied to them. They assumed Arab dress and the veil as a prudent as well as polite gesture, but they did not hood their minds or hide their femininity.[20] They became icons for a liberation that the increasing occidentalisation of the world was going to impose on Islam, a liberation that continues to divide the Muslim world and has been identified with progress. Hester Stanhope and Jane Digby carried off their oriental lives with the panache both of a born adventuress and of a born aristocrat, qualities that made it difficult for many women to emulate them.

CHAPTER 15

Playing on Dulcimers

The Myth of Nostalgia

> You may be familiar with the great Afreet, who was going
> to execute the travellers for killing his son with a date
> stone. Morgiana, when she kills the forty robbers with
> boiling oil, does not seem to hurt them in the least; and
> though King Schabriar makes a practice of cutting off his
> wives' heads, yet you fancy they have got them on again
> in some of the back rooms of the palace where
> they are dancing and playing on dulcimers.
> (Thackeray, *From Cornhill to Grand Cairo*)[1]

I

WHEN WILLIAM MAKEPEACE THACKERAY published his *Notes of a Journey from Cornhill to Grand Cairo* in 1846, he had smelled decay, not the decay of a great society based on a religious and economic tolerance that in many ways had lessons for the more liberal West, but the death of the myth upon which western perceptions had been based. His readers were too clever to require a moral to be tacked to the fables they read, 'else I would tell you that the government of the Ottoman Porte seems to be as rotten, as wrinkled, and as feeble as the old eunuch I saw crawling about it in the sun' at the door leading to where 'none pass through but such as are sent for'. He had seen a woman drive up in a brougham to the Sultan Ahmet mosque; was this a knell, tolling for the Turkish dominion? The palace of the seraglio was no more than faded, gilded wood, 'its guards were shabby, the foolish perspectives painted on the walls half cracked off'. It resembled Vauxhall Gardens in the daytime.

In that barbarous edifice of wood and marble, he had passed a long row of barred and filigreed windows looking on the water and was curious about 'the wondrous beauties singing to their dulcimers, paddling in the fountains, dancing in the marble hall, or lolling on the golden cushions as the gaudy black slaves brought pipes and coffee'. But beneath it was the trap door of which he had been told and underneath one could see the Bosphorus running 'into which some luckless beauty is plunged occasionally, and the trap door is shut and the dancing and singing and the smoking and laughing go on as before'. It might be death for anyone on the water to pick up a stray sack floating innocently by, though it was true he had seen none, at least on the surface. And presiding over it all was the Padishah or Father of all Sovereigns on Earth, who looked like a young French roué worn out by debauch, in which 'his mother and his ministers conspire to keep him … that they may govern the kingdom according to their own fancies'.[2]

Thackeray was not romantic about travel. It was memorable only for its discomforts and absurdities. Nor had he any Romantic attachment to ancient Greece, of which his recollection was the same as that for castor oil.[3] He professed delight at the *Arabian Nights Entertainments* of which he was reminded as he landed at Smyrna. How fresh, easy and good-natured, how entertaining it all was! How delightful the notion about knowledge, 'where the height of science was made to consist in the answering of riddles! and all the mathematicians and magicians bring their great beards to bear on a conundrum!'[4] He did not share Byron's view of the East; it would be just absurd if Byron's view of the Turk was accepted as the model. A Londoner was not a spittoon for true believers, who drank champagne, wore French watches, and of whom, though dressed in scarlet and covered all over with daggers and pistols, the only sign of their legendary ferocious vitality was beating any infidel attempting to enter a mosque.

Thackeray's clubland nonchalance did not conceal his sense of superiority. Turks were a sham, Jews greasy, Arabs doltish, Armenians sly and Greeks shifty. He was not above laughing at himself and the posse of fellow travellers, a caravan of tourists as absurd in themselves as the people among whom he was travelling. They had visited Malta and Rhodes, where he admired 'noble escutcheons of superb knights who lived there and prayed, and quarrelled and murdered the Turks, and were the most gallant pirates of the inland seas and made vows of chastity; and robbed and ravished; and, professing humility, would admit none but nobility into their order; and died recommending themselves to sweet St John, and calmly hoping for heaven in consideration of all the heathen they had slain.' As for the crusades, his sympathy had always been for the Turks; he found Saladin 'a pearl of refinement' and thought Walter Scott had led the world astray about 'brutal, beef-eating Richard'.[5]

2

Cornhill to Grand Cairo was not a voyage in pursuit of ancient Greece or Rome, nor an exposé of cruel and despotic Ottomans, nor a panegyric of suffering ethnic minorities nor even a guide book. It was the chronicle of a visit to the convalescence ward of the sick man of Europe. The Romantic view of Islam had not died its natural death when Turkey joined the embrace of the Congress of Europe, and the Ottoman empire became open to tourists. Europeans, even Russians, had experienced Ottomans as allies against France, in Egypt, in the Holy Land, in the Adriatic and in Naples, where they had shared military command with the Russians. It was enough to shake the Ottoman certainties about infidels, as well as Europe's certainties about the Ottomans. Geopolitical priorities replaced questions of faith and liberty as the Ottoman empire entered the shifting world of alliances, and 40 years after the Napoleonic wars the Ottomans were leagued with some of her new allies and erstwhile foes against Russia in the Crimean War, whose causes were, like all wars, a mixture of national interests and illusion.

For a time in the later century they shook off the embrace of Europe, but not of the British, whose foreign policy was largely determined by fear for the integrity of India, when the Ottomans tried to defend their interests in Bulgaria by a reversion to the earlier policy of frightfulness. European international politics was dominated by the Eastern Problem, or how to ensure that the Ottoman empire did not break into successor states which would admit either Austria or Russia as protectors and leave the eastern approaches to Asia and the subcontinent open to dangerous rivals.

3

The memory of the Greek War of Independence and the Bulgarian atrocities seemed in the popular mind to prove that the Ottoman beast had not changed its pelt, but in the political mind western Europe was faced with a different threat. Britain's interest in India, and France's in the Levant and North Africa brought them both into an alliance with the Ottomans against Russia in 1854, but when Russia lined herself against the German empire the old alliances changed. Russia seemed not to have forsaken her Byzantine idea for Constantinople, and neglect from what had once been their now protectors, the French Republic and Britain, drove the Ottomans, led largely by junior military officers who admired efficiency in their pursuit of power, into alliance with Germany in 1914. Gallipoli was the first serious war with Turkey in which the British had engaged and it revived all Turkish fears of the redheaded *giaours* on the shores of the Bosphorus. The unexpected reversal at the hands of troops whose ancestors had annihilated the Hungarians at Mohacs field and besieged Vienna, in its turn revived the old fear that the Ottomans might put themselves at the head of a Holy War and lead India into revolt. A Mahdi, or temporal and spiritual leader with claims to world domination and spiritual control, might be found in Mesopotamian Iraq, who, with Turkish and German assistance, would raise the green banner of the Twelfth Iman, inflame the tribes of the north-west frontier and rouse the spirit of the Indian Mutiny in an all-out religious war.

Clubland, which had become the final home of the men who had administered India and had measured themselves against the Afridis and Waziris, and of Boer War veterans sniffing the air of high adventure in the veldt, now produced its last great Romantic novel of the East. John Buchan in the person of Richard Hannay voiced the ancient nostalgia for what was gone as he viewed Constantinople: 'I don't quite know what I had expected – a sort of Fairyland Eastern city, all white marble and blue water, and stately Turks in surplices, and veiled houris, and roses and nightingales ... and sweet music.'[6] What he claimed to have found was a land of intrigue, plots and vague messianic conspiracies.

The conclusion of that war marked the end of the Ottoman empire, which had been on the retreat for more than a hundred years. It also marked the end of the Ottoman Caliphate, and the emergence of a modern and democratised Turkey under Kemal Ataturk. Constantinople, the heir to Byzantium, turned its historic churches from mosques to museums and the political capital moved to the Anatolian heartland at Ankara, to balance the Greek origins of the old capital by the more ancient Hittite past of the new. The shrouded and sinister Topkapi palace was, with its stupendous views of the three waters, of the Marmora, the Bosphorus and the Golden Horn, turned into a pleasure garden, a parade ground for crowds gaping at a view rendered familiar by celluloid images. Istanbul, adopting its Greenmantle, became a huge film set for the machinations of international criminals and James Bond. The inner city of the Theodosian walls lost its gardens and farms, which were replaced by overcrowded suburbs; the bridge across the water to Galata was crowded by commuters, and its once elegant European quarters were as packed with buildings of indistinction as south London. The emergence of a Turkey in western clothes meant that travellers needed a new empire of the imagination to explore, and they found it in sea and sand. They replaced the lost cities of ancient Greece and Rome as the major attraction.

The Ottoman empire is now one with Nineveh and Tyre, but the echoes of a former grandeur, which once attracted Yeats, are resonant across the waters. They reach to Cyprus, birthplace of Venus, crusader kingdom, home of Othello and uneasy home to two divided peoples. Secular Greeks advertise her attractions by a well-endowed Venerean sublimation lazily splashing her way through limpid waters; secular Turkey by pines and ruined castles framed against snow-topped mountains. Hushed behind the advertiser's jingle are the muted brass and kettledrums of a vanished empire and a sinister army. They grow more sinister still, and loud, as the view stretches across Anatolia into the Arab world, which has escaped from the rule of viziers, pashas and beys, and their brief colonial successors, into a world of secular dictators, backed by complaisant assemblies elected by the murmur of mullahs.

4

These dictators are, to the western imagination, the modern tyrants, whose only restraining leash is the Koran and the Hadith, and the fear of latter-day crusaders. The Kingdom of Jerusalem, now a secular republic, is all that remains of crusader enthusiasm, but it is not a crusader state, for it is dominated not by the cross but by the star of David. One Abrahamic faith is poised against another, the star assuming much the same role in the traditional Muslim mind as the cross. It is not the faith that the Prophet, peace be upon him, but not upon them, decreed as the final revelation. Once the two other Abrahamic faiths were essentially brothers of the book. Now the exemplary tolerance of Islam is being sorely tested.

The Romantics only understood this dimly. Byron saw Christianity not as true faith but as a kind of school of good behaviour, a Christian school being a more suitable place for his bastard daughter than the atheistic care of the Shelleys. Shelley for his part just saw Christianity, indeed all creeds, as the protective ideology of princes, priests and the privileges of power. Byron credited Islam with many of the good points Christians attributed to themselves. Muslim men were good company, courteous, reliable and strictly moral, but once roused they could be as fierce as any Inquisitorial cleric and as ruthless as any crusader. Muslim women as much as Christian could be victims of the world dominated by males. Shelley could not forgive Muslims, any more than he could Christians, for imposing their own forms of tyranny. The struggle for the freedoms to which Greece had taught mankind to aspire, wherever it might be waged, was holy war. He did not see in the Greek liberators whom he met in Pisa the dark chthonic atavisms of the race, and he knew nothing of the passions that made Christian rebellion in her heartland seem a form of licensed terror.

5

The Romantics had a tragic sentiment of life: pleasure could be transient, love fatal, ambition frustrated and causes corrupted. But they were not fatalistic. The human mind was in constant struggle with blind destiny, or implacable gods, but humankind could win. They had learned from their favourite mentors, the Aeschylean and Sophoclean Greeks, that though the decrees of the gods were not lightly defied, defied they had to be. In seventeenth- and eighteenth-century Europe, the Gods were being taught to come down from their machines, placable and often placated. In Mozart's opera *Idomeneo* Neptune finally agrees that Idamante shall be spared a wanton death resulting from a futile vow. Gluck allowed Iphigenia to be reprieved by a last-minute access of sanity on the part of the god to whose implacable decree she was being sacrificed. (Gluck, however, recognised that not only god-like forces were at work in human affairs and produced an alternative version, in which the implacable irrationality of Agamemnon and his men eventually take her life.) Moral dilemmas, and the fatal consequences of the irrational attitudes of men rather than gods, had been the stuff of drama and opera for over a hundred years. This was the *Zeitgeist* of the West and ranged itself against the apparent fatalism of the East, which it had learned from *The Arabian Nights*.

France, which had effectively given *The Nights* to the western world in the early eighteenth century, was in the process of being distracted from religion and the disputes and bloodshed to which it had given rise, by the development of commercial and then colonial interests. The relative ease with which Spain had acquired a whole new empire in the West at a time when her seaboard neighbour, Portugal, was placing factories all over the Far East, moreover, provoked the envy of other European powers. The heavy mark-up on oriental goods charged by the European emporia of Venice and the Hansa ports could be avoided by direct dealing with the suppliers, while the Ottoman military power that had threatened Vienna was being slowly rolled back by advances on both East and West. Merchants no longer felt they had to barter for goods for they could now own the means of production.

For nearly a hundred years, while Holland, France and England were disputing the eastern inheritance, they were deceived enough to consider India as a Muslim land. Early travellers had called her Hindu temples mosques, and her gymnosophists and ascetics lingered in European letters as an indispensable part of the Muslim myth. In the work of William Beckford, Thomas Moore and George Meredith, *giaours*, perceived as djinns, and sorcerers, and thaumaturges of both sexes performed like creatures of pantomime.

6

Despite the long exposure of the East to commercial penetration, Muslim general dislike of the mercantile life meant that in its empires it was left to Jews, Armenians, Greeks and Hindus. Muslim traders may have dominated the carrying trade in eastern seas, but one Indian ruler spoke for others when he said wars by sea were merchants' affairs and of no concern to the prestige of Kings. It was not until the middle of the eighteenth century that a serious attempt was made in the West to understand the Muslim world.[7] It was partly fuelled by missionary attempts at conversion, not of Muslims but of lapsed or recalcitrant Christians. Many of these conversions, in spite of the East India Company's refusal to license missionary activity, were of the Indo-Portuguese Roman Catholics, converted by early Portuguese missionary activity.[8] Conversion in Barbary to Islam and in Malta to Christianity was usually induced by a desire to improve the fate of prisoners of war who faced perpetual slavery.[9]

It was mainly the result of the quest for encyclopaedic knowledge that a grudging interest in the eastern world began to take hold of the western mind. For free-thinkers this took the form of a search for facts and ideas that weakened the hold of traditional Christianity. With Voltaire and the critics of monarchy, they were to provide a vehicle for a satiric attack on their governing institutions. Christians, however, were seeking support for the truth of Biblical history, and for an understanding that would make relations easier with their eastern brethren. Both sought also to facilitate access to the ancient Greek and Roman world outside Europe. But seldom were they searching for a way to understand Islam better. Despite both Beckford's and Moore's use of encyclopedias and travellers' notes to create authenticity, the world that they created owed more to poetry than to fact.

The playwrights of the time saw little to interest them in the Islamic East. The most prolific, such as Metastasio and Alfieri, looked for their subjects in the same lexicon as Racine and Corneille, in the stories of ancient Greece and Rome. They looked east occasionally but it was to the Assyria of Semiramis, 2000 years BCE, to Mithridates VII, King of Pontus, to Xerxes of Parthia and of course to the Old Testament. Before Byron and Rossini, there was little perception that the predestined certainties of Islam might not preclude moral dilemmas, or that Islamic 'tyrants' might question their actions. Moral uncertainty if it existed in the work of the Carlovingian 'Roland poets' – Boiardo (*Orlando Inamorato*, 1486), Pulci (*Morgante Maggiore*, 1494) and Ariosto (*Orlando Furioso*, 1516), as well as the conventional 'Crusader' poet Tasso (*Gerusalemme Liberata*, 1593) – was more related to the time their heroes spent in combating the forces of darkness and magic rather than of Islam. Darkness, magic and Islam may have been synonomous in the common mind, but to the truly Romantic mind they were also absurd.

It was Walter Scott, who delighted in the myths of history and legend, who recognised that there was always a rational explanation for the irrationalities in both. His search for chivalry took him to one great battleground between Christianity and Islam, Malta. For him both crusaders and their opponents were deluded warriors, deluded by their faith, by their commanders or by their own ambitions, not by enchantment. Chivalry was the common bond of all, the Holy Grail itself, of men who wished to act honourably. Sir John Falstaff might end his catechism with the opinion that 'honour is a mere scutcheon' a view almost echoed by Scott's Wilkin Flammock, but Sir Walter clearly thought that although it was a quite irrational impulse it was also what distinguished heroes from villains. Ivanhoe in speeding to champion Rebecca in the unequal combat with Bois-Guilbert acted unreasonably but he had to act honourably. Bois-Guilbert acted rationally in pursuit of his desires, but dishonourably. God (and literary convention) determined who was right. Scott hoped that the spirit of chivalry had survived until 1565 and the Siege of Malta, 30 years before Tasso's *Gerusalemme Liberata*, and 40 before *Don Quixote* were written. By their gentle mockery both had decided that the times of Melec-Ric (Richard I) had gone for ever.

Scott's monarch was George IV, for whom honour was a scutcheon but who loved dressing up when Scott presented him to his Scottish people. Neither lived to see the pageantry of Eglinton, or the revival of a Venerable (and Protestant) order of the Knights of Malta or to see Scott himself canonised as the laureate of England's medieval, Christian and Romantic past.[10] That Scott is little read today marks the irrevocable decline of the influence of his ideal. Honour is indeed a scutcheon, if anyone knows what a scutcheon is.

7

> The Turk and the Arab come out of big spaces, and they have the desire of them in their bones. They settle down and stagnate and by and by they degenerate into that appalling subtlety which is their ruling passion gone crooked. Then comes a new revelation and a great simplifying. They want to live free and face to face with God ... and get back to the noble bareness of the desert.[11]

John Buchan had been private secretary to Lord Milner as High Commissioner in South Africa and imbibed much of the cultural baggage he had acquired in north and south Africa. The desert remains an attraction for the western mind that is besieged by contradictory thoughts and the conundrums of human behaviour, and which admires the simplicity of the life its denizens lead. This mind is rather Bedouin, and it was in the Bedouin lands of Arabia that *wahabism* took root and spread to the mountain deserts of south-east Asia. These were not the lands of the infinite subtleties of Islamic thought and culture which flourished in the Caliphates of Baghdad, Cordoba and Cairo, to which militant Islam does not wish to return today.

If they have their own baggage to shed – Karl Deutsch once likened its stance today to the last rain-dance of the Pawnee Indians, a nostalgia for a simple past of certainties – the West too has its own. The work the Romantics began has not yet finished.

Nostalgia for the past and for the habits of yesteryear affect all religions when under attack. Apart from Shelley, the Romantics on the whole did not attack religion but the role of priests and the power of accumulated authority the sacred texts seemed to give them. Mockery was one of their tools. They applied to Islam as they saw it some of the treatment they gave Christianity, and some succumbed – not to the enticement of religion, but to the seductions of a culture which seemed based on the gratification of pleasure. The end results of this might seem very similar to that promised to Christians – Eblis, hell and damnation – but it all subscribed to their view of the world: perdition might be at the end, but on the way one should enjoy the world. It seemed, from the perspectives of the West, easier for Muslims to do this, if you were a man.

The Romantics left their impress on modernity. They saw the natural world as a possible substitute for God. It had its own laws and was more accessible. It was better to live free of the unreasonable restrictions of authority, as receivers of the Promethean fire. Life might be tragic and the quest for freedom might often lead to death, but Romantic, even Byronic death was preferable to prostration; submission was servile; duty to neighbour was the more important divine commandment than duty to God. Disraeli had a dream that the three Abrahamic faiths had so much in common that united they would be irresistible, but united round what? The emancipation of women, and decision by the democratic interplay of a parliament, or by the consensus of a synod or *ulema*?

The current crisis of the world of the Abrahamic faiths may have more to do with land and the future of oil than the past messages of pontiffs and prophets; but their idealism is used to protect the past rather than the future. Romanticism strove to find a language that expressed the hopes of the future for people murmuring against the certainties of their history: emancipation for Greeks, Italians, women, children, the under-privileged and the human spirit generally. The causes have not changed if the nations have, so the tension between the past and the future remains the great debate of humankind. Once the crusades were called the Great Debate, and in the sense that this is between ideals and aims, they are still being waged. The Romantics were the great identifiers of this debate, which still continues.

Notes to Chapters

Preface

1 *Notes of a Journey from Cornhill to Grand Cairo*, chapter xvi: 'Cairo'.
2 Byron, *The Bride of Abydos*, 1813, canto 1 stanza 1.
3 The poems referred to as the *Turkish Tales* of Byron are *The Giaour* (1813), *The Bride of Abydos*, (1813), *The Corsair* (1814) and *The Siege of Corinth* (1816), all written and published separately.
4 Anderson, *Letters of Mozart*: Wolfgang to von Hefner, 15 September 1773.
5 In 2009, this matter is not decided and rumbles on, Islamists claiming that Allah can only refer to the God of Islam and to use it as referring to the god of other faiths is demeaning to Islam.

Chapter 1 The Empire of Osman

1 Lewis, 'Monarchy in the Middle East' in *From Babel to Dragomans*, p. 84.
2 Faroqhi, *Subjects*, pp. 225–6.
3 Keats, *The Eve of St Agnes*, stanza xxx.
4 Kinglake, 'Turkish Travelling', in *Eothen*, chapter 2.
5 Crawley, NCMH ix, p. 528.
6 Montagu, *Letters*, p. 113. Letter to Countess of Bristol, 1 April 1717.
7 De Quincey, 'Modern Superstition' in *The English Mail-coach*, p. 249.
8 Mansel, *Constantinople*, p. 258.
9 Cavaliero, *Crusaders*, pp. 138–9.
10 Clogg, *Concise History*, pp. 21–3.
11 Fletcher, *Cross and the Crescent*, pp. 151–3.

12 Lewis, 'Islam and the West' in *From Babel to Dragomans*, p. 114.

13 Hourani, *Arab Peoples*, p. 259.

14 Lewis, *From Babel to Dragomans*, p. 114.

15 Kinglake, 'The Desert' in *Eothen*, chapter 17.

16 Kinglake, 'Cyprus' in *Eothen*, chapter 7.

17 Kinglake, 'Terra Santa' in *Eothen*, chapter 11.

18 Herold, *Bonaparte in Egypt*, p. 74.

19 Sitwell, *Arabesques and Honeycombs* (1957), p. 194.

20 Herold, *Bonaparte in Egypt*, p. 175.

21 Irwin, *For Lust of Knowing*, chaps 4 and 5.

22 The translation is Dorothy L. Sayers's of 1949, canto xxviii, lines 22–7.

23 Michel Belon, *Les Observations de plusieurs singularités et mémorables*, 1554, book 3 chapter 10, quoted in Grosrichard, *The Sultan's Court*, p. 101.

24 Milton, *White Gold*, pp. 162–7.

25 Gibbon, *Decline and Fall*, vol vi, chapter 58.

26 Sharafuddin, *Islam and Romantic Orientalism*, p. xxii.

27 Grosrichard, *The Sultan's Court*, pp. 88–9. The quotation is from Jean Chardin, *Voyages en Perse*, London 1686, Amsterdam 1711. The reference is to the Amsterdam edition, vol. 2, p. 207.

28 Grosrichard, *The Sultan's Court*, pp. 85–98, quotes extensively from seventeenth- and eighteenth-century travellers in support of this widely held opinion.

29 Sharafuddin, *Islam and Romantic Orientalism*, p. 67, claims that nearly all orientalists' sources, from d'Herbelot's *Bibliothèque Orientale* (1697) to the Reverend Henley's notes on his translation of Beckford's *Vathek* (1786), repeat stories that centre on oriental tyranny of one kind or another.

Chapter 2 The Sultan in his Seraglio

1 Byron, *Don Juan*, canto 5, stanza 153.

2 Valensi, *Venice and the Sublime Porte*, pp. 31–44.

3 Valensi, *Venice and the Sublime Porte*, p. 75.

4 G. Thévenot, *Voyages en Asie et en Afrique*, Paris, 1989 and Jean Dumont, *Nouveau voyage du Levant*, Hague 1694, both quoted in Grossrichard, *The Sultan's Court*, pp. 57–8.

5   Grossrichard, *The Sultan's Court*, p. 32, quoting Voltaire, Commentary on Montesquieu's *L'Esprit des Lois*, *Oeuvres*, vol. 30, p. 409.

6   Morier, *Hajji Baba in England*, chapter 19. Morier wrote in this case of Persian as well as Turkish practice which he had observed at first hand.

7   Morier, *Hajji Baba in England*, chapter 20.

8   Byron, *Childe Harold's Pilgrimage*, canto 2, stanza 38, lines 6–8.

9   Byron, *Childe Harold's Pilgrimage*, canto 2, stanza 47, lines 1–3.

10 Byron, *Letters and Journals*, vol. 3, pp. 110–12: letters to Lady Melbourne and Thomas Moore, 7 and 8 September 1813.

11 Leake, *Travels*, i, p. 38.

12 Leake, *Travels*, iii, p. 259, quoting Pasha Ali.

13 Leake, *Travels*, i, p. 53.

14 Marandi, 'Byron's Infidel', p. 135.

15 Byron, *Childe Harold*, stanza 67, lines 7–9.

16 Morier, *Journey through Persia*, p. 325. The 'cap of terror' is in Byron, *Childe Harold*, canto 2, stanza 58, line 5.

17 Byron, *Childe Harold*, canto 2, stanza 63, lines 7–9. The encounter with Ali Pasha is in *Childe Harold*, canto 2, stanzas 57–66.

18 Captain William Martin Leake, who had been roving the Turkish world in a semi-diplomatic role since 1800, is one of the main sources of information about Ali.

19 Byron, *Childe Harold*, canto 2, stanza 62, line 9. Phyllis Grosskurth in *Byron, The Flawed Angel*, p. 96 has to accept that the homosexual overtone of the meeting between Ali and Byron is speculation, though her overall view of Byron is to suggest that it should not be excluded.

20 Byron's four days with Ali Pasha are described in detail in his *Letters and Journals* vol, I 'In My Hot Youth', in a letter to his mother of 12 November 1809, pp. 226–31.

21 Grossrichard, *The Sultan's Court*, p. 20.

22 Byron, *The Giaour*, note by Byron to line 151.

Chapter 3   *The Harem*

1   Moore, *Lalla Rookh* in *Poetical Works*.

2   Lodewijk, *The Book of Tulips*, pp. 7, 38–9. The painting is by J.B. Vanmour.

3   Loti, *Désenchantées*, chapter 2.

4   Faroqhi, *Subjects*, pp. 102–3; Lewis, *Rethinking Orientalism*, pp. 97–8; Lane, *Modern Egyptians*, pp. 136, 190.

5   Genesis, chapter xxx.

6   Montagu, *Letters*, vol. i, p. 372: letter to Anne Thistlethwayte, 4 January 1718, and an undated letter to the Abbé Conti in February that same year, p. 375.

7   Byron, *Don Juan*, canto 5, stanzas 157–8.

8   Byron, *Don Juan*, canto v, stanza 8.

9   Anderson, *Letters of Mozart*, p. 735. Christophe Bretzner, a Leipzig merchant, wrote *Balmonte und Constanze* in 1780. It was set to music and performed in Berlin in 1781.

10   Dent, *Mozart's Operas*, p. 71.

11   Ballaster, *Fabulous Orients*, pp. 61–70.

12   Anderson, *Letters of Mozart*, p. 735.

13   *The Bride of Mosta*, a popular Maltese folk tale, rendered as a modern ballad by Francis Berry, has recently been published, edited by J. Manduca, Malta, 2005.

14   The tale is Chapter 35 of *Hajji Baba of Ispahan*.

15   *Euphrasia: A Tale of Greece* in Shelley, *Collected Tales*, pp. 295–307.

16   Schoina, 'Empire Politics' in *English and American Perception of Hellenism*.

17   Montagu, *Letters*, vol. i, pp. xiv–xv, from a spurious letter from Lady Mary Montagu to Mr P—, 1 September 1717, printed in the Everyman edition, p. 148. It may have been a travel memoir in the form of a letter.

18   *The Thousand and One Nights*, Introduction.

19   Ferrier, *A Journey to Persia*, p. 139.

20   Morier, *Hajji Baba in England*, chapter 25.

21   Kinglake, 'Cairo & the Plague' in *Eothen*, chapter 18.

22   Montagu, *Letters*, vol. i, pp. 313–14: letter to Lady ———— from Adrianople, 1 April 1717.

23   Montagu, *Letters*, vol. i, pp. 367–8: letter to recipient unidentified, 17 June 1717 O.S.

24   Ballaster, *Fabulous Orients*, pp. 71–2, reads the letter as ironic, disguising a rather more than poetic passion for the recipient.

25   Loti, *Désenchantées*, pp. 75, 80–1.

26   Byron, *Don Juan*, canto 6, stanza 31; Grosrichard, *The Sultan's Court*, pp. 141–2.

27 Morier, *Journey through Persia*, p. 369.

28 Morgan, *Italy*, vol. 3, p. 194. Byron also makes the comparison with 'an Italian convent where all the passions have, alas! but one vent': *Don Juan*, canto 6, stanza 32.

29 Mansel, *Constantinople*, p. 226.

30 Montagu, *Letters*, vol. i, p. 402: letter to the Countess of Bristol, 10 April 1718. Loti, *Désenchantées*, p. 81.

31 Loti, *Désenchantées*, pp. 75, 80–1.

32 Ferrier, *Journey*, p. 74; Morier, *Hajji Baba in Ispahan*, chapter 25.

33 Morier, *Hajji Baba in Ispahan*, chapter 35.

34 MacCarthy, *Byron*, p. 123.

35 Marandi, 'Byron's Infidel', pp. 137–9.

36 Morier, *Hajji Baba in England*, chapter 51.

37 Ferrier, *Journey*, p. 71.

38 Faroqhi, *Subjects*, pp. 99–100.

39 Childs, *Lady Hester Stanhope*, pp. 68–9.

40 Ferrier, *Journey*, pp. 69–70.

41 Blanch, *Sabres of Paradise*.

42 Montagu, *Letters*, vol. i, pp. 408–9: letter to the Countess of ———— ——, May 1718.

43 Montagu, *Letters*, vol. i , pp. 380–1: letter to Lady Mar, 10 March 1718; Ballaster, *Fabulous Orients*, pp. 65–7.

44 Montagu, *Letters*, vol. i, p. 406: letter to the Countess of ————, May 1718.

45 Montagu, *Letters*, vol. i, p. 415: letter to Abbé Conti, 19 May 1718.

Chapter 4 Exotic and Erotic

1 Hazard, *La Crise*, p. 380.

2 According to the Lane version, edited by Stanley Lane-Poole, first published in London in 1906.

3 Warrack, *Carl Maria von Weber*, p. 105.

4 Words of Henry Howard, Earl of Surrey, *The Happy Life*, 1547.

5 S.T. Coleridge, *Table Talk*, 9 May 1830. Plutarch, *Lives*, vol. ii, p. 303.

6 Lane-Poole, *Nights*, vol. iv, p. 305.

7 An international conference was held in Osaka, Japan, in 2002 to mark the first volume published by Galland in 1704. The papers were

published as *The Arabian Nights and Orientalism* (ed. Yuriko Yamanaka and Tetsuo Nishio) in 2006. Many of them were disquisitions on the textual composition of the *Tales*.

8   Lane-Poole, *Nights*, vol. iv, p. 319.

9   Lane's working texts were the Cairo edition of the *Nights* published in 1835 and the Calcutta edition of the first 200 Nights published in 1814–18. A German edition printed in Breslau between 1825 and 1838 took the tales to the 703rd night at the time Lane was translating.

10   A phrase used by Lane's great-nephew, Stanley Lane-Poole, in his Preface to the *Nights*, p. xi.

11   Conant, *Oriental Tale*, p. 239.

12   Bishop Atterbury, friend of Alexander Pope, quoted by Conant, *Oriental Tale*, p. 230.

13   Conant, *Oriental Tale*, p. 230. Her final chapter is a clear account of the various genres in which oriental tales were numerous, and what purposes they served.

14   Conant, *Oriental Tale*, p. xxiv. Pages 30 to 47 describe many of the 'oriental' works translated in the eighteenth century from the French, whose most readable progeny is *Vathek*.

15   Voltaire, *Zadig*, chapter 6.

16   Johnson had, as a young man, translated the French version of Jeronimo Lobo's *A Voyage to Abyssinia*, but *Rasselas* was not intended to be more than a *roman à thèse*. Caraman, *The Lost Empire*, Introduction.

17   Conant, *Oriental Tale*, p. 243.

18   Tennyson, *Recollections of the Arabian Nights*, stanza 13, lines 3–6.

19   Raleigh, *The English Novel*, p. 109.

20   Tennyson, *Arabian Nights*, stanza 1, lines 5–11.

21   Beckford, *Journal*, p. 14.

22   Two other sources, both in Beckford's library, have been traced: *Mogul Tales* in Weber's *Tales of the East*, 3 vols, Edinburgh, 1812, pp. 58ff. *and Adventures of Abdalla, son of Hanif*, Englished by William Hatchett, 1729; Conant, *Oriental Tale*, pp. 38–41.

23   Sharafuddin, *Islam and Romantic Orientalism*, p. xxi.

24   Mavor, *Grand Tour*.

25   McGann, *Lord Byron*, vol. iii, p. 423. Comment on Byron's notes to *The Giaour*.

26   Beckford, *Vathek*, p. 221.

27   Beckford, *Vathek*, p. 231.

28 Isaac de la Peryère's *Preadamitae* appeared in Holland in 1651 supported by Queen Christine of Sweden. It was suppressed in France as being both Calvinistic and heretical, but an English translation was produced in 1656.

29 Williams, *Many Dimensions*.

30 Beckford, *Vathek*, p. 219.

31 Beckford, *Vathek*, p. 277.

32 Beckford, *Vathek*, p. 272.

33 Beckford, *Vathek*, p. 262.

34 Yeats, *Sailing to Byzantium*, iv, 1927.

35 Franci, 'The Myth of the Orient', p. 101.

36 'To make coffee when I want.' Cantata No. 211, the 'Coffee Cantata', from a poem by Picander, 1732.

37 Kinglake, 'Over the Border' in *Eothen*, chapter 1.

38 De Quincey, *Confessions of an English Opium Eater*, p. 241.

Chapter 5 Peri and Prisoner

1 Archives of the Order 1521: Grand-Master of Malta to his envoy in Vienna, 26 April 1765.

2 Casanova, *History*, vol. ii, p. 95. *Le seul complète*, the French version, published by Flammarion from Paris, is more reticent: 'vous devez deviner le ravage que ce spectacle unique et ravissant dut faire sur mon pauvre corps': vol. 1 of the *Mémoires de Jacques Casanova de Seingalt*, Paris, 1930, p. 370.

3 W. S. Landor, *Gebir*, seventh book, lines 90–4.

4 Faroqhi, *The Ottoman Empire*, p. 40.

5 Thomas Pellow left an account of his captivity in Morocco, recently re-told in Milton, *White Gold*.

6 See chapter 3, p. 37–8.

7 *Etat des Royaumes de Barbarie*: letters from a Redemptorist priest, 1700.

8 Casanova, *History*, vol. ii, chapter 4.

9 In Archives of the Order in Malta (AOM), 1464 *Lettere ai vari sovrani del Gran Maestro Perellos*, letter of 13 January 1703, to the Balì Sacchetti. The state of slaves in Barbary and Malta is the subject of many files in the archives of the Order of St John in Malta, especially

AOM 1569, which contains an account by a Redemptorist father, titled *Voyages en Barbarie*, dated 1736, and referring especially to Algiers in 1718.

10 Colley, *Captives*, p. 75 reckons that this was probably a higher figure than the average.

11 Colley, *Captives*, pp. 50 and 95.

12 AOM 1569, *Voyages en Barbarie*.

13 Colley, *Captives*, p. 83, *The Ballad of Lord Bateman*. Other tales of escape are to be found in chapter 4, *The Harem*, pp. 38–9.

14 The most recent and thorough account of slavery in seventeenth- and eighteenth-century Morocco, drawing upon Pellow's account and other surviving letters and documents, is Milton, *White Gold*.

15 Colley, *Captives*, p. 129 quoting William Chetwood's *Voyages and Adventures of Captain Robert Boyle*, 1726, p. 34.

16 Colley, *Captives*, pp. 128–30.

17 See chapter 14, *The Amiable Turk*, pp. 188–91.

18 Cavaliero, *Crusaders*, pp. 81–5, and Cavaliero, 'Decline', p. 224–38.

19 See Bromley, *Corsairs*, pp. 29–42.

Chapter 6 *Virgins Soft as Roses*

1 Byron, *The Bride of Abydos*, canto 1, stanza 1, lines 14–16.

2 Sharafuddin, *Islam and Romantic Orientalism*, pp. 215–16, who lists some of the books he had read.

3 Kinglake, 'The Desert' in *Eothen*, chapter 17.

4 Marandi's essay 'Byron's infidel', if not disproving Byron's stated facts, casts enough doubt on how well he had understood what he had read. Byron was a good observer but not a scholar, and his portrait of the Ottomans in letters and poems displays the talents of a good journalist but reveals that he subscribed to contemporary views on Turkish mores.

5 Sharafuddin, *Islam and Romantic Orientalism*, p. 224, quoting Malcolm Elwin, *Byron's Estranged Wife,* London, 1962.

6 Byron, *The Bride of Abydos*, canto 1, stanza 1, lines 5–6.

7 There were in fact five (*The Giaour, The Bride of Abydos, The Corsair* and *The Siege of Corinth*), but *Lara* (1814) was not set in Ottoman lands and is only considered oriental because of its close similarity to *The Corsair*.

8 Byron, *The Bride of Abydos*, canto 1, stanza 1, lines 15–16.

9   Byron, *The Giaour*, lines 20–1.

10 Quoted in MacCarthy, *Byron*, p. 216.

11 Byron, *The Giaour*, Byron's note no. 4.

12 Byron, *The Giaour*, lines 493–4, 496, 500–1, 506.

13 Byron, *The Giaour*, lines 739–41.

14 Byron, *The Giaour*, lines 493–4, 496, 500–1, 506.

15 Marandi, 'Byron's Infidel', pp. 142, 154.

16 Byron, *The Giaour,* line 554.

17 MacCarthy, *Byron*, p. 111. Later he said it took him a week.

18 Grosskurth, *Byron*, p. 96.

19 Byron, *The Bride of Abydos*, canto 1, stanza 4, lines 87, 97–8.

20 Byron, *The Bride of Abydos*, canto 1, stanza 4, lines 158, 175.

21 Byron, *The Bride of Abydos*, canto 2, stanza 7, line 113. Sharafuddin, *Islam and Romantic Orientalism*, p. 221.

22 Byron, *The Bride of Abydos*, canto 2, stanza 38, lines 692–3. Sharafuddin, *Islam and Romantic Orientalism*, p. 233.

23 Byron, *The Bride of Abydos*, canto 1, stanza 5, lines 151–4.

24 Grosskurth, *Byron*, pp. 183–4.

25 Byron, *The Corsair*, canto 2, stanza 7, lines 264–5.

26 Byron, *The Corsair*, canto 2, stanza 7, lines 265–6, 502.

27 Byron, *The Corsair*, canto 3, stanza 8, line 341.

28 Byron, *The Corsair*, canto 1, stanza 9, lines 224–5.

29 Byron, *The Corsair*, canto 2, stanza 14, lines 480–1.

30 Byron, *Seige of Corinth*, stanza v, lines 9–10.

31 These figures first appeared in Finlay's *History of Greece* in 1856. Sharafuddin, *Islam and Romantic Orientalism*, pp. 223–4.

32 Lines associated with the *Siege of Corinth*, 1813, lines 18–19.

33 Byron, *Seige of Corinth*, stanza iv, lines 15–16, 20.

34 Byron, *Seige of Corinth*, stanza xvi, lines 36–7.

35 MacCarthy, *Byron*, p. 119.

36 Byron, *Siege of Corinth*, stanza 17, lines 485–6.

37 Byron, *Siege of Corinth*, stanza 24, lines 746–50.

38 Byron, *Siege of Corinth*, stanza 33, lines 1077–8. The bomb, of course, is that which was dropped on Hiroshima in 1945.

39 Byron, *Siege of Corinth*, stanza 24, lines 764–6.

40 Sharafuddin, *Islam and Romantic Orientalism*, in his final chapter 'Byron's Turkish Tales' finds them penetrated by Islamic insights that suggested Byron was neither a wholly dispassionate nor a wholly hostile witness.

41   Cochran, *Byron*, p. 76.

42   Byron, *Don Juan*, canto 2, lines 881–5, 898–900, 920–1.

Chapter 7 Ghastly as a Tyrant's Dream

1   P.B. Shelley, *Hellas*, *Works*, Semichorus I, p. 268.

2   De Quincey, 'Modern Superstition', in The English Mail-coach, p. 249.

3   Grimes, 'Censorship, Violence and Political Rhetoric', pp. 98–101.

4   P.B. Shelley, *The Revolt of Islam*, 1817, Preface and Canto 1, stanzas 32 and 34.

5   Holmes, *Shelley the Pursuit*, p. 405.

6   Clogg, *Concise History*, p. 20.

7   P.B. Shelley, *Hellas*, *Works*, Preface, para 3.

8   P.B. Shelley, *Hellas*, chorus set in Constantinople at sunset, *Works*, p. 253.

9   P.B. Shelley, *Hellas*, *Works*, p. 257.

10   P.B. Shelley, *Hellas*, *Works*, p. 261.

11   P.B. Shelley, *Hellas*, *Works*, p. 262.

12   P.B. Shelley, *Hellas*, *Works*, p. 264.

13   P.B. Shelley, *Hellas*, *Works*, p. 268.

14   P.B. Shelley, *Hellas*, *Works*, p. 268.

15   P.B. Shelley, *Hellas*, *Works*, p. 270.

16   Leake, *Travels*, vol. i, p. 14.

17   Leake, *Travels*, vol. i, p. 438.

18   Leake, *Travels*, vol. i, p. 53: observation of 4 January 1805.

19   Leake, *Travels*, vol. i, p. 331: diary entry for 7 September 1805.

20   Lewis, *From Babel to Dragomans*, p. 28.

21   The hatred of Christian for Turk in the Balkans was revived during the Serbian attack on Kosovo in the twentieth century, though the 'Turks' were actually ethnic Serbs, the Albanians of whom Pasha Ali had been one.

22   Delacroix, *Journal*, pp. 22, 29: entries for 24 January, 11 April 1824.

23   Michel, *Massacre*, p. 18.

24   Passeron, *Daumier*, p. 44.

25   Brookner, *Romanticism*, pp. 82–3.

26   Delacroix, *Journal*, p. 39: entry for 11 May 1824.

Chapter 8 Look Upon My Works, Ye Mighty, and Despair

1   P.B. Shelley *Ozymandias*, lines 12–14 (1817).
2   Gibbon, *Decline and Fall*, footnote to chapter 17.
3   Colley, *Captives*, pp. 106–10.
4   Bruce, *Explorers*, p. 102.
5   The 'poet' was John Wolcot (1738–1839), otherwise known as Peter Pindar, in A *Complementary Epistle to James Bruce Esq.*, quoted in Reid, p. 306.
6   Reid, *Traveller Extraordinary*, pp. 304–8.
7   Sharafuddin, *Islam and Romantic Orientalism*, pp. xxv–6.
8   AOM 1563, *French correspondence of G.M. Zondadari*: letter to M le Maire, 25 July 1720.
9   Emanuel Schikaneder, *Die Zauberflöte*, Act 2, 1791.
10 Irwin, *For Lust of Knowing*, p. 133.
11 Irwin, *For Lust of Knowing*, p. 135.
12 Mary Shelley, *Frankenstein*, chapter 13.
13 The original author has been identified as Shaikh Murtada 'd Din (died Cairo, 1202). The French translator was Pierre Vathier. Landor, *Poetical Works*, vol. i, p. 474.
14 Landor wrote of Rose, 'Ah, what avails the sceptred race, / Ah, what the form divine! / What every virtue, every grace! / Rose Aylmer, all were thine.' *Rose Aylmer*, lines 1–4.
15 Landor, *Gebir*, book i, lines 264–5.
16 Landor, *Gebir*, book ii, line 102.
17 Sharafuddin, *Islam and Romantic Orientalism*, pp. 43–115, provides an exhaustive analysis and critique.
18 Sharafuddin, *Islam and Romantic Orientalism*, pp. 106, 112.

Chapter 9 Forty Centuries Look Down on You

1   Napoleon Bonaparte, 21 July 1798.
2   Tyldesley, *Egypt*, p. 47.
3   Herold, *Bonaparte in Egypt*, pp. 27–35, gives details of the more eminent among the members of the Commission.

4 Mayes, *The Great Belzoni*, p. 122, quoting Giovanni Battista Belzoni, who saw Luxor first on 22 July 1820.

5 Tyldesley, *Egypt*, pp. 47–9, among them the Elephantine temple of Amentohep, destroyed in 1822.

6 Herold, *Bonaparte in Egypt*, p. 260

7 Mayes, *The Great Belzoni*, p. 142.

8 The refrain of Tennyson's *Recollections of the Arabian Nights*.

Chapter 10 Barbering and Shaving

1 Robert Graves, 'The Persian Version' in *Poems, 1838–48*.

2 *The Travels of Sir John Chardin into Persia and the East Indies*, volume one containing the author's voyage from Paris to Isfahan, appeared in London in 1686. He corrected a lot of what had appeared in Paris in 1677 in Jean-Baptiste Tavernier's six volumes of his journeys in Turkey, Persia and India.

3 Morier, *Journey through Persia*, p. 273. These words actually reappear in the mouth of the Armenian, Yŭsŭf, in *Hajji Baba in Ispahan*, chapter 37.

4 Morier, *Hajji Baba in Ispahan*, chapters 37 and 74; *Hajji Baba in England*, chapter 3; Chardin in Ferrier, *Journey*, p. 74.

5 Ferrier, *Journey*, p. 78.

6 Ferrier, *Journey*, p. 60.

7 Morier, *Journey through Persia*, p. 215.

8 Ferrier, *Journey*, p. 9.

9 Ferrier, *Journey*, p. 78.

10 Morier, *Journey through Persia*, p. 156.

11 Morier, *Journey through Persia*, p. 157.

12 Moore, *Poetical Works*, Letter vi, in *Twopenny Postbag*, 1813, p. 157.

13 Morier, *Journey through Persia*, pp. 199–222.

14 Morier, *Hajji Baba in Ispahan*, chapter 21.

15 Morier, *Hajji Baba in England*, chapter 35.

16 Morier, *Hajji Baba in England*, chapter 21.

17 George Meredith, 'The Thwackings', *The Shaving of Shagpat*.

18 Williams, *George Meredith*, pp. 36–7.

Chapter 11 *Lalla Rookh and the Lyre of the Oriental Minstrel*

1   Moore, *Lalla Rookh*, in *Poetical Works*, p. 123.

2   Moore, *Irish Melodies*, in *Poetical Works*, p. 343.

3   Fleming, *Byron*, p. 142.

4   Byron, *Letters*, vol. 3, p. 101: letter to Moore, 23 August 1813. Southey's *Thalaba* appeared in 1801 and his *The Curse of Kehama* in 1810. Moore's *Lalla Rookh* did not appear until 1817, and in the meantime Byron produced his three *Turkish Tales* between 1813 and 1814, and *The Siege of Corinth* in 1816.

5   Kelly, *Ireland's Minstrel*, p. 132.

6   Moore, *Lalla Rookh*, in *Poetical Works*, p. 24.

7   Quoted in Kelly, *Ireland's Minstrel*, p. 132.

8   Victor Jacquemont, *Letters from India 1829–32*, trans. C.H. Phillips, London, 1936, quoted by Sharafuddin, *Islam and Romantic Orientalism*, p. 196.

9   Sharafuddin, *Islam and Romantic Orientalism*, p. 136, quoting *The British Review* of 1817, vol. x, p. 22.

10   Moore, *Lalla Rookh*, in *Poetical Works*, p. 15.

11   Moore, *Lalla Rookh*, in *Poetical Works*, p. 49.

12   The Book of Job, 1 verse 7.

13   Moore, *Lalla Rookh*, in *Poetical Works*, p. 15.

14   Moore, *Lalla Rookh*, in *Poetical Works*, p. 47, quoting, in his notes, chapter 83 of Sale's Koran.

15   Moore, *Lalla Rookh*, in *Poetical Works*, p. 8 (and following quote).

16   Sharafuddin's essay 'Thomas Moore's *Lalla Rookh* and the Politics of Irony', chapter 3 of his *Islam and Romantic Orientalism*, pp, 134–213, gives an almost line-by-line analysis of *The Veiled Prophet of Korassan* and *The Fire-Worshippers*, the first and last of the tales of *Lalla Rookh*, to interpret Moore's political position. The point about the *Irish Melodies* is made by Kelly, *Ireland's Minstrel*, p. 135.

17   Sharafuddin, *Islam and Romantic Orientalism*, p. 172, quoting from the ten-volume *Poetical Works*, vol. vi, p. xvi.

18   Moore, *Lalla Rookh*, in *Poetical Works*, pp. 72–3.

19   Moore, *Lalla Rookh*, in *Poetical Works*, pp. 123, 126.

20   Moore, *Lalla Rookh*, in *Poetical Works*, p. 129.

21 Moore, *Lalla Rookh*, in *Poetical Works*, p. 132.
22 Moore, *Lalla Rookh*, in *Poetical Works*, p. 135.
23 See Keats's poem, chapter 1, p. 5 of this book.
24 Moore, *Lalla Rookh*, in *Poetical Works*, pp. 136–8.
25 Moore, *Lalla Rookh*, in *Poetical Works*, p. 106.
26 Byron, *Letters*, vol. 5, pp. 249–50: letter to Moore, 10 July 1817; Kelly, *Ireland's Minstrel*, p. 136.
27 Kelly, *Ireland's Minstrel*, pp. 171–2.

Chapter 12 Scott and the Quest for Chivalry

1   Wilkin Flammock in Scott, *The Betrothed*, chapter 26.
2   Benedict of Peterborough, in Longford (ed.), *Royal Anecdotes*, p. 89.
3   Kinglake, 'Terra Santa', chapter 16 and 'Cairo and the Plague', chapter 18, in *Eothen*.
4   Scott, *Ivanhoe*, chapter 36. An account of the Templar's end is found in Partner, *Murdered Magicians*, part 2.
5   Scott, *Ivanhoe*, chapter 40 (and following quote).
6   Scott, *The Betrothed*, chapter 21.
7   Scott, *The Betrothed*, chapter 21.
8   Scott, *The Talisman*, chapter 11.
9   Scott, *The Talisman*, chapters 5, 12 and 13.
10 Graham Greene, reviewing Cecil B. de Mille's *The Crusades* in *The Spectator*, 20 August 1935 in *The Pleasure Dome*, London, 1972, p. 18.
11 Scott, *Letters*, vol. 12, p. 46: letter to William Laidlaw, 2 February 1832.
12 Sultana, pp. 149–50. Sultana presents the story of *The Siege of Malta* as far as possible in words of Scott rather than of Vertot from whom Scott helped himself liberally.
13 Sultana, p. 156.
14 Sultana, p. 157.
15 Sultana, p. 164.
16 Johnson, *Sir Walter Scott*, vol. ii, p. 1232: Scott to Robert Cadell, 26 January 1832.
17 Scott, *Journal*, 1 December 1831.
18 Sultana, p. 152.
19 Scott, *The Betrothed*, chapter 25.
20 Anstruther, *Knight*, p. 30.

Chapter 13 *Tancred and Eva*

1 Disraeli, *Endymion* (1880) chapter 81.
2 Froude, *The Earl of Beaconsfield*, pp. 42–3.
3 Disraeli, *Tancred*, book 3, chapter 4.
4 Disraeli, *Tancred*, book 6, chapter 2.
5 Disraeli, *Tancred*, book 6, chapter 3.
6 Disraeli, *Tancred*, book 5, chapter 3.
7 Disraeli, *Tancred*, book 3, chapter 7.
8 Kuhn, *Politics of Pleasure*, pp. 225–34, argues at length that this overtly homoerotic friendship arose from the two men being caught in the spell of male friendship, true to their blood, which for semites took precedence over the demands of politics or business.
9 Disraeli, *Tancred*, book 6, chapter 6.

Chapter 14 *Isabella, Hester and Jane*

1 Beckford, *Journal*, 29 December 1788.
2 Gladstone, *The Bulgarian Horrors and the Question of the East*, London 1861, p. 61.
3 Beckford, *Journal*, 22 December 1788, p. 196.
4 Thackeray, *George II* in *The Four Georges*, p. 350.
5 Edgeworth, *Popular Tales*. The quotation is in the last paragraph of the tale. Ballaster, *Fabulous Orients*, p. 372.
6 See chapter 5, p. 77.
7 Beckford, *Journal*, p. 208: 20 January 1788.
8 Casanova, *History*, vol. ii, chapter 4.
9 Brookner, *Romanticism*, p. 103.
10 Llewellyn and Newton, *People and Places*, pp. 5–6. The artists were Giovanni Schranz (1794–1882) and Luigi Brocktorff, both painters of landscapes and seascapes. Both artists had painted the city from the sea. Preziosi hoped to get 'inside' Constantinople.
11 Pardoe, *Beauties of the Bosphorus*, part 1, p. 4.
12 Scott, *The Bride of Lammermoor*, chapter 25.
13 Blanch, *Loti*, p. 123.
14 Blanch, *Loti*, p. 133. His *Journal Intime* was published in Paris in 1925.

15   Loti, *Désenchantées*, pp. 204, 217.

16   Loti, *Désenchantées*, pp. 250, 253.

17   Kinglake, *Eothen*, chapter 8, *Lady Hester Stanhope*. All subsequent references to Kinglake are from the same chapter.

18   Childs, *Lady Hester Stanhope*, pp. 68–9.

19   Jane Digby has attracted many biographers, the most recent of whom is Mary S. Lovell: *A Scandalous Life*, p. 252, quotes her diary of 2 December 1860.

20   Though Jane Digby did adopt womanly dress when travelling without her sheikh.

Chapter 15 *Playing on Dulcimers*

1   Thackeray, *Cornhill to Grand Cairo*, chapter 6: 'Smyrna'.

2   Thackeray, *Cornhill to Grand Cairo*, chapter 7: 'Constantinople'.

3   Thackeray, *Cornhill to Grand Cairo*, chapter 5: 'Athens'.

4   Thackeray, *Cornhill to Grand Cairo*, chapter 6: 'Smyrna'.

5   Thackeray, *Cornhill to Grand Cairo*, chapter 8: 'Rhodes'.

6   Buchan, *Greenmantle*, chapter 10: 'The Garden House of Suliman the Red'.

7   Cavaliero, *Strangers*, p. 3.

8   Cavaliero, *Strangers*, pp. 84–6.

9   *Voyages en Barbarie*, no pagination.

10   Alexander, *Medievalism*, pp. 34–49, examines this in detail in pp. 24–49.

11   Buchan, *Greenmantle*, chapter 15: 'An Embarrassed Toilet'.

Writers, Artists and Composers Mentioned in the Text

Bach, Johann Sebastian (1685–1750), celebrated the spread of the passion for coffee in Europe in the late seventeenth and eighteenth centuries in a Coffee Cantata, *Schweig stille, plaudert nicht*, BWV 211, written between 1732 and 1734.

Beckford, William (1759–1844). Heir to the fortune of a Lord Mayor of London, Beckford lived for a time in Switzerland, where he wrote *Vathek* anonymously, in French. It was translated with learned footnotes by Samuel Henley (qv) and appeared in English in 1786. Beckford claimed authorship. He only met real Muslims while they were on embassies to Spain and Portugal, which encounters are described in his *Journal* between 1787 and 1788 (published in 1954).

Belzoni, Giovanni Battista (1778–1823). Paduan circus strong man, who on coming to England trained as a hydraulic engineer and went to Egypt where he became an inspired explorer and collector for the British Museum. In 1821, he produced his *Narration of the Operations and Recent Discoveries ... in Egypt and Nubia*, followed by an exhibition of Egyptian antiquities.

Bruce, James (1730–94). Scottish laird and traveller, he wrote *Travels to the Source of the Nile* (published in 1790). He had been appointed consul in Algiers and had explored the north African littoral. But when he went to find the source of the Nile he bypassed Egypt, travelling as a *hakim* or medicine man, and his account of Ethiopia (Abyssinia), though accused of being full of tall stories, proved a suitable corrective to Johnson's (qv) *Rasselas*.

Burckhardt, Johann-Ludwig (1784–1817). Swiss Arabist and traveller, who rediscovered Petra and whose *Travels in Nubia* (1819) inspired Belzoni (qv) to make more substantial discoveries in lower Egypt.

Burton, Richard (1841–96), had visited Mecca disguised and undiscovered, and paraded himself as an expert in Islamic lore. In his unexpurgated version of *The Arabian Nights* he tried to put back the sex that Edward Lane (qv) had removed to spare maidenly blushes.

Byron, George Gordon, Lord (1788–1824), visited the Ottoman empire, mainly Greece, from 1809 to 1811, which experience appeared in *Childe Harold*. From his time there, he wrote what are called his *Turkish Tales*: *The Giaour* and *The Bride of Abydos* (1813), *The Corsair* (1814) and *The Siege of Corinth* (1816). Ottoman lands figure in *Don Juan* (1819–24), who enters the sultan's harem, and in *Beppo* (1818) and *The Maid of Athens* (1810). He died in Greece, trying to unite the fractious Greeks against the Ottoman.

Casanova, Giacomo (1725–98). This notorious womaniser held a diplomatic position in the Venetian embassy in Constantinople some time in the 1750s, during which time, so strict were the laws of the harem, his only exposure to women was in the role of a voyeur.

Chardin, Jean or John (1643–1715), started life as a Parisian jeweller who took his trade to Persia and became jeweller to the Shah, made his fortune and retired to London, where he was knighted for services to the East India Company. The narrative of his time in Persia, *Voyages de M Chardin*, published in Amsterdam in 1711, was the principal source of information on the country in the English-speaking world at its time.

Coleridge, Samuel Taylor (1772–1834), his *Kubla Khan*, published in 1816, was probably the genesis of oriental Romanticism, a poem with drug-induced dreams of the cloudy lands of Mongol China, Persia, the Levant and Abyssinia.

Defoe, Daniel (1660–1731). Defoe's protagonist in *Robinson Crusoe* (1719) was taken prisoner by Salé pirates, and put into private servitude. He escaped as he feared that his captor entertained sodomitical intentions, believed to be the peculiar vice of North Africa.

Delacroix, Eugène (1798–1863), painted the iconic *Massacre at Chios* in 1824, a 'shocker' that highlighted Ottoman atrocities in the war with Greece. He was later attracted by the savage splendour of Muslim society and the wildlife of Algeria, encouraging the French to think of formal annexation and colonisation of the country.

Denon, Vivant (1747–1825), was an aristocrat who accompanied Napoleon to Egypt in 1798. His *Voyages dans la Basse et la Haute Egypte* (1802, two volumes) is a graphic account of the country the French army uncovered.

D'Herbelot de Molainville, Barthélemy (1625–95). This French encyclopaedist collected and translated Arabic texts to form his monumental *Bibliothèque Orientale*, which first saw the light of day in 1697. It was the vade mecum for all oriental scholars in Britain and in France, including Edward Gibbon (qv) and was republished more than once in the eighteenth century, the most comprehensive edition being that produced in The Hague in 1776.

Digby, Jane (1807–81). A notable beauty who contracted a series of marriages and liaisons round Europe including King Ludwig I of Bavaria, finishing at age 46 with an Islamic marriage to an Arab sheikh, whom she supported from her considerable fortune, under canvas and in monogamy, until her death.

Disraeli, Benjamin (1804–81). *Tancred*, written in 1847, was part of a trilogy of political novels, of which *Coningsby* and *Sybil* are the companion pieces. Each novel is independent of the other and, in *Tancred*, Disraeli tries to tackle the subject of religious compromise and reconciliation between the three Abrahamic faiths as a contribution to explaining and settling the Eastern Problem which was to preoccupy him as Prime Minister.

Edgeworth, Maria (1768–1849). Irish novelist who included in an early collection of tales *Murad the Unlucky* (1804), a morality tale for children set in the time of Suleiman the Magnificent.

Galland, Antoine (1648–1715), translator of *The Arabian Nights Entertainments* (1704–17). He was a protegé of Colbert, charged to collect Arabic material for the French East India Company (*Compagnie des Indes*).

Gibbon, Edward (1737–94), gave considerable space in his *Decline and Fall of the Roman Empire* to Muhammad and Islam, though possessing no Arabic. He relied greatly on the work of d'Herbelot (qv) though he was neutral as between the claims of Christianity and Islam, believing both faiths to be deceitful.

Haydn, Joseph (1732–1809), wrote his first comic opera for Eszterhaza, *L'Incontro Improvviso* in 1764, about a Persian princess captive in Egypt. It, like Mozart's (qv) *Il Seraglio*, has a buffoon character called Osmin.

Henley, Samuel (1740–1815), was an American loyalist who left his professorship in Virginia to teach at Harrow, eventually becoming vicar of Rendlesham. He was obsessed by literary and biblical curiosities and published Beckford's (qv) *Vathek* in 1786, with elaborate footnotes, implying that it was his own work.

Ingres, Dominique (1780–1860). Romantic French painter fascinated by the Turkish bath as the nursery of classically nude figures. In *Le Bain Turc* (1862), he painted his own wife, and made many portraits and sketches of odalisques to perpetuate the myth of Oriental sensuousness.

Johnson, Samuel (1790–84), wrote *Rasselas, Prince of Abyssinia* in 1759, as an allegory of the vanity of human wishes. It appeared at about the same time as Voltaire's (qv) *Candide*.

Kinglake, Alexander (1809–91), visited the Ottoman empire in the 1830s, journeying through the Balkans, Turkey, Syria, Palestine and Egypt, visiting Lady Hester Stanhope (qv) en route. He wrote about his journey in the first classic account of these parts in *Eothen* (1844) and went on to be a historian of the Crimean War (1854–56)

Landor, Walter Savage (1775–1864), published his epic poem *Gebir* in seven books in 1798, the year Napoleon invaded Egypt. It was a fictitious, heroic saga of North Africa, in which Prince Gebir of Spain invades the realms of Queen Charoba of Egypt. Magic and soothsaying are much involved. (See also Reeve).

Lane, Edward William (1801–76), was an oriental scholar resident in Cairo, where he wrote *The Manners and Customs of the Modern Egyptians* in 1836, followed by a translation of *The Arabian Nights* in 1838–40. He was bitterly attacked by Richard Burton (qv) for mutilating (de-sexing) the text.

Leake, William (1770–1860). An artilleryman first sent to train Ottoman gunners, he was the first emissary to Ali Pasha of Yannina in 1804, later returning in 1809 as resident at his court when Byron came. His *Journal of a Tour in Asia Minor* (1824) established his reputation as orientalist and numismatist.

Loti, Pierre, was a pseudonym for Louis Viaud (1850–1923). A French naval officer stationed for some time on the Bosphorus, where he may have contracted a romantic relationship with a harem wife. His novel *Aziyadé* (1879) hints at this, while *Désenchantées* (1911) tries to give a more sympathetic account of harem life in the Ottoman capital.

Marsh, Elizabeth (1735–85), was seized by Moroccan corsairs and enslaved. She successfully protected her chastity and wrote of her experiences in *The Female Captive* (1769).

Meredith, George (1828–1909), was married to Thomas Love Peacock's widowed daughter, and wrote his first novel *The Shaving of Shagpat* in 1850, as a satirical 'take' on his father-in-law's work, being a magical and absurd tale of a magical Persia. It was much admired by George Eliot, and launched him on a prolific literary career.

Montagu, Lady Mary Wortley (1689–1762). An earl's daughter, Lady Mary married Edward Wortley Montagu in secret, and in 1716 she accompanied him to Constantinople, where he represented the Court of St James. Her *Turkish Letters* were published posthumously in 1763 and were for a long time the principal source of information about life in the Ottoman empire. After her return to London she became a leading member of London society and a wit. She caught smallpox in 1715, was badly marked and is credited with introducing from the East the practice of inoculation against the disease.

Moore, Thomas (1779–1852). Irish poet, friend and biographer of Byron, Moore was inspired by Byron's *Turkish Tales* to produce his own oriental romantic fantasy, *Lalla Rookh* (1817), which established his European reputation.

Morier, James Justinian (1789–1840). A naturalised Smyrniot Jew, accompanied Sir William Harcourt's embassy to Persia in 1808, which was memorialised in his account of the journey in 1812. He went on to write two picaresque novels about Persia, *Hajji Baba of Ispahan* (1824) and *The Adventures of Hajji Baba in England* (1828). A later work *Ayesha* (1834) introduced the Turkish word *bosh* into the English language.

Mozart, Wolfgang Amadeus (1756–91), captured the appetite in Vienna for plays about Turkey in his *Il Seraglio* (*Die Entführung aus dem Serail*) in 1782. Low life is portrayed like low life everywhere (as in Haydn's *L'Incontro Improvviso*), but the Turk is no longer abominable but a perfect Christian gentleman.

Ockley, Simon (1678–1720), was vicar of Swavesey and an orientalist. Author of *A History of the Saracens* (1718), he was one of the first translators of the Koran in an attempt to bring about a better understanding of Islam in the West.

Pellow, Thomas (1704–?), was enslaved from age 11 in Morocco, became a renegade, rose to military rank and escaped to England, where he 'wrote' *The History of a Long Captivity … in South Barbary*, printed in 1740.

Pococke, Richard (1704–65). Though in holy orders, travelled extensively in the East, producing his *Description of the East and Other Countries* in two volumes between 1743 and 1745. It was used as source material by Edward Gibbon (qv).

Preziosi, Amadeo (1816–82), was a Maltese water-colourist who settled in Constantinople to portray the city in the early nineteenth century.

Quincey, Thomas de (1785–1859), was an opium eater like Coleridge, whom he knew. He had disturbing dreams of Nilotic mud and oriental horrors, which he recorded in *Confessions of an English Opium Eater* (1822).

Reeve, Clara (1729–1807), wrote *The Progress of Romance* (1785) from which the story of Charoba, queen of Egypt, was the inspiration for Landor's (qv) *Gebir*.

Rossini, Giaocchino (1792–1868), wrote two comic operas taking off Neapolitan attitudes to Muslims: *L'Italiana in Algeri* for Venice in 1811 and *Il Turco in Italia* for Milan in 1814. His serious opera *Maometto II* was adapted for Naples in 1820 from a play by Voltaire and was rejigged as *The Siege of Corinth* in 1826 to capture Parisian enthusiasm for Greek independence.

Sale, George (1697–1736). A lawyer and orientalist, was the first layman to translate the Koran (1774). Though not in orders, he vetted translations of the New Testament for use among Arabic-speaking Christians in the Levant, and a vehicle for the conversion of Muslims.

Scott, Walter (1771–1832), explored his interest in the relations between faiths and the conflict of chivalry and modernity in four Crusader novels: *Ivanhoe* (1819), *The Betrothed* and *The Talisman* (1825) and the unfinished *Siege of Malta* (started in Naples in 1832). Only *The Talisman* actually takes place in the Holy Land and is basically a panegyric about the Islamic hero, Saladin.

Shaw, Thomas (1694–1751), spent 13 years in Algiers as chaplain to the factory there. He dedicated and presented his *Travels and Observations relating to several parts of Barbary and the Levant* (1738) to George II.

Shelley, Mary Wollstonecraft (1797–1851), wrote a story of a frustrated escape from a harem, *Constantine and Euphrasia*, which appeared in *The Keepsake* in 1838. It was another harem escape story but written well after Greece had secured her independence and was more concerned with the sufferings of women generally than with those of harem women particularly.

Shelley, Percy Bysshe (1792–1822). Unlike Byron, Shelley never visited the East but he was an ardent supporter of Greek independence, and through his acquaintance with Prince Mavrocordato in Pisa he wrote his last completed work about the war, *Hellas* (1822). His earlier work *The Revolt of*

Islam (1818), also known as *Laon and Cynthia*, was only indirectly about Islam, the revolt of the title being the French one set in an eastern setting, the title being intended to mislead the reader that part of the poem was about incest.

Southey, Robert (1774–1843), later Poet Laureate, produced the fantasy narrative poem *Thalaba the Destroyer* in 1801, situated in a magical north Africa. It held Shelley enthralled at Oxford.

Stanhope, Lady Hester (1776–1839), was the niece and former social secretary of William Pitt the Younger. She left Europe in 1810, settling by 1814 in modern Lebanon, then Syria. She established herself as a prophetess, living in some splendour among Syrian Arabs as a character to be reckoned with, and the cynosure of visitors to the Holy Land. The most prominent was Alexander Kinglake (qv).

Tennyson, Alfred (1809–92), wrote his Romantic poem on the golden prime of good Haroun Alraschid in *Recollections of the Arabian Nights* (1830).

Thackeray, William Makepeace (1811–63), made a journey from Cornhill to Grand Cairo and his *Notes* on this journey, appearing in 1846, helped to perpetuate the view that the Orient was a backward, sinister but rather amusing place.

Volney, Constantin (1757–1820). A French savant who spent four years in Egypt and Syria and whose *Ruines ou Méditations sur les Révolutions des Empires* (1791) inspired Napoleon's interest in Egypt and the Levant.

Voltaire, François Marie Arouet (1694–1778), was a prominent critic of the Ottoman empire as the embodiment of oriental tyranny. His *Zadig* (1748) was a satire on Zoroastrian Persia, human imperfectibility and the fate of honest men.

Weber, Carl Maria von (1786–1826). A cousin of Mozart's (qv) wife, adapted one of the Arabian Nights tales in 1811 as *Abu Hassan*. It is light-hearted and had a happy ending, like both Mozart's and Haydn's eastern fables.

Wood, Robert (1717–71), was under-secretary of state for the southern region, and an oriental traveller who produced two lavishly illustrated books on Pergamon and Baalbek in 1753. He was a patron of James Bruce (qv).

Bibliography

ALEXANDER, Michael, *Medievalism, the Middle Ages in Modern England*, New Haven, 2007.

ANDERSON, Emily, ed., *The Letters of Mozart and his Family*, London, 3rd edition, 1989.

ANSTRUTHER, Ian, *The Knight and the Umbrella: An Account of the Eglinton Tournament, 1839*, London, 1963.

BALLÁSTER, Ros, *Fabulous Orients, Fictions of the East in England, 1662–1785*, Oxford, 2005.

BECKFORD, William, *Vathek, An Arabian Tale*, London 1781/82, in *Shorter Novels of the 18th Century*, London, 1903.

—— *The Journal ... in Portugal and Spain, 1787–1788*, ed. B Alexander, Stroud, 2006.

BLANCH, Lesley, *The Wilder Shores of Love*, John Murray, 1954.

—— *Sabres of Paradise*, London, 1960.

—— *Pierre Loti, Portrait of an Escapist*, Lndon, 1983.

BRADFORD, Sarah, *Disraeli*, London, 1982.

BROMLEY, John S., *Corsairs and Navies, 1660–1760*, London, 1987.

BROOKNER, Anita, *Romanticism and its Discontents*, London, 2000.

BRUCE, James, *Travels to Discover the Source of the Nile in the years 1768, 1769, 1770, 1771, 1772, 1775*, seven volumes abbreviated in *The English Explorers*, London and Edinburgh, 1875.

BUCHAN, John, *Greenmantle*, London, 1916.

BURUMA, Ian and MARGALIT, Avishai, *Occidentalism: a Short History of Anti-Westernism*, London, 2004.

BYRON, Lord George, *Letters & Journals*, edited by Leslie A. Marchand, vols 1, 3, 5, London 1973–76. (See also McGANN, Jerome.)

CARAMAN, P., *The Lost Empire*, London, 1985.

CASANOVA, Giacomo, *History of My Life*, vol. 2, trans. W.R. Trask, London, 1967.

CAVALIERO, Roderick, 'The Decline of the Maltese *Corso* in the 18th century', *Melita Historica*, vol. 2, no. 4, 1959.

—— *The Last of the Crusaders*, London, 1960.

—— *Strangers in the Land, The Rise and Decline of the British Indian Empire*, London, 2002.

CHEW, S.C. *The Crescent and the Rose*, Oxford, 1908.

CHILDS, Virginia, *Lady Hester Stanhope*, London, 1990.

CLOGG, Richard, *A Concise History of Greece*, Cambridge, 2002.

COCHRAN, Peter, 'Byron and Islamic Culture', *The Keats-Shelley Review*, No. 21, 2007, pp. 65–78.

COLES, Paul, *The Ottoman Impact on Europe*, London, 1968.

COLLEY, Linda, *Captives: The Story of Britain's Pursuit of Empire, Soldiers and Civilians Held Captive 1600–1850*, New York/London, 2002.

—— *The Ordeal of Elizabeth Marsh, A Woman in World History*, London, 2007.

CONANT, Martha Pike, *The Oriental Tale in England in the 18th century*, New York, 1908.

CRAWLEY, C.W., 'The Near East and the Ottoman Empire, 1798–1830' in *War and Peace in an Age of Upheaval, 1793–1830*, vol. ix of The New Cambridge Modern History, 1965.

DELACROIX, Eugene, *Journal*, trans. Lucy Norton, ed. H. Wellington, Oxford, 1951.

DENT, Edward J., *Mozart's Operas*, Oxford, 1960.

DISRAELI, Benjamin, *Tancred or The New Crusade*, London, 1847.

EDGEWORTH, Maria, *Murad the Unlucky* from *Popular Tales*, London, 1802.

Etat des Royaumes de Barbarie: letters from a Redemptorist priest, 1700. Manuscript in the Archives of the Order in Malta.

FAROQHI, Suraiya, *The Ottoman Empire and the World Around It*, London, 2004.

—— *Subjects of the Sultan: Culture and Daily Life in the Ottoman Empire*, London, 2005.

FERRIER, R.W., *A Journey to Persia: Jean Chardin's Portrait of a Seventeenth-century Empire*, London, 1966.

FLEMING, Anne, *Byron the Maker; Truth or Masquerade*, vol. 1, *Byron in England*, Lewes, 2006.

FLETCHER, Richard, *The Cross and the Crescent, Christianity and Islam from Muhammad to the Reformation*, London, 2004.

FRANCI, Giovanna, 'The Myth of the Orient Passes Through Ravenna', *Journal of Anglo-Italian Studies*, vol. 3 (1993).

FROUDE, J.A., *The Earl of Beaconsfield*, London, 1914.

GIBBON, Edward, *The Decline and Fall of the Roman Empire*, London, 1776 to 1778.

GRIMES, Kyle, 'Censorship, Violence and Political Rhetoric: The Revolt of Islam in its Time', *Keats-Shelley Journal*, New York, vol. 43, 1994.

GROSRICHARD, Alain, *The Sultan's Court: European Fantasies of the East*, trans. Liz Heron, London, 1998 (original *La Structure du Serail*, Paris, 1979).

GROSSKURTH, Phyllis, *Byron the Flawed Angel*, London, 1997.

HAZARD, Paul, *La Crise de la Conscience Européenne*, Paris, 1935.

HEROLD, J. Christopher, *Bonaparte in Egypt*, London, 1963.

HOLMES, Richard, *Shelley, the Pursuit*, London, 1974.

HOURANI, Albert, *A History of the Arab Peoples*, London, 1991.

IRWIN, Robert, *For Lust of Knowing: The Orientalists and their Enemies*, London, 2006.

JOHNSON, Edgar, *Sir Walter Scott, The Great Unknown*, vol. 1, 771–1821; vol. 2, 1821–1832, London, 1970.

KELLY, Linda, *Ireland's Minstrel: A Life of Tom Moore, Poet, Patriot and Byron's Friend*, London, 2006.

KINGLAKE, Alexander, *Eothen*, London, 1844.

KUHN, William, *The Politics of Pleasure: A Portrait of Benjamin Disraeli*, London, 2006.

LANDOR, W.S., *Poetical Works*, ed. S. Wheeler, Oxford, 1937.

LANE, Edward William, *The Manners & Customs of the Modern Egyptians*, Everyman edition, no date., originally in two vols, London, 1837.

LANE-POOLE, Stanley, *The Arabian Nights Entertainment*, trans. Edward William Lane, London, 4 vols, 1925.

LEAKE, William, *Travels in Northern Greece*, 4 vols, London, 1835. (Facsimilie reprint, Amsterdam, 1976.)

LEASK, Nigel, *British Romantic Writers and the East*, Cambridge, 1992.

LEWIS, Bernard, *From Babel to Dragomans: Interpreting the Middle East*, Oxford, 2004.

LEWIS, Raina, *Rethinking Orientalism: Women, Travel and the Ottoman Harem*, London, 2004.

LLEWELLYN, B. and NEWTON, C., *The People and Places of Constantinople*, London, 1985.

LODEWIJK, Tom, *The Book of Tulips*, London, 1979.

LONGFORD, E. (ed.), *Royal Anecdotes*, Oxford, 1981.

LOTI, Pierre, *Désenchantées* (Eng. trans. as *Disenchanted* by Clara Bell), London, 1911.

LOVELL, Mary S.A., *Scandalous Life: The Biography of Jane Digby*, London, 1995.

MacCARTHY, Fiona, *Byron, Life and Legend*, London, 2002.

MANSEL, Philip, *Constantinople, City of the World's Desire, 1445–1924*, London, 1997.

MARANDI, Seyed Mohammed, 'Byron's Infidel and the Muslim Fisherman', *Keats-Shelley Review* No. 20 (2006), pp. 133–55.

MAVOR, Elizabeth, *The Grand Tour of William Beckford*, London, 1986.

MAYES, Stanley, *The Great Belzoni, the Circus Strongman who Discovered Egypt's Treasures*, London, 2003).

McGANN, Jerome J., *Lord Byron, The Complete Poetical Works*, vol. ii, Oxford, 1981.

MICHEL, P.-H., *The Massacre of Chios*, London, 1947.

MILTON, Giles, *White Gold; The Extraordinary Story of Thomas Pellow and North Africa's One Million European Slaves*, London, 2004.

MONTAGU, Lady Mary Wortley, *The Complete Letters of Lady Mary Wortley Montagu*, vol. i, 1708–20, ed. Robert Halsband, Oxford, 1965.

MOORE, Thomas, *Poetical Works*, London, no date *c*.1870.

MORGAN, Sydney, *Italy*, 3 vols., London, 1821.

MORIER, James, *A Journey through Persia, Armenia and Asia Minor to Constantinople in the years 1808 and 1809*, London, 1812.

—— *The Adventures of Hajji Baba of Ispahan in England*, Oxford, 1925.

—— *The Adventures of Hajji Baba of Ispahan*, London, 1927.

PARDOE, Julia, *The Beauties of the Bosphorus*, London, 1837–39.

PARTNER, P., *The Murdered Magicians: The Templars and their Myth*, Oxford, 1981.

PASSERON, Roger, *Daumier*, Oxford, 1981 (original *Daumier, Témoin de son Temps*, Fribourg, 1979).

PLUTARCH, *Lives*, trans. John Dryden, London, 1910.

QUINCEY, Thomas de, *The Confessions of an English Opium Eater*, London, 1907.

—— *The English Mail-coach and Other Essays*. London, 1912.

RALEIGH, Walter, *The English Novel*, New York, 1904.

SAID, Edward W., *Orientalism*, New York, 1978.

—— *Culture & Imperialism*, London, 1993.

SCHMIDT, Margaret Fox, *Passion's Child, The Extraordinary Life of Jane Digby*, London, 1977.

SCHOINA, Maria, 'Empire Politics and Feminine Civilisation in Mary Shelley's "Euphrasia" a Tale of Greece', *Anglo-American Perceptions of Hellenism*, ed. T. Rapatzikou, Cambridge Scholars Press, Newcastle, 2007.

SCOTT, Sir Walter, *The Letters of Sir Walter Scott*, ed. H. Grierson, London, 1932.

—— *The Journal*, ed. W.E.K. Anderson, Oxford, 1972 and Edinburgh (paperback) 1982.

SHARAFUDDIN, Mohammed, *Islam and Romantic Orientalism: Literary Encounters with the Orient*, London, 1994.

SHELLEY, Mary, *Collected Tales and Stories*, ed. Charles E. Robinson, Baltimore, 1976.

SHELLEY, P.B., *Works*, Wordsworth Edition, Ware, 1994.

SITWELL, Sacheverell, *Arabesques and Honeycombs*, London, 1957.

SULTANA, Donald, *The Seige of Malta Rediscovered*, Edinburgh, 1977.

THACKERAY, William M., *Notes on a Journey from Cornhill to Grand Cairo*, London, 1846.

—— *The Four Georges*, London, 1923.

TYLDESLEY, Joyce, *Egypt, How a Lost Civilization was discovered*, London, 2005.

VALENSI, Lucette, *Venice and the Sublime Porte: The Birth of the Despot*, Ithaca, 1993 (original *Venise et la Sublime Porte*, Paris, 1987).

Voyages en Barbarie by a Redemptorist Father (1718). Manuscript in Archives of the Order in Malta.

WARRACK, John, *Carl Maria von Weber*, London, 1968.

WILLIAMS, Charles, *Many Dimensions*, London, 1931.

WILLIAMS, David, *George Meredith, His Life and Lost Love*, London, 1977.

YAMANAKA, Yuriko and NISHIO, Tetsuo (eds), *The Arabian Nights and Orientalism, Perspectives from East and West*, London, 2006.

Index